MW00697566

BATTLE SCARS

BATTLE SCARS

Twenty Years Later: 3d Battalion 5th Marines Looks Back
at the Iraq War and How it Changed Their Lives

CHIP REID

CASEMATE

Philadelphia & Oxford

Published in the United States of America and Great Britain in 2023 by
CASEMATE PUBLISHERS
1950 Lawrence Road, Havertown, PA 19083, USA
and
The Old Music Hall, 106–108 Cowley Road, Oxford OX4 1JE, UK

Hardcover Edition: ISBN 978-1-63624-355-9
Digital Edition: ISBN 978-1-63624-356-6

A CIP record for this book is available from the British Library

Printed and bound in the United Kingdom by CPI Group (UK) Ltd, Croydon, CR0 4YY
Typeset in India by DiTech Publishing Services

For a complete list of Casemate titles, please contact:

CASEMATE PUBLISHERS (US)
Telephone (610) 853-9131
Fax (610) 853-9146
Email: casemate@casematepublishers.com
www.casematepublishers.com

CASEMATE PUBLISHERS (UK)
Telephone (0)1226 734350
Email: casemate-uk@casematepublishers.co.uk
www.casematepublishers.co.uk

Front cover image: Marines carrying PFC Mike Meyer on a stretcher after he had been shot
eight times during the battle of April 4, 2003. Meyer was certain he was going to die, but quick
action by a team of Devil Docs helped save his life. (Baltimore Sun)

In Memory of the Fallen

In the Memorial Garden at Marine Corps Base Camp Pendleton in Southern California is a plaque that begins with these words: "They say that a man dies twice: first when he leaves his body—and second, when his name is spoken for the last time."
This book is dedicated to the four Marines and one Navy Corpsman of 3d Battalion, 5th Marine Regiment, First Marine Division, who lost their lives during the invasion of Iraq in 2003. It is my hope that their names will never be spoken for the last time.
In the order in which they lost their lives, they are:

Hospital Corpsman Michael V. Johnson
Major Kevin G. Nave
Corporal Erik H. Silva
Staff Sergeant Riayan A. Tejeda
Lance Corporal David E. Owens, Jr.

Compared to the carnage in later years of the Iraq war, the loss of five Marines might not sound like a very large number. But as I have discovered, every Marine combat death has monumental repercussions, as the loss reverberates and ripples through the battalion and through communities back home.
From day one Marines are taught that their fellow Marines are their brothers, and that they are responsible for each other's well-being. That bond is critical to creating a cohesive unit, but it also makes losing a Marine comparable to the devastation of losing a family member.

Contents

Preface

On Thanksgiving Day 2021, while driving from my home in Washington, D.C. to the Philadelphia suburbs for a family dinner, a souped-up pickup truck roared past me on I-95. It had temporary plates and two Marine Corps stickers, one on the rear window and one on the bumper. I thought: "Isn't that just like a Marine. He just bought the damn thing and it's already plastered with Marine Corps stickers."

That got me thinking about the most challenging, gratifying, jaw-dropping, and frightening story I covered in my 33 years as a journalist—the slightly less than six weeks I spent embedded with 3d Battalion, 5th Marine Regiment (3/5 for short), during the invasion of Iraq in 2003, as a correspondent for NBC News.

For years I had thought that one day I would escape the journalism rat-race and write a book, but I hadn't settled on a topic. "That's it!" I thought as the pickup disappeared out of sight. For the 20th anniversary of *Operation Iraqi Freedom* in 2023, I would write a book about the Marines of 3/5.

As I drove, I thought of questions I wanted to ask them. Where are they today and what are they doing? Do they have families? How did their lives change due to their first combat experience? (It was the first combat for almost all of them.) What did they learn as Marines that helped them prosper in civilian life? Did they struggle with Post-Traumatic Stress Disorder (PTSD)? What do they think about the war today?

When I returned home, I reached out to some of the Marines I had occasionally stayed in touch with and started asking questions. I found their stories fascinating and powerful—and they were eager to tell them. They clearly did not want their service and their sacrifice to be forgotten.

At first, I thought I could get a good cross-section with about a dozen Marines, but word spread about my project and requests to be included started pouring in. Eventually I interviewed more than forty Marines, plus several wives and grown children, whose experiences and insights were often as engrossing as those of the Marines.

Almost all the interviews were done over Zoom and were professionally transcribed so that I could be sure to quote my interviewees accurately. A few chose to write their answers and email them to me. I have extensively quoted from the interviews and emails, because I think it's important to hear their stories in their own words.

There was quite a bit of profanity in several of the interviews. Some Marines have a hard time getting through a sentence without the F-word, the MF-word, the S-word, or some other creative ornamentation. I don't see it as my place to censor them, so I have quoted them in their own endearing words.

Almost all the Marines I interviewed are retired, but I usually refer to them simply as "Marines." As I heard repeatedly: "Once a Marine, always a Marine." And "There is no such thing as a former Marine."

Some served a single four-year term of service, but quite a few stayed in for the twenty years (some even longer) required to receive a pension. Only a handful were still on active duty when I spoke with them.

I was often surprised, sometimes stunned, by their honesty, how deep they reached to tell me their stories. On several occasions I heard the words "I've never told this to anybody who's not a Marine, but ..."

I was deeply gratified that they still trusted me after all those years. Many of them talked about arriving home from Iraq and discovering that their families knew all about where they had been and what they had done because they had been glued to NBC and MSNBC, waiting for my frequent updates on their progress along the road to Baghdad.

Whenever I appeared on TV, I was later told, the phone tree would "light up" with wives, mothers, and other loved ones speaking only two words before hanging up: "Chip's on!"

Of course, their passionate interest in my reports had nothing to do with me—it was because they were desperate for information about their Marines. Where were they? What were they doing? Were they in danger?

Had anyone been injured—or, heaven forbid, worse? When were they coming home? They hoped to catch a glimpse of their Marine in the background of my live reports—or even better—to see and hear him in an interview. I interviewed as many Marines as I could convince NBC and MSNBC to put on the air.

One of my most prized possessions is an immense photo book with "Marines" stamped on the front in gold letters. It contains dozens of letters and family photos from the Marines' wives, girlfriends, fiancées, parents, grandparents, etc., thanking me and my crew for enduring battlefield conditions to report on their men.

I say "men" because of the 1,100-plus Marines in 3/5, they were all men. Under Marine Corps rules at that time—the rules have loosened somewhat since then—women were not permitted to serve in front-line combat units.

This book is modeled, to some degree, on Tom Brokaw's best-selling book *The Greatest Generation*. That renowned book is a tribute to the dozens of World War II veterans Brokaw profiled—and to all who served in that war. Brokaw was in the anchor seat at NBC News when I was reporting from the battlefield in Iraq.

In that same vein, this book is a tribute to the dozens of Marines I interviewed, and to everyone who served in the Iraq War. Many of the Marines I interviewed also served in Afghanistan, so I think of this book as a tribute to all who served in those wars.

World War II and the Iraq War, of course, have very different places in American history. World War II saved the world from fascism and dictatorship. The Iraq War, by contrast, is a war that many Americans, especially young ones, know little about. Many Americans who do know about the war believe it never should have happened.

I had serious reservations about the war in Iraq even before it began. But I believed then, and I believe even more strongly now, that the stories of those who fight our wars should be told. Even if a war is unpopular, even if you think it was a mistake, our men and women in uniform put their lives on the line and answered their nation's call.

In writing a tribute to the Marines of 3/5, I believe it's important to honor not only their service, but also their sacrifice—in battle and in the two decades since. Indeed, there is quite a bit of sacrifice in the pages that follow, including death in battle; death by tragic accident; life-changing injuries; and the whole panoply of nightmarish symptoms of Post-Traumatic Stress Disorder. Also, of course, addiction, divorce, and suicide, which tend to plague the armed forces to a greater degree than the non-military public.

But there is also much that's positive and life-affirming in this book: heroism in battle; the intense, life-long camaraderie among Marines; patriotism and belief in one's mission; life-changing traits learned as Marines; and the Post-Traumatic *Growth* that often follows PTSD.

For the most part, I have told the 2003 Iraq invasion story chronologically, from Kuwait to Baghdad, while interspersing that account with stories from the past 20 years about Marines who were affected by specific battles and other incidents along the way. It took only 22 days for the Marines of 3/5 to fight their way to Baghdad, but the effects on those who fought in that war have lasted two decades.

This is not a book that must be read sequentially. Some readers might prefer to scan the Contents for stories, topics and events that interest them, which might then lead to other topics of interest. Some readers might be drawn to descriptions of battles and heroic deeds, for example, while others might be drawn to the descriptions of PTSD and the life-affirming effects of Post-Traumatic Growth.

Many of the Marines I interviewed appear in more than one chapter. Unless otherwise noted, the ranks I attribute to them are the ones they had in 2003 in Iraq.

As the convoy moved toward Baghdad and the Marines came under attack almost daily, I was awed by the fact that men as young as 18 and 19 were charging forward under machine-gun fire and making instantaneous life and death decisions at an age when my biggest worries were who to take to the high school prom and what courses to take in college. I developed enormous respect for their courage and devotion to duty. That respect only increased during my time writing this book.

From someone who doesn't have a military bone in his body, this is my small contribution to ensuring that the service and sacrifice of our men and women in uniform—even in unpopular wars—are not forgotten.

Introduction

Mr. Magoo Goes To War

On February 14, 2003, my girlfriend Nina—now my wife—and I took a walk on a beach in central California. I would be flying to Kuwait soon to become an embedded journalist with a battalion of U.S. Marines in the invasion of Iraq, and we were squeezing in a short vacation before I left.

It was not a very romantic Valentine's Day. The weather fit the mood: chilly, bleak, and gray. Nina was distraught about the upcoming war, and about my volunteering to be in the middle of it. She tried one more time to convince me not to go, and I tried to explain why I had to go.

I told her again, that as an NBC News Correspondent it was my job to cover the news regardless of the danger. I said it was also a good way for me to honor her father, a highly decorated Marine in World War II.

She didn't buy it. She was worried about my safety. "You can't do this!" she said in a moment of exasperation. "It's like Mr. Magoo going to war!"

She had a point. I was about to turn 48, more than twice the age of most of the Marines I would be embedding with, and I had worsening arthritis in my back and knees. I had never been to war, had never owned a gun, and had never even been in a fist fight. Not exactly a battlefield resume.

When I was 18 in 1973 the Vietnam War was winding down, and I had a draft card and a low lottery number. I was classified 1-A, which meant that in the (unlikely) event that President Nixon decided to reverse course and order a troop build-up, I probably would have been wading through rice paddies in short order—the last thing I wanted to do with my life. Like many of my friends, I had even considered applying for conscientious objector status. The thought of serving in the military was abhorrent to me.

But here I was 30 years later volunteering to go to war. And I could hardly wait. I saw being embedded as an extraordinary opportunity to experience a world I had only seen in movies, while also fulfilling my duty as a journalist—to keep the millions of viewers of NBC News and MSNBC, and the families of the Marines I would embed with, informed about the war.

Word finally came on February 24, my 48th birthday. The Pentagon wanted all media embed teams to report as soon as possible to Kuwait, the war's launching point.

I was prepared for this moment so it took only minutes to finish packing for what might be months overseas. Everything I needed, including flak jacket and helmet, fit in one duffle bag and one backpack. I flew that same day from Los Angeles, where I was based at the time, to London, where I met John Zito, a very talented, easy-going NBC News producer based in New York, who had been assigned to be my producer in Iraq.

We flew to Cyprus, then Abu Dhabi, and finally Kuwait City, where I connected with my good friend and NBC colleague David Bloom at the airport. David had worked tirelessly for months with a team of NBC producers and technicians to design and build what came to be known as "The Bloom Mobile"—a Humvee bristling with communications gear that allowed his reports to be broadcast live while his team raced across the desert toward Baghdad.

My team's satellite dish was quite different. It opened like a peacock's tail and was so delicate and unstable that a strong gust of wind could knock it out of commission.

On the day that Bloom and I went our separate ways (his team embedded with the Army, my team with the Marines), he said to me with a smile: "Race you to Baghdad?" David was wonderful to work with in every way, but he had a competitive streak like a world-class athlete. I accepted the challenge, even though "winning" that race depended in no way on our own efforts.

Tragically, David never made it to Baghdad. A little more than two weeks after the war began, he died of a pulmonary embolism.

In an on-air tribute to David, I explained how the entire NBC News team had stood on David's shoulders in preparing to cover the war. For example, he had put together a massive three-ring binder of research materials and gave copies to the rest of us without our even asking.

When I admired the futuristic combat boots he was wearing, he told me they were specially designed to protect the wearer from landmines. In theory, they deflected the blast. They were extremely expensive, but David convinced the bean counters at NBC to buy another pair and he gave them to me. Again, without my even asking. Fortunately, I never discovered if they actually work.

His death was a devastating loss, not only for his wife Melanie and three young daughters, but for all his NBC colleagues, especially those of us in Iraq. I felt enormous pressure to help fill the journalistic void created by his absence.

Training for Combat

After arriving in Kuwait, I learned why there had been such a rush to get us there—not because the invasion was imminent, but because the Pentagon had decided that all embeds needed several more days of training—in addition to the week-long "Hostile Environment Training" we had already undergone in the Blue Ridge Mountains of Virginia.

Compared to what Marines endure, our training in Kuwait was luxurious. We stayed in a Sheraton Hotel that had room service, a restaurant, a bar, and a pool. There were no screaming drill sergeants, no death marches, no getting psychologically torn down to be built back up. If we had been required to go through anything remotely like Marine Corps boot camp, I doubt that any of the journalists would have received a passing grade.

All embeds were required to attend a series of detailed lectures on such topics as: how to live like Marines; what to do if we were attacked with conventional, chemical, or biological weapons; how to stay safe during combat; and how to stay the hell out of the way of the Marines when they're fighting.

We were also thoroughly briefed on the Pentagon's guidelines for reporting from a war zone. There were five basic rules:

1. Do not report on precise locations without authorization.
2. Do not report on future operations.
3. Do not report on the size of individual Marine units.
4. Do not report classified information.
5. If a Marine is killed, DO NOT/DO NOT/DO NOT report his identity until the family has been notified.

Violating any of those rules could land you in the next helicopter heading back to Kuwait City.

Otherwise, we had the same basic press freedoms we had back home. A Marine briefer told us: "We WANT you to show casualties so people can see the horrors of war. It is not a pretty profession."

For our protection we were given gas masks and charcoal-lined MOPP suits (Mission Oriented Protective Posture), otherwise known as chemical weapons suits. They looked like less-bulky versions of children's snow suits. Their purpose was to protect us from Saddam Hussein's allegedly vast stores of chemical weapons.

The Bush Administration had justified the Iraq war largely on the existence of WMDs—Weapons of Mass Destruction. Most of the journalists, though, had studied the evidence carefully during the debate over going to war, and were skeptical about whether Saddam really had them. Old mustard gas cannisters from the Iran–Iraq war? Yes, they had plenty of those. But not much more.

We wore the MOPP suits anyway, out of respect for the Marines who were required to wear them 24/7—an order that was later relaxed and then rescinded as it became clear the weapons did not exist.

Despite our doubts about the existence of WMDs, the Marine briefers did their best to frighten us. One told us: "If you get nerve gassed and you take your Atropine, you'll be fine. Unless you have permanent nerve damage." And while teaching us about another drug that was provided to us, known as CANA (Convulsive Antidote Nerve Agent), a briefer advised us to inject it "only if a chemical weapon causes your entire body to twitch out of control."

We also joined the Marines in what they called "lightning drills," in which officers would shout, without warning at any time of day or night: "Gas! Gas! Gas!" That was the signal to immediately zip up our MOPP suits and put on our gas masks. During one drill I fumbled around with my gas mask for so long that a Marine who was judging my performance said matter-of-factly: "You're dead, sir." It was one of several times that I felt like Mr. Magoo.

"When the Bullets Start Flying You're on Your Own"

There was one more thing that a senior Marine officer wanted us to know before we crossed the border. His actual words were: "When the shit hits the fan, you're on your own," but I cleaned it up a little for the title of this section.

What he meant was that if we ever found ourselves in a dangerous spot during a firefight, it was not the job of the Marines to save us. They had more important jobs to do and helping us could jeopardize their safety. They were under orders not to endanger the mission by coming to our aid. It seemed reasonable to me. The last thing I wanted was for a Marine to get hurt or killed because he was watching out for me.

But on the rare occasions when I did find myself in a potentially vulnerable position, there always seemed to be a Marine or two looking out for me.

One such occasion occurred during an ambush by Iraqi snipers. As bullets started hitting vehicles in the convoy, the Marines jumped into a ditch by the side of the road where they could return fire from a position of cover. My cameraman, Joe Klimovitz, and I joined them.

We were low enough that we were out of the line of fire, but bullets were slamming into a concrete wall behind us. That's when I had the bright idea to tape a 10- or 15-second "stand-up," a short on camera snippet explaining what was happening—an action sequence that would liven up that night's story on NBC.

I asked Klimo to stay where he was—deep in the ditch and out of any danger, while I crawled a few feet up the side of the ditch. I then stood up slightly in a crouch so that the camera could see both me and the building behind me where the snipers appeared to be. When I raised my helmeted head a few inches too high a small chorus of Marines bellowed: "Get the fuck down!" I thanked them later. We all laughed about it. Mr. Magoo strikes again.

Another incident occurred shortly after the convoy pulled into a field where we were to camp for the night, in an area where there were reports of large numbers of Iraqi fighters. I was sitting in the cab of a seven-ton truck (so named not because it weighs seven tons, but because it can carry seven tons of cargo) being driven by 22-year-old Lance Corporal Bill Rodriguez, a laid-back Marine (when he wasn't in battle) with a wry sense of humor.

Shortly before pulling into camp, Rodriguez had repeated the same "you're on your own" message that senior officers had told us before crossing the border. "Just so you know," he told me, "if everything goes to hell, I'm not going to be able to save your ass. I have a job to do."

Not long after that, we heard an explosion of gunfire nearby. Rodriguez grabbed his M16 rifle, jumped out, and started running toward the action. After I started to follow him, he turned around and told me to stop, grabbed my arm, and hustled me to the rear cargo area of the truck. "Get in!" the 22-year-old ordered the 48-year-old. He told me to hide under some gear. I did, and so did my satellite technician Rob Grant.

While in the back of the truck I used my satellite phone to call the NBC control room in New York to offer a live report with the sound of gunfire in the background. While I was waiting to go on the air, I rehearsed what I was going to say, which included the line "My satellite technician and I are cowering in the back of a truck." Grant politely asked me if I could say "we have taken cover" instead of telling millions of people that we were "cowering."

I rode in Rodriguez's truck on several occasions, and that was not the only time he took a moment to make sure I was safe. Sometimes I obeyed him, sometimes I did not. Some stories are too important to cover from a safe location. But I felt indebted to him and have stayed in touch with him and his mother, and I met his much-doted-upon daughter Geena when they visited D.C. I told his mother that part of her son's job in

Iraq had been keeping me alive. She loved hearing that. I can't honestly say there was a moment when Rodriguez kept me from getting shot, but he did shove me in a safer direction on more than one occasion.

Embedding With Our Battalion

On March 11, nine days before we crossed the border into Iraq, the journalist embeds were given our final vaccinations—anthrax and smallpox—and we all were required to sign legal documents releasing the Pentagon from liability if we were killed or injured.

Titled "Release, Indemnification, and Hold Harmless Agreement and Agreement Not to Sue," the key words were: "The embedding process will expose media employees to all hazards of a military environment, including but not limited to the extreme and unpredictable hazards of war."

After signing our lives away, we loaded into a convoy and headed for a camp north of Kuwait City where we at long last embedded with our unit: 3d Battalion, 5th Marines. Commonly referred to as 3/5, the battalion has an illustrious history and is one of the most highly decorated in the Marine Corps. The battalion distinguished itself in such storied battles as Belleau Wood in World War I, Guadalcanal, Peleliu, and Okinawa in World War II, Inchon and Chosin Reservoir in Korea.

Over the next ten days, while awaiting the order to cross into Iraq, we hopscotched from one camp to another, each one closer to the Iraq border, and each more primitive than the last. The first two camps, Matilda and Grizzly, were surprisingly civilized—with huge tents for sleeping and eating. We watched the Marines play baseball and joined them for an evening of entertainment—a raunchy Marine talent show. Marines would give the Navy a run for their money in cursing like a Sailor.

At Camp Grizzly one evening, Lieutenant Colonel Sam Mundy, the battalion's commanding officer, invited me and my three-man crew to dinner—producer John Zito, cameraman Joe Klimovitz ("Klimo"), and satellite technician Rob Grant.

As we stood in the long line outside the mess tent, Mundy stepped back each time other Marines approached, allowing them to go ahead of us.

He explained that Marine officers by custom allow their lower-ranking brethren to eat first, a nod to the fact that during combat it's the grunts fighting on the front lines who are most in need of sustenance.

I found Mundy to be surprisingly soft-spoken for a man about to command more than a thousand men in combat. The only time he raised his voice at dinner, just slightly, was when I said I had heard that his father had been the Marine Corps Commandant in the 1990s. Sounding a bit irked, he responded: "Who told you that?"

Mundy was enormously proud of his father, but he clearly wanted to be recognized for his own accomplishments. In fact, he would be recognized throughout his career for his accomplishments. He retired as a lieutenant general (three stars), after having been Commander of Marine Corps' Special Operations Command, and Commander of Marine Forces Central Command, two of the top jobs in the Corps.

Mattis, Dunford, and Mundy: A Line-up Like the 1927 Yankees

Lieutenant Colonel Mundy was only one of the exceptional leaders in the line of command of our battalion. Mundy reported directly to Colonel Joseph Dunford, who later became Commandant of the Marine Corps and Chairman of the Joint Chiefs of Staff for four years under Presidents Obama and Trump. During our training in Kuwait Colonel Dunford spoke to the embeds about how to behave on the battlefield, how to stay safe, and most importantly—how to stay out of the way when the bullets and bombs start flying.

Completing this line-up—the Marine version of the fabled 1927 Yankees team that included Babe Ruth and Lou Gehrig—Dunford reported to Major General Jim "Mad Dog" Mattis (a nickname he reportedly hates). Mattis is one of the most accomplished and admired generals of modern times. Renowned for his strategic brilliance, he retired with four stars and later became Secretary of Defense for two tumultuous years under President Trump. Unlike most of Trump's top advisors, Mattis did not quake in fear when the President disagreed with or criticized him. He had the Marine-bred courage to stick to his guns.

While waiting for the order to cross into Iraq, the Marines trained constantly. They did countless push-ups and held regular pull-up contests. Some Marines astonished us with their strength and abilities. They practiced marksmanship with all kinds of weapons, including M16 rifles, machine guns, grenade launchers, TOW missiles, and Javelin missiles. Senior officers studied battle plans on immense maps drawn in the desert sand. Important targets were represented by Tabasco bottles. We were allowed to watch but were strictly forbidden from videotaping or reporting any of it.

A few days before the order to cross the border was issued, General Mattis spoke to a crowd of journalist embeds. He reiterated that we would be given no information on battle plans, adding that even if they could tell us, it wouldn't do us much good. "Plans change all the time," he said, which struck me as the military version of Mike Tyson's famous quip: "Everybody has a plan until they get punched in the mouth." Mattis, sensing that some of us were going into this assignment with some trepidation, also gave us a much-needed pep talk, which ended with the words: "If you're crazy enough to be here, you're welcome here."

Part One

From Kuwait to Baghdad at the Tip of the Spear

CHAPTER I

The Ground War Begins

Before dawn on March 20, 2003, my NBC News team and I were awakened by a Marine who told us to pack quickly, zip up our chemical weapons suits, put on our flak jackets and helmets, and grab our gas masks. The war, we assumed, was finally about to begin. With a flurry of butterflies in my gut we waited for the next order. And waited. And waited.

It didn't take long to learn that "hurry up and wait" is an everyday event in war—and for good reason. As General Mattis had told us, plans change constantly, and it's crucial that units be ready to move on a moment's notice. You don't want to be the Marine—or embedded journalist—who is frantically packing as the convoy starts to roll.

My NBC News team had planned to join the Marine convoy in our own Humvee, which had been modified for our use at a Kuwait City body shop. The powers-that-be at NBC headquarters in New York wanted us to have some independence from the Marines and having our own vehicle would provide that.

I thought it was a terrible idea. I wanted to be with the Marines so I could see and hear and report on their reactions to this incredibly important moment in their lives. I also thought driving our own vehicle was asking for trouble. That was confirmed when Zito and I practiced driving our Humvee with night-vision goggles—an ability that was essential in this mission—and we discovered our talent for driving it into a ditch. I worried that we wouldn't be able to keep up with the highly trained Marine drivers and that we would be left behind in the Iraqi desert. They certainly weren't going to wait for us to catch up. Driving our own Humvee, I feared, would be a good way to get us killed.

Fortunately, on the last night before the order to cross the border into Iraq, then-Colonel Dunford visited the units under his command, saw our Humvee, and didn't like what he saw. An order soon came down that no civilian-driven vehicles would be permitted on the battlefield with the Marines. I quietly rejoiced. I hope that someday I'll have the opportunity to personally thank General Dunford (he retired as a four-star general) for, quite possibly, saving my life.

After several hours of waiting, we were told to report to the field headquarters vehicle of Lieutenant Colonel Mundy. He informed us that because Dunford had banned our Humvee from the battlefield, we would be assigned to Amphibious Assault Vehicles, otherwise known as AAVs. It was exactly what I had been hoping for. We would be with the grunts—experiencing what it's like for Marines to go to war for the first time.

Loaded down with gear, I became exhausted as I trudged toward our AAV, which was near the front of the line and looked like it was a mile away. The Marines were already on board, and I feared they might leave without us. The war was not going to wait for a couple of journalists. And with all that gear it was impossible—for me, anyway—to run.

NBC News had provided us with enormous—and extremely heavy—flak jackets, that covered our bodies from the neck all the way to the hips. I'm sure the executives in New York were motivated by a desire to keep us safe but wearing these suits of armor was a huge burden—and doubtless part of the reason I was popping Advil like Skittles. At times I couldn't bear to put it on. Wearing it was so backbreaking that I sometimes chose risk over safety.

The Marines' flak jackets were much lighter than ours—just a Kevlar vest and two lightweight ceramic SAPI plates (Small Arms Protective Inserts), one on the chest and one on the back. Some Marines removed the back plates, insisting that they would never turn their backs to the enemy. It's an argument that makes little sense, of course, because an ambush can come from any direction—or all directions at once, as we would soon discover.

The Marines refer to Amphibious Assault Vehicles as "Amtracs" or just "tracs"—short for their original name "amphibious tractors." Producer John Zito and I had been told to squeeze into one trac, already jam-packed with about 20 Marines, while Joe Klimovitz and Rob Grant crammed into another.

When we finally arrived, the last to board, I was surprised that the Marines seemed happy to see us, not at all irritated that they had to crowd together even tighter. They were in such a state of nervous excitement that nothing would have phased them.

After another long wait, as dusk fell, we began to inch forward. It was like traffic on the 405 in Los Angeles at rush hour, as hundreds of vehicles of every imaginable size and shape, from tanks to trucks, Amtracs to Humvees, waited their turn at the bottlenecks.

I would try to describe it, but I can't match the description by then-Second Lieutenant Casey Brock when he painted a picture of that once-in-a-lifetime moment in a Zoom interview almost 20 years later:

> What a unique experience the invasion of Iraq was in 2003. I don't know when that's ever going to happen again. Horizon to horizon it was just combat vehicles and tanks. I know I'll never see that again. Not many Marines in modern times have witnessed an entire Marine Expeditionary Force going on the offensive, moving as one, leveraging all the power that the Marines have to offer. It was surreal. It was awe-inspiring.

Saddam Hussein's troops had built massive sand berms along the border to try to stop the invasion. But Marine engineers made that effort futile. They used bulldozers to carve paths through the berms.

As the traffic jam turned into a single column, we picked up speed. The high-pitched, grinding scream of dozens of those steel behemoths must have been terrifying to anyone within miles—especially anyone in our path. A couple of Marines opened the steel lid of the passenger compartment, allowing us to stand on our seats for a stunning, panoramic view. It was a moonless and cloudless night, and in the distance, we could see bombs and missiles lighting up the night sky like the Fourth of July. A Marine told me the light show was courtesy of artillery units who were clearing the way for the ground forces.

There was little conversation—it was almost impossible to hear each other. But the exhilaration on the Marines' faces as they took in the view said more than words. This is what they had been waiting for, through boot camp, the School of Infantry, and all the other grueling physical and mental challenges. It had all been worth it—they were charging into battle as United States Marines. Private First Class Ben Putnam later told me that he played The Marines' Hymn ("From the Halls of Montezuma to the Shores of Tripoli") on his harmonica as his Amtrac stormed across the border.

I dialed the NBC control room in New York on my satellite phone. They were desperate for live reports from the front lines, and I was on the air within seconds. I described the surreal scene at length and before I hung up, I heard the anchor say to the millions of American viewers of NBC News: "As Chip just told us, the ground war has begun."

A short time later the hazy forms of several people suddenly appeared ahead, about fifty yards to our right. A young Marine raised his M16 rifle and appeared to take aim. An officer looked through his night-vision binoculars and screamed for everyone to hold their fire. The people were camel herders, not enemy troops. He then turned to the young Marine, got in his face, and gave him a lecture like a drill sergeant.

The Amtrac was so noisy that from six feet away I couldn't hear what he said, but I assumed it was a much more animated version of a rule that General Mattis had shared with the embeds during his pep talk: "When in doubt, we don't shoot."

We sped north all night. Most of the Marines slept. It's part of their training—when you get a chance to sleep, do it—because it might be a long time before you get another chance. I didn't have the good sense to sleep and stood for hours, staring in disbelief at a scene I had never imagined I would get to see.

Amtracs are a far cry from the comfort of Amtrak trains back home. Dating to the 1970s, they are still the Marine Corps' primary troop carrier. Because they have tracks, like tanks, they feel like they're rumbling over rocks at high speed when they're really going over hard desert sand at about 20 miles an hour. Producer John Zito described riding in an Amtrac as "being in a trash can dropped down a flight of stairs." That's not far from the truth, but it's remarkable what the Marines accomplish with them.

Amtracs were designed as amphibious troop transports, to take Marines from ship to shore. They were not designed to go from Kuwait all the way to Baghdad. But with frequent repairs by Marine mechanics who knew these machines as well as they knew their M16 rifles, they made it to Baghdad and well beyond.

I frequently heard from Marines that they get "the short end of the stick." In other words, they don't get the levels of funding and the expensive, modern weaponry that the other services get. But rather than complain about it, they make do with what they've got, and take pride in doing so much with so little.

The battalion's first assignment was a potentially catastrophic one. Soon after crossing the border, we saw several clusters of enormous flames shooting into the night sky. They were Gas and Oil Separation Plants (GOSPs) in Iraqi oil fields. They had been sabotaged by Saddam Hussein's forces as part of his "scorched earth" defense. We were heading straight for them.

When we arrived at the first GOSP, several pipelines and oil wells were burning furiously. Some Marines feared it was a trap—that the Iraqis might have planted bombs that could turn the entire plant into an inferno. One Marine told me he had heard that if the GOSP had detonated, one-third of the battalion's Marines could have been killed or injured. That's almost 400 men.

Commanding Officer Mundy later told me that there was no such catastrophic estimate. He attributed any such talk to speculation or rumor. But he did confirm that senior officers had been worried that the burning plants might have been wired for demolition. Fortunately, there was no detonation, and the Iraqis encountered at the GOSPs put up almost no resistance. More than a hundred enemy prisoners of war (EPWs) were taken into custody.

Because 3/5 was a tip-of-the-spear combat unit whose mission was to proceed toward Baghdad with all possible speed, the tasks of extinguishing the fires and dealing with the prisoners were left to follow-on units. Our battalion fell back into formation and continued moving north.

Back on the main road, Iraq's Highway 1—which at times was paved, at other times sand and dirt—we passed hundreds of Iraqi men wearing civilian clothes. The roadside was littered with discarded uniforms. These "enemy" soldiers seemed happy to see us. Many smiled and waved, some even blew kisses. More than a few made eating motions—the universal sign language for "we're hungry"—and some Marines tossed MRE (Meals Ready to Eat) packages.

For the next several days, as the convoy moved steadily north, there was little resistance. Small Marine units consisting of several vehicles periodically detoured onto sideroads to "hunt for bad guys," but they always seemed to come up empty. Some Marines started to complain of boredom. They were here to fight, not roll effortlessly to Baghdad.

Each night at dusk the convoy would move into a 360-degree defensive position in a large field near the main road, where the Marines would eat, clean and repair vehicles and gear, and get a few hours of sleep. It was during these early days on the road to Baghdad that we learned what General Mattis meant when he told us that if we "live like Marines" and never act like we deserve special treatment, the Marines would accept us.

"Living like Marines" included learning new ways to engage in basic human functions such as eating, sleeping, and answering nature's call.

For the remainder of my time with the Marines I ate nothing but MREs. Over the years they've been called "Meals Rejected by Everyone," or "Meals Rarely Edible." I confess that I liked MREs, maybe because my expectations were so low after watching so many war movies featuring such gourmet creations as K-rations, SPAM, and hard tack.

Everybody had their favorites. Or maybe I should say everyone had MREs they could stomach, and others they could not. Gunnery Sergeant Octaviano Gallegos would trade anything for an entrée known as "the five fingers of death"—five small hotdog-shaped pieces of mystery meat. I would trade anything for the cheese tortellini, which I swore was one of the best things I had ever eaten—which gives a good idea of my level of culinary sophistication.

The MREs even had a flameless heater. Adding a splash of water to the package caused a chemical reaction that triggered a heating element. A hot meal in 60 seconds in the middle of the desert—with no fire. It seemed like a modern miracle.

But the best thing about MREs was the sides and desserts. You never knew what you were going to get. They included crackers and peanut butter, which Operations Officer Craig Wonson says he lived on for weeks; cheese spread and crackers, chocolate chip cookies, pound cake, M&Ms, and my favorite—strawberry "dairy shake" powder. I have no idea what was in it, but if you worried about what was in MREs you would have starved to death.

A single MRE, including all its components, has about 1,260 calories. The recommended daily intake is three MREs for a total of about 3,800 calories. That's an enormous amount of food, but the daily life of combat Marines is so strenuous that many of them, perhaps most, lost weight in Iraq—despite eating like sumo wrestlers. I ate like a glutton and lost fifteen pounds.

Marines have a long history of sleeping in trenches they dig themselves with small foldable shovels. The purpose is to get below ground level in case enemy forces fire upon them while they sleep. It also gives them a foxhole to fight from. For young, fit Marines it was no big deal. But for soft, desk-jockey embeds like me, digging through the hard-packed desert sand was exhausting and left my hands blistered. Many Marines called it "digging a grave" because that's what the sleeping trenches looked like—just the right size to fit a body.

Our small shovels came in handy when answering nature's call too. Just walk out into the desert (or stay near camp if you're nervous about who might be out there), dig a hole, do your thing, and fill the hole back up. It felt very natural—the same thing warriors, pioneers, and explorers have been doing for eons.

Embeds were prohibited from carrying weapons, but a couple of Marines I had gotten to know decided that my knowledge of guns was lacking. If they were wounded, they reasoned, and I was the only person close enough to defend them, they wanted me to know how to use their weapons. During an hour-long tutorial with a Beretta M9 pistol I was taught how to aim, shoot, operate the safety, keep it clean, and how to take the gun apart and put it back together.

Another important Marine tutorial came courtesy of First Sergeant Miles Thetford, after he watched me try to fill my water bottle from a "water bull"—a 400-gallon water tank towed by a truck. I was Mr. Magoo at his worst. Thetford said it looked like I was trying to fill a Coke bottle with a fire hose. More water was spilling on the ground than going in the bottle, which meant less water for Marines to drink. Thetford very kindly showed me how to "milk" a water bull without wasting water.

After three days of unimpeded forward movement, on Sunday March 23 we crossed the Euphrates River, a name that brought to mind words from the Bible: the Garden of Eden, Babylon, Mesopotamia. We were in the Fertile Crescent between the Tigris and the Euphrates Rivers, but there was nothing fertile about what we were seeing.

Some Marines were shocked that this barren, war-scarred desert might be near where the Book of Genesis locates the Garden of Eden. There wasn't much time to think about it—just a quick, mind-boggling moment—before they returned their focus to the job at hand, moving as quickly as possible toward Baghdad while scanning the scrub desert for any sign of enemy troops.

One other thing the battalion was on the lookout for: warehouses, factories, or other facilities that might store or manufacture weapons of mass destruction. From the Pentagon's point of view, it would have been a very large feather in the cap for any military unit that found evidence supporting the Bush Administration's claims about WMDs.

The battalion did find and inspect several warehouses. One was packed to the rafters with weapons of destruction—but not mass destruction. It was full of landmines—thousands, perhaps tens of thousands, piled haphazardly on top of each other in columns six to ten feet high in one dusty, dingy room after another. They had been there a long time—perhaps since the Iran–Iraq war in the 1980s.

A Marine officer told me he was disappointed they didn't find WMDs but was pleased that these mines had never been planted in the ground where they could have inflicted unimaginable harm on civilian populations.

CHAPTER 2

First Combat

At 1:30am on March 25, five days after crossing the border, I was sound asleep when a Marine startled me awake with a shout just inches from my face. "Stand to, Marine!" he roared. I had never heard that expression before and was groggy and confused after only two or three hours of sleep.

"What does that mean?" I asked innocently, while noticing that all the Marines around me were already packing their gear. The Marine responded with a tirade of curse words. In the darkness, he thought I was a Marine, and that I was being a wise-ass or, much worse, disobeying an order. Sitting up quickly, I said: "I'm not a Marine, I'm the news guy!" He went silent for a moment while letting off some steam. He then calmly stated: "Get up. We're moving out."

During the five days since the battalion crossed the Iraq border, there had been little sign of enemy forces. But on this day, the Marines of 3/5 would finally find what most of them had been looking for—a fight.

At first light the convoy started moving slowly north. There had been reports of Iraqi forces in the area and the Marines were hyper-alert, with M16s, machine guns, and missile launchers at the ready. A few tanks led the way. The lead vehicle behind the tanks was a Humvee carrying five men belonging to the Combined Anti-Armor Team, known as the CAAT team. One of their top jobs was to defend the tanks against enemy attack.

The team was led by First Lieutenant Brian Chontosh who was sitting in the front passenger seat of the Humvee. Lance Corporal Armand McCormick was driving. Outside, on the Humvee's hard back, was

20-year-old Lance Corporal Robert Kerman, who had been asked to join the team that day because Chontosh—who fully expected an ambush—wanted "another pair of eyes." And it didn't hurt that Kerman was an expert marksman.

Standing on the floor of the backseat with his upper body in the turret, Thomas "Tank" Franklin was manning the .50-caliber machine gun, a fearsome weapon that can fire well over five hundred five-inch rounds in a minute. Franklin was given his nickname for an obvious reason—he was built like a tank. Finally, sitting in the back seat was radioman Ken Korte.

McCormick had been in the Humvee's turret on previous days while Franklin drove. But on March 25 they switched positions—McCormick drove, and Franklin moved to the turret. A very fortunate switch on this day because, according to McCormick: "Tank happened to be the best machine gunner in the battalion."

McCormick was one of the Marines who had been complaining about the lack of action in the previous days. "We were bored," he later told me. "We were lethargic. Exactly what they tell you never to be when you're fighting a war." He was "falling asleep"—and was about to get a wake-up call.

After covering only two or three kilometers, "everything seemed calm," Franklin recalls. "But I had a bad feeling." Chontosh was the first to notice cause for alarm. A sand berm less than 50 yards to their right, running parallel to the road, looked suspicious. It looked manmade. It also looked like it had been constructed very recently. He radioed Blue One, code name for the tanks immediately ahead of him. He also called the command vehicle, farther back in the convoy.

"All of a sudden," Franklin says, "it was just chaos." In an instant, the tanks and other lead vehicles were engulfed in a storm of bullets, rocket-propelled grenades (RPGs), and mortars.

From his standing position in the turret Franklin could see it all— hundreds of enemy soldiers. "They were freaking everywhere. I was swinging the turret this way, and then that way, burning through ammo." An RPG flew in front of him and hit a tank less than 30 feet away, doing little damage. Another streaked close behind him. "It was the scariest sound I ever heard," he says, "that high-pitched scream."

Close behind the Chontosh team was another Humvee, driven by 21-year-old Corporal Scott Smith. Hospital Corpsman Michael "Doc" Johnson, a widely admired 25-year-old Navy medic, was in the back seat. Lance Corporal Frankie Quintero was standing on the floor of the back seat, his upper body in the turret, manning a TOW missile launcher. Quintero remembers Johnson smacking him in the leg a couple times, and saying, "Hey man, be careful up there." The chatter on the radio included some of the usual joking around but was dominated by warnings to be alert.

Quintero, with a better view due to his elevated position, noticed some dust clouds ahead near the lead tank. For a moment he thought: "What the heck is that?" Within seconds he realized what the commotion was—they were under attack.

Smith says they had been sharing a bag of Skittles when the world around them suddenly exploded. The tanks stopped to return fire, blocking the path of Chontosh's and Smith's Humvees, leaving them in "a very, very bad kill zone," as Quintero later described it. The radio crackled: "Contact right!" immediately followed by "Contact left!" Quintero saw no fighters to the left, so he rotated the turret and his TOW gun to the right. At that moment someone shouted over the radio: "RPG! RPG! RPG!"

A split second later a rocket-propelled grenade ripped through the right side of their lightly armored Humvee. Quintero didn't see it, but felt it slam into his abdomen with such force that it propelled him upward, onto the top of the Humvee. In his peripheral vision he saw the missile hit Johnson in the head and push him out of the vehicle and into the road. In that chaotic moment, driver Smith says, "I literally lost my mind." He started screaming into the radio: "Johnson's dead! Johnson's dead!"

The Marine Corps does not have its own medics. Instead, Navy medics, known as Hospital Corpsmen, or just corpsmen, are assigned to Marine units. The Marines also call corpsmen "Devil Docs," a variation on the Marine nickname "Devil Dogs." When Marines are injured in battle, the cry of "corpsman up!" brings corpsmen running to their aid, often under fire. They save others' lives while risking their own. What a cruel irony it was then, that Corpsman Michael Johnson, a man who had volunteered to save lives, was the first member of 3/5 to lose his life in 2003.

The RPG that killed Johnson and severely injured Quintero did not detonate. If it had, it's likely all four men in the Humvee would have been killed instantly or seriously injured. Powered by a white-hot propellant, the RPG entered the Humvee with such explosive force that it momentarily knocked out the two Marines in the front seats—team leader John Puckett and driver Scott Smith, who remembers he was awakened by missile debris burning on the back of his neck.

They quickly regained consciousness and Puckett climbed up to check on Quintero, who was in excruciating pain, holding his abdomen. "How bad is it?" Quintero asked Puckett. Instead of answering, Quintero says, Puckett grabbed Quintero's M16 and started firing. Quintero remembers thinking, "Man, that's not good, that's not really what I want to hear." He remembers being cradled by a Marine and carried to a new location, where Quintero hoped he was out of the line of fire.

Lieutenant Brian Chontosh and his team were also trapped in the kill zone. With tanks in front of them, the rest of the battalion behind them, and enemy fighters firing from berms on both sides, there appeared to be no way out.

From the moment I met Chontosh he stood out. He looked like the guy on a Marine Corps recruiting poster, with the pent-up energy of a coiled rattlesnake, or maybe the Tasmanian Devil cartoon character who careens across the landscape like a tornado. Many Marines talk about him with a sense of awe, even reverence, like he's a mythological figure. One Marine who was in his platoon in 2003 still calls him a "God of War." "We all trained for war," he says, "but Chontosh was built for it. He was just born that way." Chontosh's machine gunner, Thomas Franklin, later said: "Watching Chontosh in combat, it was almost like he was untouchable."

So, in retrospect, it's not surprising that Chontosh, in this seemingly hopeless moment, did something so unbelievable that it seems straight out of a Hollywood movie. He ordered McCormick to turn right and drive toward the berm, straight into the heart of the enemy attack. McCormick instantly obeyed the seemingly outlandish order, slamming the pedal to the floor. "We were flying," McCormick says, "as fast as I could get that Humvee rolling."

Marines who witnessed that moment say it was an act of insane courage—or perhaps just insanity. Scott Smith, driving the Humvee behind Chontosh, couldn't believe what he was seeing. "They turned directly into the fire!" he recalled years later, still stunned by the memory. "I could not comprehend that. It was like driving into the mouth of a dragon or into an image of hell!"

Chontosh's machine gunner, Tank Franklin, recalls his first thought as the Humvee made the turn: "Are you fucking kidding me?" But he never stopped firing, mowing down enemy fighters in their path, and destroying an entrenched Iraqi machine-gun position on the berm.

As they sped across the rough terrain Lance Corporal Kerman was hanging onto the hard back of the Humvee like a bucking bronco rider. Kerman was new to 3/5. He had expected to join a different battalion with his buddies from boot camp, but was assigned to 3/5, in part because his father had served in 3/5 in Vietnam. "I hated my life," Kerman later said. "I didn't have any friends."

As a "boot," a 20-year-old Marine fresh out of boot camp, he was looked down upon, teased, hazed a bit, and given unflattering nicknames. Chontosh admits that Kerman was so young and fresh-faced that he nicknamed him "Xena, the warrior princess." But that's just typical Marine trash talk. In fact, Chontosh says, Kerman was "a super cool dude." And if Lieutenant Chontosh thought that—Kerman was golden. But in his own mind, Kerman saw himself as "the new guy who couldn't do anything" and he was champing at the bit to prove himself.

Closing in on the berm Chontosh noticed a dip—a passageway to the back side, where they could attack the enemy from the rear. "Take it," he yelled, just before shooting two Iraqis guarding the path. McCormick roared through the opening and crashed the Humvee into a dry irrigation ditch on the other side of the berm. It was full of Iraqi fighters. Chontosh jumped out. "Let's go!" he shouted.

McCormick says Chontosh, as an officer, only had an M9 handgun—so Chontosh grabbed McCormick's M16 rifle and jumped into the trench— running and shooting at enemy fighters as he sprinted. McCormick threw a box of machine-gun ammo to Korte and told him to feed the ammo belts for Franklin who was firing non-stop. McCormick and Kerman jumped into the trench and joined Chontosh.

The Iraqi fighters were so stunned at the sight of the Marines invading their safe haven—and so terrified of Franklin's deafening .50-caliber machine gun—that most of them ran. The ones who didn't were shot by Chontosh, Kerman and McCormick as they raced down the trench.

Franklin covered them with the .50-caliber machine gun but had to be careful—because his three fellow Marines were so close on the heels of the Iraqis that he worried about hitting them. "I didn't want to shoot my guys," Franklin says. "I'm covering them the best I can and Chontosh was pointing at where to shoot. 'Dude, I want to shoot them,' Franklin said to himself, 'but I don't want to shoot you!'" Rounds from an Iraqi sniper were kicking up sand all around Franklin, but he kept firing, even though his position in the turret left him exposed. "I wasn't going to abandon them just because somebody was taking shots at me," he later told me.

As Chontosh, McCormick and Kerman continued their run-and-gun down the trench, Kerman looked behind and saw three Iraqis giving chase. He turned and fired six rounds at the pursuers, missing from a mere 30 yards.

He was flabbergasted. He was an expert marksman, the best in his company at boot camp. He looked at his weapon and immediately diagnosed the problem. In the chaos, he had picked up somebody else's M16. The sight was calibrated differently than his gun. He quickly made a mental adjustment—calculating that he had to aim at their knees to hit them in the chest. He fired three shots. All three Iraqis went down.

Chontosh described to me what happened next: "McCormick was shooting dudes that were coming up over the top of us, and we just went down the trench until our ammo was out. When my ammo ran out, I picked up an AK-47 and shot that. There were plenty of dead people and weapons. We just kept moving, just kept going, picked up another AK-47 and shot that one." Franklin recalls seeing Chontosh, far down the trench, holding two AK-47s taken from dead enemy soldiers—one in each hand.

Chontosh, McCormick and Kerman continued running another 150 to 200 yards, shooting with whatever abandoned weapons they could find. When they rounded a bend in the trench and passed out of sight, Franklin says he became terrified for them. "I was like, holy shit! I sure hope they come back."

Moments later Chontosh stopped because, as he later explained it, he suddenly realized the "geometry" was bad. They were now directly on the other side of the berm from the main Marine force, which was no doubt fighting its way over the berm. Most of the battalion had no idea that Team Chontosh was in the trench on the backside of the berm. "We had to get the hell out of there before we got hit by friendly fire," McCormick says.

On the way back to the Humvee, McCormick found an Iraqi RPG that had not been fired. He handed it to Chontosh and said he should fire it so that an Iraqi couldn't use it. Neither man knew how to shoot it. McCormick told him: "At least you've been to a fucking weapons course." Chontosh quickly figured it out and fired. His citation for the Navy Cross says he "used it to destroy yet another group of enemy soldiers." Taking nothing away from his heroics that day, Chontosh says the citation got it wrong. "It was a terrible shot," he says, and McCormick agrees: "It just tumbled down the trench and never exploded."

As they ran back to the Humvee, Kerman turned and saw that they were, once again, being pursued—this time by five Iraqis. He recalls stopping and screaming: "Fuck this shit!" He turned around, quickly assumed the prone shooting position as marksmen are trained to do for maximum accuracy, and again made the mental adjustment necessary with this particular M16.

He took two shots and the two Iraqis in front went down. As two other Iraqis hit the dirt and aimed at him, he hit each of them. He took a breath and aimed carefully at the fifth and pulled the trigger. Five bullets, five down. Kerman remembers Chontosh staring at him in disbelief after the calm display of marksmanship. In just minutes he had gone from "the new guy who couldn't do anything" to a 20-year-old who would soon be awarded the Silver Star.

Kerman remembers that at that moment everything suddenly became quiet. All the Iraqis in the trench had been shot or had run away. They surveyed the carnage and estimated that they had killed more than two dozen Iraqis in about ten minutes, while somehow avoiding any injuries themselves.

Chontosh, McCormick and Kerman returned to the Humvee and jumped in, joining Franklin and Korte. Their work was not done. "Our job wasn't to be dismounted infantry," Chontosh later told me. "Our job was to be security for the tanks." They went looking for the tanks.

Farther back in the convoy, Corporal Wes Smith's machine-gun squad was taking fire. At just 21, younger than several men in his squad, Smith was serving in the billet of a sergeant, a clear indication that his superior officers had confidence in his decision-making abilities. But Smith admits that his first big decision in battle was a poor one that could have gotten men under his command killed.

As the ambush began, Smith says, an Iraqi appeared out of nowhere and aimed a rocket-propelled grenade at his team's Amtrac. The driver slammed on the brakes and shifted into reverse, accidentally backing over the edge of an irrigation canal and causing the vehicle to flip onto its side. The Marines piled out the roof hatch and into the canal, where they instantly came under fire. "We felt like sitting ducks," Smith recalls.

"I was not thinking strategically at this point, and I was just real excited," he says. "My first move was that we had to decide where to set up the machine guns. I looked at the team and said, 'let's go over here.'" He pointed to a location where they could take the fight to the enemy, but where they would also be exposed. One of his men looked at Smith and said: "I'm not doing that. We're not doing that. We need to set up right here and set up defense instead of going on offense right now." Smith relented, even though the Marine had disobeyed an order.

Looking back, Smith says: "He made the right call, my call was the wrong call. It was a very aggressive call where we really didn't have any backup or support. Setting up a more defensive position and waiting for somebody to come help us after they finished the company-wide skirmish was definitely the right move."

I asked Smith why the other Marine had felt empowered to disobey his order. "Because he was my friend," Smith said. "If he wasn't my friend, he probably wouldn't have challenged me. I think he saved a handful of lives, which would have been my fault." Smith's squad successfully fought off the enemy ambush on their position while avoiding casualties.

It was a near disaster that Smith says was a turning point in his career as a leader. "Every time I make a decision now, I try to put myself in somebody else's perspective and say: 'Is this the decision Wes Smith should be making right now?'" Smith went on to earn the respect of his Marines, and says being a strong leader sometimes means being able to admit you were wrong.

A short distance up the road from Smith, Hospital Corpsmen tending to Quintero, who had been hit in the abdomen by the same RPG that killed Johnson, quickly determined that his internal injuries would be fatal if he didn't have surgery soon and made an urgent call for a medevac helicopter. Staff Sergeant Fred Keeney tried to carry Quintero to a medevac landing zone, but being lifted was so painful that Quintero begged to be put down. Keeney could hardly believe Quintero was able to walk, or at least stumble, in his condition. Someone came running with a stretcher which they used to carry Quintero the rest of the way to a CH-46 helicopter.

Quintero says he remained conscious during the early stages after his injury, but some of his memories are dreamlike. He remembers thinking it was "pretty cool" that one of the Marines carrying his stretcher was Sergeant Major Joe Vines, the top enlisted officer in the battalion. He also recalls several Marines stopping by with words of encouragement while he waited for the helicopter. One Marine by the name of McCullough stands out in his memory. "When he came up to me, he shouted: 'Oh man! You get a Purple Heart!' He got all excited for me," Quintero says.

His most vivid memory is of the medics on the helicopter. They were working on him so frantically that he assumed he was on the verge of death. "I knew it," he says. He remembers making his peace, looking to the heavens, and thinking: "I'm ready. If this is how it's going to happen, then this is how it's going to happen. If you're going to take me, take me."

"You know when they say that your life flashes before your eyes? It's true," Quintero later told me. "Every childhood memory—growing up in Laredo, Texas and Nogales, Arizona, my mom and dad, playing baseball, everything flashed quickly."

As Quintero was being flown to a field hospital the battle was still raging farther up the road where Chontosh and his team found their tank battalion and joined them in another skirmish. Within minutes they received an urgent message over the radio: return to the main battalion immediately. The artillery platoon was about to start firing and Chontosh and his team were in the target zone. Chontosh was reluctant to leave enemy fighters in the field who might ambush them later, but he understood the necessity of allowing the artillery unit to do its job. "So we did what we could with those bad guys," Chontosh says, and high-tailed it back.

When they arrived, the scene of carnage was stunning. In addition to the many Iraqis they had killed behind the berm, there were scores of Iraqi bodies closer to the road. Many panicked Iraqis had run over the berm to get away from Team Chontosh, and straight into the main body of the battalion. In all, more than 100 Iraqis had been killed and about 50 taken prisoner.

The captain of India Company, Ethan Bishop, recalls climbing on top of the berm to view the aftermath of the battle in the trench on the backside of the berm. "There were bodies everywhere. It looked like a scene from the Civil War. I almost felt bad for the other side," he later told me. "The Marines in that fight were very lethal," he said, referring to Chontosh and his team.

The Iraqi force had included many professional Iraqi soldiers, but there were also some prisoners who claimed to be conscripts. They told interrogators they were present only because Saddam Hussein's troops had threatened to kill them and their families if they did not fight.

Chontosh received the Navy Cross—second only to the Medal of Honor—for his actions that day. McCormick and Kerman received Silver Stars. Franklin and Korte received Commendation Medals. Several Marines told me that Franklin also deserved a Silver Star. McCormick said the result of the battle in the trench would have been much different without Franklin's mastery of the .50-caliber machine gun. "All of us would be dead," he told me.

Like many people who are called heroes, Chontosh downplays his exploits that day. "I was just doing my job," he says now. "I did the same thing every other Marine would have done. It was just a passion and love for my Marines." He gives credit to his team for saving his life—and his reputation. "If it wasn't for them," he told *Military Times*, "I would be the lieutenant reported as a case of what not to do."

There is no question that Chontosh and his team deserved their medals, according to Chontosh's senior officer at the time, Captain Bob Piddock, who was commander of 3/5's Weapons Company. The list of casualties would have been much longer, he says, if they had not taken such decisive and courageous action. Piddock was farther back in the convoy during the battle of March 25, in the command vehicle, monitoring the action by radio. When he learned the details of what Chontosh and his team had done, he was extremely impressed, but not terribly surprised. He told me that they certainly acted courageously, but they also relied on their Marine training.

The Marine Corps, Piddock explained, teaches young officers that quick, accurate decision-making is the essential requirement for victory in battle. To attain that goal, all officers are taught two fundamental concepts of combat.

The first is the "70 percent solution," which means that if you wait until you have 90 or 100 percent certainty that a maneuver will succeed, it will likely be too late. An officer needs to act when he has roughly 70 percent of the potential information. "Take violent, aggressive action at 70 percent certainty," Piddock says. "Do not wait for 100 percent certainty, because there is no certainty."

The 70 percent solution acts in concert with a second essential Marine teaching—the OODA Loop. It was famously designed by U.S. Air Force Colonel John Boyd to help pilots prevail in air-to-air combat, but it caught on with other branches, including the Marines. OODA stands for: Observe, Orient, Decide, Act. The key is to decide and act before the enemy does.

The OODA Loop concept has been widely used in fields where beating an opponent to the punch is essential—including business, litigation, law enforcement, cyber security, self-defense, boxing, martial arts, and of course, combat.

Chontosh's quick decision-making—even though based on limited information—changed the course of the battle. When his Humvee crashed through the berm and into the ditch in the first minutes of the battle, the enemy forces—who massively outnumbered Team Chontosh—were so stunned that many of them ran for their lives.

Of course, this isn't to suggest that Chontosh and his team were consciously thinking of the "70 percent solution" and the "OODA Loop" at that moment, Piddock says, but those concepts are so thoroughly drilled into young officers that they become instinctual: Don't wait for certainty and take violent aggressive action before the enemy does. That basic rule of combat was to become a recurring theme on the road to Baghdad.

CHAPTER 3

Two Days from Hell

Storms of Biblical Proportions

By early afternoon, March 25 had already been like a rollercoaster ride to hell and back. The Marines of 3/5 had endured a massive ambush and the first taste of combat for almost everyone; suffered the loss of Corpsman Michael Johnson, and the near-fatal injuries of Lance Corporal Frankie Quintero; and many had killed people for the first time. They had also shown their military superiority with a bloody, one-sided rout of Iraqi forces and several examples of selfless heroism.

But March 25 was not done with them yet, and March 26 was lying in wait with its own grim surprises.

Soon after the battle on the morning of March 25, the wind suddenly picked up and the sky turned a hellish color of reddish orange. Some Marines wondered if, in this land of the Bible, it was an omen of some sort. They had been warned about the possibility of sandstorms in the Iraqi desert, but no warning could have prepared them for what was about to happen.

A sandstorm with the force of a hurricane sent Marines running for cover while choking on thick, swirling orange dust and sand. It got in their eyes, ears, noses, mouths, and throats. Visibility was reduced to almost nothing as they struggled in the fierce wind to put on whatever protection they could find—kerchiefs, goggles, gasmasks.

Some Marines said they felt like sitting ducks, because the enemy would be virtually invisible if they attacked during the storm. Adding to their woes, some of their weapons had become jammed by sand and dust.

The Iraqis were experiencing the same conditions, of course, but Marines worried that the enemy might have the upper hand because they'd been dealing with sandstorms all their lives.

As the wind subsided, it was followed by a second storm of near-biblical proportions. It didn't just rain buckets—it was more like standing under Niagara Falls. It didn't last long but it turned the desert into a sea of deep mud. Several Marines had boots sucked off their feet as they slogged through it.

Following the sandstorm and the deluge, came a third strange meteorological phenomenon: the darkest night any of them had ever seen. The reason was not clear, but one perceptive Marine postulated that the downward force of the monsoon-like rain was so strong that it propelled the remaining sand and dust upward, where it completely blocked the light of the moon, stars, and any other ambient light. Even night-vision goggles were almost useless, showing only vague shadows.

The Deaths of Two Iraqi Girls and the Screams of Their Mother

Nearly twenty years later, Sergeant Elber Navarro says the scene that night is still seared into his memory—the mud, the total darkness, the reports of advancing enemy troops, and the chaos and horror that followed.

"I remember I couldn't see my hand in front of my face," Navarro says. "I was trying to position my Marines in a defensive position, and I couldn't see where they were. It was chaotic."

Some Marines had thermal imaging scopes, marginally more effective than night vision goggles because they detect heat—in particular, body heat—rather than light.

Navarro remembers some Marines with thermal scopes anxiously whispering, "You got enemy coming up on your lines!" Thinking they were under attack, somebody opened fire, he says, "and then the whole line opened up." Red tracer fire momentarily lit up the sky. It lasted only a few seconds before screams of "cease fire!"

Navarro listened intently in the silence and heard the worst sound imaginable. "I remember hearing crying," he says. "It was children.

I knew we just killed some kids." As the crying grew quieter and then ceased, it was followed by the blood-curdling screams of a woman in agony, probably, he assumed, their mother.

Navarro said then and still insists today that the children had been used as human shields by enemy fighters. "I made it a point to tell my guys the enemy killed those kids. We didn't. In essence we did because we pulled the trigger. But they put those kids in that situation, not us. They did that to those kids."

In an interview in 2003, when he was 22, Navarro told me for an NBC News story that even though he knew it was not his fault, he was probably going to hear the mother's screams for the rest of his life. He was right. Twenty years later, he is still tormented by her screams.

Jason Arellano, a lance corporal in Navarro's squad, was nearby on that night. He remembers thinking, "I'm losing my mind," when he heard what sounded like children. "Maybe it's the wind." His heart sank when he realized it was one or more young girls crying in pain.

Then he heard the woman's spine-chilling screams. Like Navarro, he too guessed that it was the mother. Arellano, who now has four young children, says it's still a devasting memory, but that eventually he "came to closure over those little girls, knowing there was nothing else we could have done."

Corporal Rob Witt was in the same squad, and therefore in the same area as Navarro and Arellano. He recalls that seconds before the shooting began, he heard "something that made no sense." He told me it sounded like the voices of young girls. He thought they might have been giggling. After the guns were silenced by screams of "cease fire," he heard a female voice. She was "screaming bloody murder," he says, "one of the worst screams I've ever heard in my life." He still sometimes hears that scream in his nightmares.

Afterward, the Marines were ordered to stay put. Officers feared that if they walked into that impenetrable darkness there would be an ambush waiting.

The first Marine to venture out at first light was Gunnery Sergeant Octaviano Gallegos, one of the most respected Marines in the battalion, who later retired as a sergeant major, the highest rank an enlisted Marine can achieve. He found the bodies of two girls, about eight and ten years old, and told me that their faces were covered by "moon dust" leftover from the sandstorm, making them look like delicate porcelain dolls.

He was heartbroken by what he saw and felt the need to place the two girls, who were several feet apart, together. He also covered them—especially their faces—with a poncho, so that young Marines who had never seen anything so awful could be spared the horror. "For an 18-year-old to see that could be devastating," he says.

It was crushing for him too, of course, and still is today. "The memory doesn't go away," he says. It became particularly difficult after he had a daughter of his own, Emma, who was about the same age as the older of the two Iraqi girls. "I remember when Emma was younger, I used to go into her bedroom to watch her little chest rise when she was sleeping," he says. "And it would take me back to watching the little Iraqi girls lying there not breathing."

No bodies of Iraqi fighters were found at the scene, even though the Marines who fired insisted they had been there. Some Marines surmised that the Iraqi men's bodies had been taken away by surviving Iraqi fighters, but the girls' bodies had been left behind as a form of psychological warfare against the Americans. Some Marines, though, still wonder if they had been shooting at phantoms in the pitch-black night, and if perhaps the girls and their mother lived in a nearby village. Sadly, they will never know exactly what happened.

There is perhaps no Marine who was more deeply affected by the deaths of the two girls—and particularly by the screams of their mother—than 20-year-old Lance Corporal Chad Huffstutler, who drove one of the Amtrac troop carriers.

When we began our Zoom interview nearly twenty years later, Huffstutler shared with me he had some "boundaries"—one in particular—that he preferred not to cross. He didn't say what it was. But after a while he told me that the interview was going so well that he had changed his mind—he wanted to talk about the topic that he had initially said was out of bounds. It came as no surprise to me when he said it was the accidental shooting deaths of the two Iraqi girls.

Huffstutler has been plagued by PTSD for years. He says the accidental killing of the two girls is not the only traumatic event he experienced in

Iraq. He also served with 3/5 in Fallujah in 2004, an extremely bloody period in which he experienced a daily dose of the horrors of war. He lost several friends there, and survivor's guilt is also a factor in his PTSD. But he says the loss of the two girls is the incident that still affects him the most.

Huffstutler's primary PTSD symptom is an inability to fall asleep. "The screams that night and into the morning, that's what really haunts me," he says. What makes the screams especially hard for Huffstutler to take is that it's not the only time he has heard the screams of a mother who lost a child. There is a heartbreaking series of tragedies that have piled on.

One horrifying instance occurred a few years after he left the Marine Corps, when Huffstutler was working as a police officer in Tennessee and responded to a report of a shooting. When he kicked in the door of the house, he discovered the body of a woman who had committed suicide with a handgun. Her two-year-old daughter was standing nearby.

At that moment, the child's grandmother—the mother of the dead woman—arrived. When the officers told her that her daughter was dead and her toddler granddaughter had witnessed it all, she wailed—a blood-curdling lament like the one Huffstutler had heard in Iraq.

A few years later—at another crime scene—he witnessed the screams of yet another mother who had lost a child. The cumulative effect was becoming more than he could bear.

But that was not the end of it. Tragically, the worst was still to come. "Fast forward a few years later and I lost my own child," he told me, holding back tears. He did not elaborate, and I did not ask him to. There was too much pain on his face and in his voice to continue. And it had all begun on that horrific night in 2003. "That scream in Iraq, the scream of a mother who has lost a child, has played very heavily in my head over the years," he said in a quiet, aching voice that reflected two decades of torment.

A couple of days after the deaths of the two girls, my producer located five of the Marines who had been involved in the incident, including Navarro and Arellano. They were between the ages of 19 and 23 and were understandably distraught, but they were eager to be interviewed because they wanted to tell people back home how heart-broken they were, and to make clear that it was a horrible accident. They blamed the Iraqis for using the girls as human shields.

Not wanting to harm my relationship with the commanding officer, Lieutenant Colonel Sam Mundy, I told him I intended to interview the five Marines on camera. He asked me to wait for him to run it up the chain of command—which I presumed to mean that he wanted to talk with Colonel Joe Dunford, or perhaps General Jim Mattis.

Mundy got back to me quickly. He reiterated that his orders were to allow us to report the news—"the good, the bad, and the ugly" as he put it—without interference. Always gracious, he thanked me for letting him know in advance.

I interviewed the five Marines as a group for a story that aired on NBC News. Their tears revealed how devastated they were by what had happened, but they wanted their families, fellow Marines, and the American people to know that they believed they were not at fault. The fault, they insisted, lay with Iraqi soldiers who, they believed, had put the girls in that position.

A Freak Accident and the Death of Executive Officer Kevin Nave

On March 26 the battalion awoke, as usual, before dawn. The Marines spent the next several hours cleaning weapons and other equipment that had become caked with mud and sand during the storms, towing vehicles that had become stuck in the quicksand-like mud and quietly mulling over the horrors of the day before.

At dusk, when we would usually be digging in for the night, we were told to pack up quickly and get ready to roll. The convoy moved north at an unusually slow pace, stopping after only a few miles in another large field, where we dug in, once again, in almost total darkness. We were told it was a refueling stop, during which our vehicles would be driven to tanker trucks farther back in the convoy. While that operation took place, the front-line Marines had the opportunity for a badly needed few hours of sleep.

I listened to vehicles coming and going for a while and then drifted off for a short time. I was awakened by the sound of Marines shouting and running nearby. I climbed out of my sleeping bag, put on my night vision goggles, and headed toward the commotion. Someone told me there had been a horrible accident. An Armored Combat Earthmover, called an ACE, the Marine version of a bulldozer, had accidentally run over Major Kevin Nave while he slept. He was killed instantly. Gunnery Sergeant Russell Cederburg, who had been sleeping near Nave, was severely injured when the vehicle ran over his legs.

As it was explained to me, Nave and Cederburg were sleeping next to their Humvee—as Marines are trained to do. It's the safest place to be because other drivers know to give parked vehicles wide berth. But when their Humvee was moved for refueling, they were almost impossible to see in the extreme darkness.

Lieutenant Colonel Mundy told me that Nave had been his right-hand man, and his left-hand man, but said words can't express how big a loss it was. Everybody loved Nave. As executive officer he was the second highest-ranking officer in the battalion, but he loved to be with the grunts. He treated everyone with respect.

He was the Marine I knew best because, on top of all his other responsibilities, he had been given the almost impossible task of turning me and my crew into "instant Marines." He was an incredibly patient teacher.

The day before, Nave had invited me to ride along in his Humvee. He was on the radio most of the time, dealing with lots of minor crises and helping to coordinate battalion movements. In the moments between calls, I asked him a barrage of questions, and not once did he show the slightest irritation.

Due to the demands of war, it took three days to find an opportunity for a combined memorial service for Kevin Nave and Michael Johnson. On Saturday March 29 we were awakened at 2:30am, earlier than usual. In the frigid cold of an early morning in the desert, Marines set up two Battlefield Crosses, the iconic symbol of honor and respect for those who die in battle. Johnson's and Nave's rifles were placed upright, the tips of the barrels thrust into the ground. Their helmets were placed on top of the guns' stocks, and their boots were placed on the ground in front of their rifles. Two American flags completed the soul-stirring display.

The Marines who could get away from other duties gathered, and at sunrise the service began. After a chaplain offered some remarks, Commanding Officer Mundy praised Nave, calling him "the glue that held the battalion together," and concluding with this: "Knowing Kevin as well as I did, he died doing what he loved most, being a Marine out here with other Marines."

Sergeant Major Joe Vines gave a tribute to Johnson. "I'm sorry I can't offer any quick answer to the pain," he said. He praised Johnson's devotion to the other Hospital Corpsmen and the Marines whose care was in his hands. "He took care of his team," Vines said.

They recited the Lord's prayer, carefully folded the two American flags, and concluded with a moving rendition of "Amazing Grace." It was an emotionally overwhelming ceremony. Some of the Marines quietly wept. But after just 30 minutes it ended abruptly, and everyone promptly returned to their warfighting responsibilities.

Sergeant Elber Navarro later told me there never seems to be enough time to mourn on the battlefield. "It's always 'you'll mourn later.' Well, later never comes. You can't mourn because you have a mission. And that stuff comes back later, unfortunately." The inability to fully mourn the lives of those lost on the battlefield, Navarro explained to me, is just one of many unavoidable aspects of combat that contribute to PTSD.

CHAPTER 4

The Battle at Devil's Ditch

A Fierce New Enemy with One Goal: To Kill Americans

After a skirmish early in the war, in which several Iraqis were killed but there were no American casualties, I remember overhearing a Marine who said: "Thank God those guys can't aim." In the early days of the war that was, to some extent, true. Many of the Iraqi fighters, especially the conscripts, did not appear to be well trained.

That impression changed on April 4, fifteen days after the war began. In a battlefield near Salman Pak, about 30 miles southeast of Baghdad, the enemy fighters were much more professional. Many were not even from Iraq. They had come from other Middle East nations with one thing in mind, according to Marines who later interrogated some of the prisoners. They were in Iraq to kill Americans.

"Their level of ferocity was alarming," Corporal Eric Olson later told me. "That was a barroom brawl. They weren't like the guys we saw in southern Iraq, who would often shoot, scoot and run away. These guys were determined. It was an extremely intense firefight." It was a grueling battle that lasted about seven hours, on a brutally hot and humid day.

Twenty years later, Olson remembers with crystal clarity the moment the ambush began. The convoy was moving up Highway 6, approaching the outskirts of Baghdad, when he felt a tug on the shoulder of his flak jacket. Olson was sitting, but the Marine next to him was standing on the bench, keeping watch from the hatch of their Amtrac. "You've got to see this," his fellow Marine said.

Olson and some other Marines immediately stood up. Ahead, in the middle of the highway, was a Marine M-1 Abrams tank—one of the most indestructible vehicles on the planet—on fire. Thick black smoke was billowing skyward. Wounded tank crew members were in the road. The always heroic Navy Corpsmen—the Devil Docs—were attempting to treat them or drag them to safety while under fire. "That sent chills up our spines," Olson told me. "Because they'd taken out a juggernaut, one of the heaviest things we've got."

Olson and his squad were ordered to exit the vehicle immediately and engage the enemy on foot. They ran in a staggered formation as enemy troops fired at them. "I remember taking cover behind a shrub. I could see bullets snapping twigs inches from my head and hearing the whiz and the smack," Olson told me.

As he rose to continue running, Olson says, everything seemed to slow down. That is how many Marines have described their reaction to coming under attack. "It was like we were moving through oatmeal, or quicksand. You couldn't move fast enough." He could see the puffs of rifle shots from enemy fighters in the field ahead. He could see bullets flying. But strangely, he couldn't hear them. Everything went completely silent. "It was unreal," he says. I later learned that it's a phenomenon called "auditory exclusion," a temporary hearing loss resulting from extreme stress. Fortunately for Olson, it lasted only a moment.

As they had trained so many times, the squad continued running and shooting in their staggered formation toward the enemy fighters. But to reach them they had to cross a twenty-to-thirty-foot metal bridge spanning an irrigation canal—later dubbed "Devil's Ditch" by some Marines—leaving them fully exposed. "I distinctly remember it," Olson says. "It was like a movie scene. Bullets impacting all around us, exploding off the bridge."

"I'm going to get shot here," Olson remembers thinking as he raced across the bridge and ducked behind a small berm of hard sand with another Marine. They looked at each other with expressions that meant: "What the hell was that?!" Two enemy fighters were firing at them from about 40 meters away. Bullets were pounding the berm, just inches above their helmets.

Olson got a look at one. "I'll never forget the look on this guy's face," he says. He had a big black beard, a black Ninja-style uniform, and a shiny new AK-47—unlike the old, beat-up weapons that some Iraqi soldiers had in earlier battles farther south. Olson checked the grenade launcher affixed to his M16, flipped off the safety, aimed, and fired. "It was probably the best shot of my life," he says. The shooting from the two enemy fighters ceased.

Steady fire from both sides continued through the afternoon and into the early evening. The enemy troops were tougher and more competent than those of previous ambushes, but still no match for the Marines, whose advantage in fitness, training, weapons, and marksmanship steadily wore down the enemy. Finally, after about seven hours of steady combat—by far the longest battle yet—the last enemy fighters were killed, surrendered, or escaped.

A post-battle analysis concluded that there had been several hundred enemy fighters. About a hundred had been killed in action and about fifty taken prisoner. Dozens of those killed and about half of those captured carried foreign passports—mostly from Sudan and Syria, plus smaller numbers from Egypt and Jordan.

The prisoners were interrogated through allied Iraqi interpreters who traveled with the battalion. Some of them said they had come to Iraq to fight for Islamic Jihad. They wore new, black uniforms and carried state-of-the-art weapons, a clear indication, Marine officers told me, that they were no longer fighting just Saddam Hussein's troops. The Marines were also fighting international terrorist organizations.

The day after the battle, senior Marine officers took me and my crew on a tour of a large facility nearby that appeared to be a military training center. There were hundreds of new handguns, AK-47s, and machine guns, still in clear plastic packaging, along with a large supply of black "Ninja" suits. The center was near the city of Salman Pak and had been used to train both Iraqi and foreign fighters, the Marines said. In previous years the facility was believed to have been a center of chemical weapons research, but as with every property inspected by the Marines on the way to Baghdad, no weapons of mass destruction were found.

Shot Eight Times and "Waiting for the Lights to Go Out"

Private First Class Mike Meyer always wanted to be in the military. He felt a calling to serve. As a senior in high school, when his friends were applying for jobs or to college, he applied to the U.S. Marines. "I wanted to shoot guns. I wanted to be tough. I wanted to be the best of the best," he says. This from a kid who says he was "the prom king, the class clown, and pretty much everything in between," though he concedes it wasn't hard to stand out while growing up in the small town of Elgin, Texas.

The nation was already at war in Afghanistan when Meyer signed up, so he knew he might soon be heading overseas. He was right. In rapid fire succession he went from boot camp to infantry school to Kuwait— 18 years old and a Private First Class. "About as bottom rung as you can get," he says.

On March 28, 2003, eight days after crossing into Iraq, he sent a letter to his parents that was full of confidence and pride:

> We got ambushed and our platoon totally kicked ass. I shot one man twice in the chest who didn't put his AK down when they were surrendering. It was either him or me.
>
> The word is we will be home around May, so I hope y'all are ready for a birthday bash. And I will be casually drinking from the keg! I figure I've been shot at I deserve a beer!
>
> Y'all shouldn't worry about me. The air support, mortars and artillery are amazing. Anything that's moving will be destroyed by the time we even get near it. Hey mom tell everyone at church I'm doing good and that their prayers are working! And keep praying for us. Lord knows I'm praying. And dad, tell everyone at work I got me one of those terrorist killing bastards and I've got his bayonet to prove it! Well, I gotta go. Love y'all and be home soon.

Meyer did his best to convince his worried parents that everything was going to be okay. But exactly one week later he would be lying in a field, bleeding profusely, after having been shot eight times. When he wrote the letter there was no way for him to know that farther up Highway 6, on the outskirts of Baghdad, the enemy fighters would be of a very different caliber—trained fighters from foreign countries. The Marines would come to call them foreign terrorists, or simply "Jihadis."

On April 4, Meyer's unit was in reserve, farther back in the convoy than usual, when they got word that one of the tanks at the head of the convoy had been taken out in an ambush. Up to this point, the frequent enemy ambushes had been quickly subdued, with some of the enemy fighters shooting and running away. "We weren't really expecting to be called into this fight, but we were," Meyer says. "So that was something new."

As the gunfire up ahead continued, his platoon was ordered to move toward a short, metal bridge that spanned a small irrigation canal. On the other side of the bridge was a field where enemy fighters were well concealed behind tall grass, and were firing from "spider holes," deep holes that the enemy had dug by hand. "It really hit us then that this is not what we're used to," Meyer said. "This is some pretty good fighting going on."

Meyer and his squad were ordered to cross the bridge. "I remember running across and I saw dead enemy fighters lying there," he says. Unlike previous battles, no one appeared to be surrendering or running away. These fighters were different. They had different uniforms, many were dressed in black, they had better weapons, better training, and a different attitude—they seemed perfectly willing to fight to the death.

On the other side of the bridge Meyer's unit took cover behind a berm on the edge of the field. They knew the field was full of fighters—they could see the puffs of smoke from their weapons. But because they were so dug in, Meyer's platoon had a difficult time finding targets.

Suddenly, they heard the repeated "whistle ... boom, whistle ... boom" of mortars flying over their heads, exploding in the field, fired by a Marine unit somewhere behind them. Still, the enemy did not come out of hiding. Ordered to move along the ditch to a different position, they still could not see the enemy fighters—only a trail of dead enemy bodies left behind by the Marine unit that had preceded them.

Then came another welcome sound. The "thump, thump, thump" of one of the most lethal weapons in the Marine repertoire—Cobra attack helicopters. "The coolest thing I've ever seen," Meyer says now. He could see the pilots turning their heads, searching for—and finding—targets. With air support and good cover behind the berm, Meyer remembers thinking "we're going to be okay."

Moments later came a command that would change his life. His unit was ordered to go into the field to sweep out any remaining fighters. "It was the most surreal moment of my life," Meyer says. "Walking through a field basically hunting human beings, knowing if you don't find them first, they're going to kill you." As he walked through the tall grass his senses were razor sharp: "You feel everything. You hear everything."

Meyer heard a soft click and instantly recognized it—the sound of a gun safety being flipped to off. He turned toward the sound and started to lift his rifle. "I remember the flame coming out of the end of the AK-47," he says. The shooter, in a spider hole, was only five to ten feet away. The first two rounds hit the bullet-proof plate on his chest, made of a high-tech ceramic which saved his life. "The next thing I know I'm on the ground," he remembers. The bullets had hit him with such force that he couldn't breathe. More bullets hit him. One exploded through his left arm, another through his hand. He tried to crawl away but could barely move his arms. Two more bullets hit him, one shattering the humerus bone in his right arm, the other his big toe. "I was thinking Jesus Christ, this guy's still shooting me as I'm trying to crawl away."

Another bullet ricocheted off his helmet. The concussive force was so powerful he thought he'd been shot in the head. That's why blood was pouring out his mouth, he thought. But that injury had actually been caused by a grenade—thrown at the shooter by a fellow Marine. Tiny pieces of shrapnel had ripped into the lower part of Meyer's face and lodged in the roof of his mouth.

There was no doubt in Meyer's mind, he says now, that he was about to die. He prayed, telling God, "Hey, I'm coming. Forgive me for my sins." He thought about his family and "waited for the lights to go out."

At that moment a Navy Corpsman he remembers as Doc Para, ran to him and rolled him over. "I remember seeing his face when he looked at me," Meyer recalls. "He was just like, 'oh, my God.'" There was blood everywhere. Para dragged him to a slightly safer location. Other Marines staged a perimeter around him to protect him, while another Corpsman, Doc Fuentes, attached an IV line.

After the Devil Docs frantically worked on him for a while, he heard Doc Fuentes tell Captain Ethan Bishop: "I think he's going to be okay."

"It wasn't until that point that I thought I might have a chance to live," Meyer says. "For the entire time I thought I was going."

He remembers being placed on a stretcher. "They carried my bleeding body across the field and across the bridge," he says. It was the same bridge that crossed a canal—the one that came to be known as "Devil's Ditch"—where enemy fighters had been hiding. The same bridge that was at the center of so much bloodshed that day. The same bridge where another Marine, Corporal Erik Silva, had been killed earlier in the battle.

Meyer was shot multiple times and survived, but Silva was killed by a single bullet that barely missed his bulletproof vest, striking him in the chest. Several Marines interviewed for this book—including Meyer—still suffer from survivor's guilt as a result of Silva's death. Again and again, Marines told me that losing a fellow Marine in combat is like losing a brother. As a consequence, the emotional and psychological effects of every life lost are unfathomable.

Meyer remembers the details of his near-death experience very clearly because he was conscious the entire time. After being carried across the bridge, he was placed on a Blackhawk helicopter heading to Kuwait where doctors performed surgery to stabilize him. The next stop was Landstuhl Hospital at Ramstein Air Base, a U.S. base in Germany, for more surgery. Then to the Bethesda Naval Hospital in Maryland for several more operations. Finally, he flew to his family's home in Elgin, Texas to convalesce, while making frequent out-patient trips to the Brooke Army Medical Center in San Antonio.

In September 2003, Meyer traveled to Camp Pendleton for the 3/5 homecoming. Some Marines were stunned to see him. One, upon spotting him, shouted: "Dead man walking!" "They thought I was dead when I left that battlefield," he says. "And I don't blame them. I was shot so many times." Eight times, to be exact. "There was even a cause of death written up for me," he says. Cause of death: multiple gunshot wounds.

Meyer later learned that the shooter had been shot several times by his fellow Marines but was still alive and considered a threat, so the same Marine who had thrown the grenade that had also injured Meyer's face, jumped into the shooter's hole and stabbed him several times with his bayonet. Papers were found on his body indicating that he was from Syria. One Marine later told Meyer that the shooter was smiling as he died, probably because he thought he had killed an American.

Meyer still lives with constant pain but doesn't like to complain so it's hard to get him to talk about it. When asked, he talks about how lucky he was to survive, and how the heroic Devil Docs and his fellow Marines saved his life.

The list of Meyer's personal heroes also includes one Marine who wasn't present. When Meyer first arrived in Kuwait, he says, a Gunnery Sergeant named Jackson noticed that he was wearing an outdated flak jacket that could not possibly have stopped a bullet from an AK-47. It was Jackson who found the high-tech ceramic SAPI plate (Small Arms Protective Insert) that stopped the two bullets that hit Meyer's chest. "That ended up saving my life," Meyer says.

As for his mental state, Meyer says he was diagnosed with post-traumatic stress, but insists it's only "a little bit" of PTS and doesn't consider it to be a "disorder" like PTSD. He says the reason it's only a minor case is because his injuries ended his military career, so he didn't have to return to combat again and again, as so many of his brothers-in-arms did. "That's probably what saved me from having really, really bad PTSD," he says.

The primary thing he struggles with is survivor's guilt, over the fact that Erik Silva died during the battle of April 4, and he lived. "Coping with the luck of who gets killed and who doesn't, that's probably my biggest issue," Meyer says. "I got shot eight times, shrapnel, and everything else, and I can still do day-to-day activities."

At a party soon after he came home, he broke down sobbing after hearing a news report on TV about Marines who had just been killed in Iraq. He didn't even know them, but they were his brothers. Twenty years later he still has a tough time whenever he reads or hears reports about Marines losing their lives.

Meyer also has nightmares—odd dreams that always involve somebody or something shooting at him. In one strange dream he was being chased by tiny Corvettes—his favorite car—with little machine guns on top.

His Marine sense of humor is still intact. He jokes that 18-year-olds make the best Marines "because they think nothing can happen to them." And he gets a kick out of going to the dentist because he likes hearing the hygienists' panicked reactions when they look at the x-rays and see the "ton of little shrapnel" still in his face.

Despite it all, he says he has no regrets. "I'm very thankful I went into the Marines. I'm very thankful I fought in Iraq. Looking back at that war, what I cherish most, is the Marines that I fought with. I'll never have that same brotherhood, that mentality of survival, of relying on someone, that I had in those days. That's what I cherish."

Today Meyer is enjoying life in Texas, where he owns two pawn shops in the Fort Worth area. He went to Texas A&M University where he met his wife and has been married for 15 years. They have three young children, two girls and a boy.

He coaches the kids' T-Ball teams but admits that his combat injuries limit what he can do. Because the bone in his upper right arm was shattered, he can only throw underhand. "I have to explain it to the other kids' fathers who think I'm a sissy," he says with a laugh.

They probably don't think Meyer is a "sissy" after hearing the explanation of why he throws that way.

A 21-Year-Old Lance Corporal Earns the Navy Cross

The only medal higher than the Navy Cross is the Medal of Honor. During 3/5's march to Baghdad only two Marines earned the Navy Cross: 29-year-old Brian Chontosh, and 21-year-old Lance Corporal Joe Perez.

It's interesting that neither man grew up wanting to be in the military or had an illustrious family military history. Perez says he "wasn't super patriotic or anything like that. I wasn't sure where I was going or what I wanted to do. I was kind of in a rut."

Perez had taken a semester off from the University of Houston and was waiting tables and bartending. He had been studying business in school but had no idea what he was going to do with his life. So, he decided to join the military. The attacks of 9/11 might have played some role in his decision, he says, but it was primarily just a chance to do something totally different for a few years.

He knew next to nothing about the military and decided to join the Army because, he thought, "the Army is the one that does the fighting." He went to the Army recruiting office three times, but no one was in.

The third time the Marine recruiter next door came out of his office. "I've seen you come in three days in a row—what's up?" he asked. "I'm trying to join the Army but they're never here," Perez responded.

The Marine recruiter invited him in. "He, of course gave me his spiel," Perez says, "and I was like 'Oh, man, that sounds awesome. Sign me up.'" Perez says he's the kind of person who's either all in or all out. With the Marines, he was all in.

After joining, he says, it was like a whirlwind, just the kind of big change he was looking for. He remembers getting off the bus at Marine Corps Recruit Depot, San Diego in civilian clothes and standing in formation on the yellow footprints painted on the pavement, the same footprints that countless Marine recruits have stepped on.

Next stop—boot camp. Perez was a few years older than most of the guys and had the advantage, he says, of having grown up in a rough neighborhood. "There was physical violence growing up. I got hit a lot when I was a kid," he says. Unlike some, he says, he quickly figured out that "boot camp was just a game." After boot camp came the School of Infantry and his assignment to 3/5. Just six months after joining the Marines, Perez was in Kuwait waiting for the order to go to war.

He remembers an important moment before crossing the border, when his platoon commander, a staff sergeant named Gonzalez, called the men together. This would be the first combat for all of them, and there was some nervousness in the ranks. "Guys, I know you feel a bit overwhelmed," Gonzalez said, as Perez remembers it. "Some of you may be feeling stressed out about what's going to happen in combat. Just understand that the Marine Corps has trained you sufficiently to execute this mission."

Perez didn't know if that was true or not, but he says that important little speech gave him "a sense of confidence that maybe we weren't in over our heads." Now, looking back, he says Gonzalez was right—they were sufficiently trained to execute the mission. In stressful situations, he says, the training automatically kicked in. "It all just came together."

It all came together in a very big way in his first combat—the April 4 battle in which they fought not only Iraqi troops, but well-trained foreign fighters. Perez was the point man for the lead squad in his platoon, making him the most exposed member of the platoon. The presidential citation for his Navy Cross describes his actions in typically formal language:

> He led the charge down a trench destroying the enemy and while closing and under tremendous enemy fire, threw a grenade into a trench that the enemy was occupying. While under a heavy volume of fire, Lance Corporal Perez fired an AT-4 rocket into a machine-gun bunker, destroying it and killing four enemy personnel ... In an effort to link up with 3d Platoon on his platoon's left flank, Lance Corporal Perez continued to destroy enemy combatants with precision rifle fire. As he worked his way to the left, he was hit by enemy fire, sustaining gunshot wounds to his torso and shoulder. Despite being seriously injured, Lance Corporal Perez directed the squad to take cover and gave the squad accurate fire direction that enabled the squad to reorganize and destroy the enemy.

Perez described it to me from his point of view, and without all the military formality. With Perez in the lead, his squad was "slogging through mud" in an irrigation ditch, moving as quickly as possible to reach the point where they could start sweeping through the field—where enemy fighters were out of view in deep hiding places.

He had already run about a kilometer through the mud while wearing a bulky chemical weapon suit and carrying full gear, weapons, and plenty of ammo. "I remember being exhausted. I was tapped out," he told me. "I remember putting my hand down on the berm because I thought I was going to pass out."

At that moment two enemy combatants popped up from their spider holes. "I just took my time, leveled my rifle, and took care of those two guys," he says. After being ordered to push ahead to make room for another Marine unit, they started taking machine-gun fire from a larger bunker. In addition to his M16 rifle, Perez was carrying an AT4 shoulder-fired rocket launcher. "I took a rocket shot at the bunker," he says. "There were three guys in there. They were done."

Next came an order to close the gap between platoons, "so that we weren't letting guys squirt through our lines." Leading his squad, he started running on top of a knee-high berm when he looked down to his right. "There was a guy sitting under a bush with a machine gun. I immediately hit the deck and everybody else instinctively did the same," he says. "I was the only one that was high enough on the berm to see the guy, so I shot him a couple times."

"I was like, okay, cool. We're good. I got up to start moving again and took three or four steps and I saw another guy under a bush with a PKM [a Russian-made machine gun]. I looked him straight in the face," Perez says. "He looked scared. I probably looked the same way. As I'm running, I pull up my rifle to take shots at him. As I did, he pulls the trigger and lets it fly. And that's when he caught me in the vest, mostly in the vest." From just six feet away, five or six rounds hit the high-tech ceramic plate in his bullet-proof vest, saving his life.

Perez says he was astoundingly fortunate because the first bullet hit him at belly button level. Most ceramic plates don't cover that area, they only cover the chest. But he was wearing an extremely large plate because that's all that was available when got his vest. Most Marines don't like the large ones because they're heavy and bulky. "But now looking back on it," Perez says, "I'm like, thank God." A bullet to the abdomen from extremely close range could have caused massive internal damage—and might have been fatal.

But Perez's luck wasn't perfect. Two bullets hit his body. One grazed his back, the other blasted through his shoulder. He did a quick self-assessment. "I can breathe, I don't have a chest wound. I'm fine," he thought. "I can't move my injured arm, but I can move my other arm."

Marines near him were calling for a Doc. "I said don't worry about Doc. I'm fine. Give me a grenade." Perez had used his grenade earlier and needed another one now because the man who shot him was still alive on the other side of the knee-high berm. "I kept telling them: 'Give me a grenade! Give me a grenade!'"

Perez didn't want any of the Marines behind him to throw it. "If they thew it short it would land in my lap," he says. "I'd seen enough people fumble grenades in boot camp." Someone tossed him a grenade. Perez pulled the pin and lobbed it over the berm, killing the man who had almost killed him.

After a Navy Doc tended to his shoulder, Perez was placed on a stretcher and carried to a medevac helicopter—sadly, the same flight that carried the body of Erik Silva.

Perez was sent to Camp Pendleton to recover from his shoulder surgery but was eager to get back to Iraq. "I felt like I let my guys down," he says. "I just wanted to be back out there." He rejoined them that summer for the last two months of the deployment.

Perez did not experience emotional or mental difficulties following that first deployment, but the next one was different. The second battle of Fallujah, in late 2004, was the bloodiest period of the Iraq War for U.S. forces. "I came back emotionally drained," he says.

It was close-quarters urban combat. "You don't know what's going to be popping up behind any door," he says. "The death was much closer. It's like up in your face. When you see guys get shot or killed the effect is more amplified in that setting." He also had a "very rough" Afghanistan deployment in 2010 that affected him quite a bit. "A lot of PTSD," he says, including nightmares and heavy drinking.

When Perez left the Marines, he was determined not to be like the guys he knew who resisted getting help. "I knew already that I had some stuff going on and I didn't want it to hamper me for the rest of my life," he wisely decided. So, he paid a visit to a nearby Department of Veterans Affairs medical center. [There are about 170 VA medical centers nationwide.] After hearing about his combat experience, the woman who did the intake interview exclaimed: "Oh my God, we're taking you over to the mental health area right now!"

Perez was "all in" when he joined the Marines, and "all in" when it came to dealing with his PTSD. "I did the treatment," he says, "and I was fully committed." For three months he went to the VA once a week. "My mental health specialist was really awesome," he says. She gave him homework, which he took seriously. "I don't think you're ever cured of PTSD," he says. But therapy helped him understand what was happening and taught him coping mechanisms. The bottom line, he says: "I think it really helped."

Perez completed his college degree and a master's degree but doesn't really use what he learned in his work. He owns a small coffee shop and is planning to open another business. He describes himself as "a very solitary person," happy to spend most of his time with his wife, who he's been with since right after his 2003 deployment, and young daughter. Perez cares about his business but says his family is his purpose in life.

As for that Navy Cross, he insists he didn't deserve it. He's read citations of people who received the Navy Cross in Vietnam and World War II and says that what he did doesn't come close to what they did. "I didn't feel like it was for me," Perez says. "It was like a collective, what we did together as a group." He knows that's a cliché, because so many other medal recipients say it. But he is adamant that he means it.

Solving a Battlefield Mystery

During our interview on Zoom, Captain Ethan Bishop, commanding officer of India Company, told me that one of his sergeants—Nathaniel Donnelly—saved his life during the long firefight of April 4. But when I told Donnelly that, he said he didn't know what Bishop was talking about. He said it was probably a case of mistaken identity.

How could one Marine say that another Marine had saved his life, and the alleged lifesaver have no memory of it? It was very strange and, I decided, a mystery worth looking into.

As Captain Bishop tells the story, he and some of his Marines were using a sand berm as protection from enemy gunfire near that infamous metal bridge that crossed Devil's Ditch. "I remember Sergeant Donnelly running back across the bridge for some unknown reason," Bishop told me.

The reason was unknown to Bishop because, in the fog of war during a ferocious battle, Bishop was not aware that he and his men were being fired upon from the rear. Donnelly saw what was happening and recognized that his fellow Marines were in extreme danger. Donnelly ran across the bridge, completely exposed, threw a grenade into the ditch, then opened fire, killing everyone in an enemy machine-gun nest. Bishop saw what Donnelly had done and only then realized how vulnerable he had been. He later described Donnelly to me as his "savior, of sorts."

When I described to Donnelly the incident Bishop was referring to, he realized that Bishop was right. "Wow, yeah, that was me," Donnelly responded in an email. "I had no idea that the enemy gunfire was targeting the CO [the commanding officer]—I just knew the enemy was shooting at 'us'—learn something new every day!" he told me.

What makes the story even stranger—and even more fortuitous for Bishop—is that Donnelly wasn't even supposed to be in Iraq in 2003. In late 2002, Donnelly was in Costa Rica living the good life. After eight years in the Marine Corps, he was on what's known as "terminal leave"—using up his accumulated leave time before being discharged. One evening between Christmas and New Year's Eve in 2002 he was at a party with American military and diplomatic personnel in Costa Rica and someone shared with him the news (probably classified, Donnelly admits now) that 3/5, the battalion from which he was soon to separate, was preparing to deploy to Iraq.

He was shocked, and immediately decided to do whatever it took to re-join his unit. "I wasn't going to stay in for eight years as an infantryman practicing for the game," Donnelly later told me, "and then here comes the game and I'm sitting on the sidelines." He caught a flight to Los Angeles and went straight to Camp Pendleton, where he and a 3/5 friend went to the battalion office and found his official discharge papers. He had only one or two days left before he would have been officially retired. They put the papers through a shredder. "Welcome back," his friend told him.

He had already turned in all his gear, and what was left in the storage room was "crap," Donnelly says. He found two boots that didn't match but were, luckily, his size, and grabbed the last camouflage uniform on the shelf, which was a couple of sizes too big.

When Donnelly boarded the plane Captain Bishop was there to check in his Marines, and was stunned to see Donnelly, who was not on the list. He was supposed to have ended his active service by then. "I just claimed stupidity at that point," Bishop told me. "And we put Donnelly on the manifest."

Of course, Bishop had no way of knowing it at the time, but allowing Donnelly to break the rules and board the plane was one of the best decisions he ever made. It might have saved his life during the battle of April 4.

The Hybrid Marine—A Hospital Corpsman Takes Up Arms

There's a lot that's unusual about Jeff "Doc Porno" Parnakian. The first thing is his nickname. Soon after being assigned to 3/5, a gunnery sergeant was taking roll and hesitated on Parnakian's last name. He either couldn't pronounce or—more likely—decided to use it to get a laugh. "Doc Jeff (pause) Pornography?" he asked. "Everyone started laughing," Parnakian recalls. "And that's how Doc Porno stuck. It doesn't have any weird sexual thing to it. It's just funny."

He is proud of his service as a hospital corpsman and takes special pride in the courage it takes to do the job—to run under fire to the aid of wounded Marines and Sailors. Since the creation of the U.S. Navy Hospital Corps in 1898, Hospital Corpsmen have received 22 Medals of Honor, 199 Navy Crosses, and 984 Silver Stars. (Technically speaking, the Marine Corps has been part of the Navy since 1834.)

I asked him how it feels to hear the words "corpsman up!" as a battle is raging—the signal for him to run to the aid of someone in distress. "That's like the Super Bowl moment for a corpsman," he said. "The Marines see enemy fighters to shoot at, that's their Super Bowl moment. Mine is being able to do my job, and my job is to keep these guys alive and allow them to continue in the fight and complete the mission. And I felt that was a really awesome place to be. I loved it."

Corpsmen carry handguns and receive their own version of Marine Corps basic training. But their primary role is to act as medics. They are not medical doctors, but they receive extensive training in emergency medicine. They would be perfectly at home in a hospital emergency room or working as Emergency Medical Technicians (EMTs).

But being a corpsman wasn't enough for him, so he decided to turn his role upside-down. "A lot of corpsmen go into this job being essentially a noncombatant," he said. "You wait around until someone gets wounded. And I took things a little different. I like to be proactive. I used to call it 'preventive medicine.' If I'm standing around, I'm a wasted body."

Unlike most corpsmen, Parnakian carried an M16 rifle in addition to a 9mm handgun. He says the Marines respected him for being willing to step up and learn how to fight like a Marine. "Just like I was teaching them how to do IVs and tourniquets, I wanted to cross-train with their jobs." He says he wanted to be "a better team member" for his fellow Marines, "a better warrior to help them out. I couldn't just sit around and wait for someone to get hurt."

In his dual role he had the best of both worlds. As a kid he had wanted to be a Marine, and here he was fighting like a Marine, while also getting the training he would need to be an EMT as a civilian. "I was really good at being a corpsman, and at the same time the closest thing to a Marine I could be."

Parnakian was an active combatant during the seven-hour battle on April 4, 2003. "I shot a lot of rounds that day," he says. He remembers being treated like one of the Marines, especially when his squad was ordered to sweep through the field looking for enemy fighters. "We went over the berm and rushed all the way to their fighting holes," he says. He and a fellow Marine doubled up for a "buddy rush," running across the field, leapfrogging until they found an occupied hole. They killed the enemy fighters and, after removing their bodies, used the hole for their own protection.

He spent a lot of time that day doing the work of a corpsman too, but because so many more enemy fighters were injured than Marines, almost everyone he worked on was an enemy prisoner. Corpsmen are required to tend to enemy fighters too, after caring for any wounded Marines. "We had just been trying to hurt these guys, and now I'm patching them up," he said. "It's a weird conundrum."

CHAPTER 5

Winning the Hearts of the Iraqi People

The Marines demonstrated their military superiority repeatedly on the road to Baghdad, decisively winning every battle along the way. But they had mixed success in another mission—winning the hearts of the Iraqi people.

From the viewpoint of Iraqi civilians, the Marine convoy must have been terrifying—gigantic war machines bristling with futuristic weapons, and Marines so heavily armed that they must have looked like monsters from another world.

The trepidation was mutual because the Marines had learned never to let down their guard. The battalion was ambushed frequently, and some of the attackers wore civilian clothing. Some of those were probably conscripts, but others were Iraqi troops in disguise.

A maxim often attributed to General James Mattis, commanding officer of the First Marine Division in 2003, succinctly expresses the Marines' hypervigilant state of mind: "Be polite, be professional, but have a plan to kill everybody you meet." It's a popular saying, found on tee shirts available on-line, and even on some Marines' business cards.

But while it was necessary to be vigilant, and to fight with a vengeance, the Marines had another, very different, official role. As decreed by President Bush, a major purpose of the war was to free the Iraqi people from the rule of a brutal dictator. And that role became even more central to the military's mission after it became clear that Saddam Hussein did not possess weapons of mass destruction.

Some Marines I spoke with had little interest in getting to know the Iraqi people. They were there to fight and win a war. Period. But for others—especially the senior officers—helping the Iraqi people was a big part of why they were there. Sometimes the battalion went out of its way to create opportunities to get to know the Iraqi people, and to try to convince them that they were there to help.

One such event occurred in the town of Ash Shumali, about a hundred miles from Baghdad, on April 1, 2003. Before dawn, some of the battalion's hospital corpsmen and a small group of Marines loaded large amounts of supplies into a small convoy for what they described as a "humanitarian mission."

I rode to the event with Commanding Officer Sam Mundy, who told me he didn't know what to expect. The plan was to quote, "win over the hearts and minds of the Iraqis" with food, medicine, and kindness. But they were also prepared for battle, just in case, with about a hundred heavily armed Marines who went along for the ride.

As we arrived in the small town it was obvious from the facial expressions and body language of the Iraqis that they were terrified. Through an interpreter, townspeople explained to the Marines that officials of Saddam's Baath Party, who had left the area a few hours earlier, had told them that the Americans would kill all males between the ages of 18 and 40.

After Mundy explained through an interpreter that they were there to offer food and medical aid, the Iraqis seemed immensely relieved. The Marines set up an area for the Navy docs to treat patients and saw between 200 and 300 Iraqis, most of whom had relatively minor problems such as skin or eye infections. One good sign: among the patients there were no signs of any recent war injuries. The Marines also distributed boxes of food. "The people seem to be happy that we are here," Mundy told me during the event. "The kids are smiling and running around looking for candy."

In quiet moments between battles, many Marines also made individual efforts to connect with, and ease the fears of, Iraqi civilians. Some Marines humanized themselves to Iraqis they met, by showing photos of their families. Others took off their helmets and said greetings in rudimentary

Arabic. Some threw MREs to Iraqis who signaled that they were hungry as we rolled by.

One heartwarming moment involved Sergeant Joe Harris. It happened after a quick, relatively easy battle in a small town. After the fight, Harris and a group of Marines walked through the town looking for any remaining Iraqi fighters. They were heavily armed, dirty, sweaty, and a little bloody. It was a Shiite city, which means the people were almost surely not supporters of Saddam Hussein who was a Sunni. The men the Marines had been fighting earlier almost surely did not live in this village. They were most likely Iraqi soldiers from Baghdad or Sunni cities farther to the north.

As Harris and his squad patrolled the town they encountered an Iraqi couple with young children who hesitantly approached them and offered food and water. The Marines were also hesitant because they—as always—had their guard up. The father was holding a baby about six months old and indicated to Harris that he wanted him to hold the baby. While telling the story to me, Harris became very emotional. "I took the baby, I held the baby, and I kissed the baby," Harris said. "I think the father was showing us that he trusted us. If he was willing to let me hold his infant child, then surely, we could trust him enough to drink his water."

For Harris, it was one of the defining moments of the war. "I've got to believe we helped that guy," Harris concluded. "And so, when people ask me if the war was the right thing to do, I don't know. But I know that we did help a lot of people while we were there."

After telling me the story, Harris wiped his eyes and mentioned that he's been thinking about the war a lot more lately. "I think about it every day. And we're hard on ourselves as Marines. I think one reason that I didn't reach out for more assistance when I came home and was feeling like I was walking around on Mars, was because even though this was major combat, it wasn't D-Day. We didn't storm Normandy. So, we're always trying to convince ourselves that it was worthwhile."

During our interview, Private First Class Ben Putnam recalled how grateful the Iraqi people were to the Marines. "In almost every town that we visited," Putnam told me, "we were treated like their liberators.

The families would come out. They'd offer date cakes. And nothing was poisoned. They'd bring us food. They'd say thank you. We felt like we were there for them, for the right reasons."

Putnam described a time in the city of Al Diwaniya when an Iraqi man approached him with tears in his eyes. "Tell your commander that I say thank you," the man said through an interpreter. "I've not been able to sleep at night, afraid that Saddam's men will come and take me or take my children."

"This grown man was just sobbing," Putnam said, "because for the first time that he can remember he's able to get a night's sleep, and I don't think any of the aftermath of the war can take that away."

CHAPTER 6

Arrival in Baghdad

A Surprisingly Warm Welcome

At dawn on the morning of April 8, 2003, with the battalion bivouacked on the outskirts of Baghdad, I took a walk around camp to get a sense of the mood. There was a palpable feeling of anticipation, and vigilance was high—but apparently not high enough.

Walking by a small crowd of Marines I heard Sergeant Major Joe Vines giving them a piece of his mind. Physically imposing, with a rich baritone voice, he had an acute knack for keeping Marines' attention. He was telling them how disappointed he was that the overnight watch had not been sufficient because there had been gaps in the 360-degree perimeter that Marines always establish around camp. Judging from the looks on the Marines' faces, I was sure it wouldn't happen again.

Later that day news came that a surveillance aircraft had spotted about a thousand Iraqi fighters gathering in a nearby field. The Marines dispatched Cobra helicopters and sent a column of military vehicles—only to discover that the Iraqis were all civilians and had gathered to show their support for the Americans. They were giving the "thumbs up" sign and shouting "Welcome Americans!"

As the convoy slowly rolled toward Baghdad that day there was no resistance. I had been told by 3/5's senior officers that they had planned to raid a series of buildings, but the engagement was canceled because the Iraqi soldiers had disappeared overnight. All along the road there were Iraqi positions that had been hurriedly abandoned. Many of their supplies had been left behind. Before scurrying away the Iraqis had burned some of their encampments, including tanks and armored personnel carriers.

There was one remaining barrier on the road to Baghdad—the Diyala River. Marine Corps engineers constructed a pontoon bridge strong enough to allow tanks to roll over it. Some of the Amphibious Assault Vehicles crossed the river in the way that they were designed—like boats. According to the First Marine Division's official history, an Iraqi prisoner said: "When we saw the tanks floating across the river, we knew we could not win against the Americans."

On April 10, 2003, 3d Battalion, 5th Marines entered Baghdad and went directly to Sadr City, a massive public housing project. The approximately one million people in this area belong to the Shiite branch of Islam and had been treated poorly, often brutally, by the Sunni government of Saddam Hussein. Just days before we arrived, local officials had unofficially changed the name from Saddam City to Sadr City, in honor of a Shiite leader widely believed to have been assassinated on Saddam's order in 1999.

When the Marine convoy pulled into the wretched area, the stench was overwhelming. It reeked of garbage and sewage. But the Marines hardly noticed because there was something else that grabbed their attention: a couple of hundred Iraqi men, women, and children lined the street cheering their arrival, with many chanting "we love America!" and "we love Bush!"

Always on alert to danger, the Marines reacted cautiously at first. But gradually they exited their vehicles to greet some of the Iraqi men, who then introduced them to their families. Several Marines shared photos of their families. Parents seemed unconcerned that their children were splashing through a stream of raw sewage trickling down a shallow trench between the two groups.

Some skeptical Marines later hypothesized that they had been welcomed so warmly because the Shiites hoped the Americans—their new conquerors—would treat them better than Saddam had. Other Marines wondered if the joyous reception was due to a simple calculation made by the Iraqis: they were less likely to be shot if they welcomed the Americans with open arms.

Whatever the truth, the Marines were aware that this was only a tiny portion of the population of Sadr City, that guns were plentiful here, and that hostility to their presence would soon surface.

A Suicide Bomber and a Sign of Things to Come

In the early evening of April 10, the day we arrived in Baghdad, my crew and I received the news that our time as embedded journalists was about to end. NBC News wanted us to join the massive media presence at the Palestine Hotel in Baghdad, where we would be available 24/7 for live reports—something that wasn't possible while traveling with the Marines.

I was reluctant to leave our battalion, in part because I had so enjoyed living with—and living like—Marines. My hesitation about leaving was also due to the fact that the story was all ours—there was no competition. We were the only TV journalists embedded with 3/5 (though there were two top-notch journalists from the *Baltimore Sun* newspaper, reporter John Murphy and photographer John Makely.)

We had no choice, though. NBC told us to join the media horde as soon as possible. On the positive side, it meant that for the first time in six weeks I would be able to take a shower, sleep in a bed, and do laundry. My producer John, cameraman Klimo, and satellite technician Rob were also looking forward to eating something other than MREs, though, strange as it may seem, I was still perfectly happy on an MRE diet. We would soon discover that the hotel was in bad shape, to say the least. There was only a trickle of running water, very spotty electricity, and the bed was even filthier than my sleeping bag, so I slept on the floor.

To get us to the hotel in the extremely dangerous city of Baghdad, the Marines organized an armed convoy of three or four Humvees, and a truck to carry our equipment. After saying our goodbyes, we set out on the eight-mile drive to the Palestine Hotel, which was a short walk from Firdos Square, where the infamous statue of Saddam Hussein had been torn down the day before.

After traveling a short distance, we approached a checkpoint controlled by Marines from our battalion. While waiting in line behind several vehicles I was writing in my notebook when I saw a flash of light out of the corner of my eye. I was in the cab of the truck, so I had an elevated view of the scene. The Marines who had been standing while inspecting Iraqi vehicles were now all lying down. I was confused—until one of them struggled to his feet and shouted: "Suicide bomber! Suicide bomber!"

An Iraqi taxi driver had exited his car, walked to the checkpoint, and blown himself up. Four Marines were wounded. Fortunately, no one was killed except the bomber. One Marine officer, clearly enraged, started screaming at the drivers in our convoy to get moving. When Klimo jumped out of his vehicle and started to put his camera on his shoulder, the officer screamed: "Put that fucking camera down!" It's the only time I can remember that we were barred from covering a story by anyone in 3/5. The scene was so chaotic, and our Marine drivers hit the gas so quickly, we had no chance to object.

Two days later I reported on the discovery of a large cache of suicide bomb vests in Baghdad. Up to that point, suicide bombings had been rare, but together with roadside bombs (otherwise known as improvised explosive devices, or IEDs), they would soon become the weapons of choice of America's enemies in Iraq.

A Late-Night Ambush Takes the Lives of Two Marines

The day after 3/5 arrived in Baghdad a platoon of about 25 Marines set out on a night patrol in Sadr City. Heavily armed, the platoon was sending a message that American forces were now in control.

As the patrol departed the command post, Corporal Jason Arellano remembers it being so dark that he thought the power grid must have gone off-line—if this impoverished slum even had a functioning power grid. The Marines were wearing night-vision goggles, making the world around them appear grainy, green, and surreal.

Corporal Wale Akintunde remembers having a bad feeling from the moment the patrol began. "I'm not normally superstitious," he told me. "But the beginning of this patrol was the first time in Iraq that I saw a black cat. I just didn't have a good feeling."

Corporal Rob Witt remembers how eerily quiet it was. The Marines' steps echoed through the empty streets. Suddenly, a red flare, or perhaps red tracer fire (Marines disagree on this point), lit the sky nearby. Then another. And another. Arellano says the red flashes appeared to be coming from an alley running parallel to the street they were patrolling. "We determined that they were tracking our movement and messaging that to others," Arellano told me. "It was really weird," said Witt. "It felt like we were being stalked."

The Marines were in two columns, one on the left side of the street, the other on the right. As they approached an intersection the Marine in the lead spotted a man around the corner who appeared to be armed. He tried to question the man in basic Arabic, but he did not respond.

Arellano and his squad leader, Sergeant Elber Navarro, went around the corner and tackled the man. "We couldn't play games at this moment," Arellano later told me. They found a gun in the man's waistband and confiscated it. Two more Marines, including Staff Sergeant Riayan Tejeda, came around the corner and asked what they had found. Navarro handed him the pistol. At that moment the Iraqi, still on the ground, shouted something in Arabic.

In an instant the quiet night erupted into ear-splitting chaos. The Marines hit the ground as a fusillade of bullets seemed to come from all directions. There was so much red tracer fire that Witt thought it looked like a *Star Wars* movie. "It was nonstop chaos," he says. Marines on the left side of the street returned fire in the direction of muzzle flashes behind a metal fence. Enemy fire also seemed to be coming from an open field to the right, but returning fire in that direction—toward the other column of Marines—was not an option.

Arellano and Witt took cover behind a brick column and fired down an alleyway where enemy shooters were hiding. An Iraqi returned fire with an RPG that went between them, missing both Marines by inches, and exploded against a building across the street. The light was so bright that their night-vision goggles momentarily blacked out.

Lieutenant Mike Prato, the platoon commander, says the Iraqis "just unloaded from almost point-blank range. We hit the ground and they were basically shooting over us. It felt like 20 minutes, but really it was just seconds. I felt like I was going to die." He remembers praying: "Let me die well." If it was his moment, he wanted to die like a Marine.

Prato saw Staff Sergeant Tejeda hit the dirt. He thought for a second that he was taking cover, but quickly realized Tejeda had been shot. He grabbed his radio and called for a medevac helicopter as other Marines rushed to the fallen Marine.

Amid the chaos, Sergeant Navarro ordered Corporal Witt and his four-man team to establish a safe landing zone for the medevac helicopter. Witt stationed his men and popped flares to light the area so they could see if enemy fighters were still close by. "The experience of waiting for a medevac while you have a Marine that's badly wounded is a horrible feeling," Witt told me. "It's a feeling of having no control. You never know when it will arrive." The helicopters took what felt like an eternity to arrive, Witt said. They had been delayed because the Marines were in a "hot" zone, and officers in charge of the helicopters feared they might be shot down when they tried to land.

During this excruciating wait, Witt became aware that a second Marine had been shot—Lance Corporal David Owens. He saw a group of Marines carry him to a less-exposed location where he could hear them desperately performing CPR.

At the same time another team was working on Tejeda. Two or three Marines took turns sucking the blood out of his mouth to try to clear an airway, while Navy corpsmen worked frantically to stop the bleeding from the gunshot wounds. Prato says they did everything possible, but despite extraordinary efforts they were unable to save him.

Corporal Akintunde had been toward the rear of his squad when the shooting began. He ran forward to join the fight and saw an unmanned M249 SAW machine gun on the ground. He laid down and used it to return fire. As he pressed his face against the weapon to aim, he felt something wet and tasted blood. He then noticed that he was lying in a pool of blood. The gun—and the blood—he suddenly realized, belonged to his good friend and former roommate, David Owens.

The medevac helicopters finally arrived. Marines hurried over, carrying Tejeda and Owens, and placed them on board. Tejeda had already died but medics were still working on Owens, who succumbed to his injuries the following day.

After the helicopter left, all became quiet again. There was nothing to do but complete the patrol and return to camp. Once back, Navarro recalls an emotional conversation with other Marines about what had happened and the loss of a much-loved brother-in-arms, possibly two. Akintunde remembers returning to camp, smoking several cigarettes alone, and crying about his friend Owens. Some Marines were so exhausted they managed to fall asleep. Others were awake all night, re-living the horror.

The next morning after a very brief ceremony for Tejeda and prayers for Owens who was still hanging on to life, it was back to work. "We were still in combat operations, so life goes on," Navarro told me years later, and repeated his lament that on the battlefield there is never enough time to mourn.

Several of the Marines involved in the short but deadly ambush of April 11 were deeply affected by the loss of their two fellow Marines. Some suffer from survivor's guilt; others still have nightmares. Several say it was a significant factor in their later diagnoses of PTSD.

Almost twenty years later, Akintunde told me he still suffers from survivor's guilt over the death of his friend David Owens. When I asked why, he became noticeably emotional. After a long pause he told a story that has tormented him ever since. It began with a personality conflict with someone in his unit—someone other than Owens. When Akintunde complained about it, his superior officer told him to switch positions with Owens who got along with everyone. Akintunde said his guilt stems from the fact that if he hadn't complained, he would have been the one behind that machine gun. "The guilt of knowing that he died, and he took my spot, that's what I struggle with," Akintunde said.

As I've discovered many times while writing this book, some Marines who lose friends in battle spend years, sometimes the rest of their lives, blaming themselves for the deaths of their Marine brothers, even when the rationale for the blame is farfetched. In truth, there are so many constantly changing factors in battle that it's almost impossible to pin blame. Enemy fighters killed Owens, not Akintunde. But it's a sad consequence of war that survivor's guilt is so common, even when it doesn't make rational sense.

Akintunde has never been diagnosed with PTSD and says his stress symptoms are not debilitating. When he watches military movies he thinks about that night, as he does on the anniversary of Owens' death. As is true for most of the Marines I've interviewed, he was hypervigilant when he came home from Iraq—for example, always facing the door in restaurants or bars, analyzing everyone who enters, and knowing where the exits are.

He sought help but was unsuccessful. "I wanted to see a therapist," he says. "But their solution was drugs, and I don't particularly care for drugs." Akintunde wanted to talk about what was bothering him, but the therapist didn't seem interested in talking. "If all you're going to do is prescribe me drugs," he said, "then I guess I'll figure this out of my own."

"The way that I deal with stuff is just reaching out to friends," he says now, especially his Marine friends, "We went through the same stuff. Talking to them has gotten me through the stuff I have issues with."

He didn't have as hard a time as some Marines because his small group of friends understood him. "People knew that if I wanted to be left alone, they left me alone," he told me. "When I wanted to talk, we'd talk. And if I got drunk and wandered off, they'd keep an eye on me and let me be."

The loss of Tejeda and Owens on April 11 and 12 deeply affected several of their fellow Marines, including Lieutenant Mike Prato, the senior officer on that night patrol, Sergeant Elber Navarro, a squad leader, and Lance Corporal Jason Arellano. Their stories are told later in this book.

Part Two

Twenty Years Later

CHAPTER 7

Consequences of Being "Trained to Kill"

While the Marines of 3/5 waited impatiently in Kuwait for the order that would send them storming into Iraq, I passed the time in conversation with dozens of them. Common topics included their gung-ho eagerness to put their training to the test on the battlefield; their hope for a quick and decisive victory so they could get back home to their families; and the paramount importance of keeping their fellow Marines safe so they could all return home in one piece.

Another topic that sometimes came up was the likelihood that it would be necessary for them to kill people. Some shared that they were not particularly looking forward to that, while others said they could hardly wait. I vividly remember one Marine, a diminutive 18-year-old Private First Class, who told me he had been bullied and teased about his size by his older brothers, even his mother, while growing up. He also told me, and anyone else who would listen: "I just want to shoot someone when I get to Iraq."

His dream, he said, was to kill someone in battle and then write home to his family and tell them all about it. He thought they would finally have no choice but to show him some respect. His senior officer, a young corporal, grew tired of hearing him talk about it and told him to keep it to himself, adding that he would be fortunate *not* to have to kill anyone.

I spent only two days with this platoon and did not come across that PFC again, so I don't know how he fared in battle. But 3/5 Marines killed so many enemy fighters on the way to Baghdad that it's likely he got his wish.

Shortly before the ground war began a senior Marine officer from another battalion was quoted in news reports as saying: "We're building them up to the point where they are emotionally ready to kill," a comment that caught me by surprise. It never occurred to me that getting Marines "emotionally ready to kill" would be part of their training.

I was also surprised the first time I heard a group of Marines walking to the chow tent in Kuwait while chanting "kill, kill, kill ... kill, kill, kill ... kill, kill, kill ..."

I asked several Marines about it, and soon understood how naïve I had been. If warriors are hesitant to kill the enemy, they're more likely to be killed themselves, and are therefore more likely to be on the losing side in combat. Training Marines to kill, to want to kill, to be eager to kill, is necessary if victory in battle is the goal.

Sergeant Joe Harris

> I'm a perfect example of it, they can take a young man from a middle-class family who has never experienced any real tragedy, never hurt anyone, never been in violent conflicts, and train them to be very efficient killers.

The Marine who most clearly explained to me the concept of being "trained to kill" is Sergeant Joe Harris, who had never even seen a dead body before he went to Iraq. A muscular guy with a V-shaped body and a bristly V-shaped beard, he's with the Austin, Texas Police Department, but looks like he should be playing linebacker in the NFL.

During our Zoom call he gave this eloquent explanation of what "training to kill" is all about:

> It is probably what the Marine Corps does better than any branch of the military in the world. When we crested that berm (on March 25) and there were dead bodies everywhere, I didn't feel anything. I felt like I was doing my job.
>
> The Marine Corps, and I think I'm a perfect example of it, they can take a young man from a middle-class family who has never experienced any real tragedy, never hurt anyone, never been in violent conflicts, and train them to be very efficient killers, doing bad things to bad people.
>
> They don't want a sociopath or a psychopath. But they take young men like Joe Harris and make him an efficient killer, while making sure he can deal with it physically and mentally.

> It starts with day one in the Marine Corps. All the training is centered around killing, especially for the infantry. There's a reason you sing songs about combat, and about killing. They're just normalizing the thought for you.
>
> We'd end a lot of exercises by chanting, kill, kill, kill, kill this, kill that, kill this. So, from everything they do emotionally and physically, they're getting you prepared for combat and prepared for war. They want you to be able to pull the trigger. I went through it. And I know that when the time came, we were jumping out of our skin to do it. I mean, we fought with passion and zeal.

Harris told me the training worked—he never hesitated to shoot. "We were taking care of business," he said.

First Lieutenant Brian Chontosh, Navy Cross Recipient

> Killing is ugly, it's violent, it's disgusting. I wish it wasn't part of what we had to do.

On March 25, 2003, moments after leading the bloody charge that earned him the Navy Cross, Lieutenant Brian Chontosh learned that his team's radioman, Ken Korte, had taken two enemy prisoners of war (EPWs) into custody back at the team's Humvee. The two Iraqis had been in the Iraqi machine gun nest that Thomas Franklin had silenced with his .50 caliber machine gun. Somehow they survived, and surrendered to Korte while the other members of Team Chontosh were clearing the trench. "EPWs from where?" Chontosh says he angrily replied when he heard about them. "We're not taking prisoners right now. We're fucking killing people."

He says he was so emotionally charged with adrenalin, and so filled with anger and hate because of the death of Doc Johnson and the injuries to Lance Corporal Quintero, that his visceral instinct at that moment was to shoot the two EPWs when he got back to the Humvee. But by the time he returned, his common sense had also returned. "A well-trained individual, with sound values in his heart," he later told me, "will return to a rational and focused frame of mind."

Shooting the two EPWs, he said, would have been a horrible idea, for two reasons. First, one of the prisoners was a regional commander who, under questioning, confessed that Iraqi fighters were being housed at a soccer stadium in nearby Al Diwaniya. Within minutes the Marines launched an attack, Chontosh says, and "blew the shit out of the stadium."

The second reason it would have been abhorrent to shoot them, the lieutenant said, is that he "could be in jail" if he had shot two unarmed prisoners. In the heat of the moment, he wanted to kill them. And then reason quickly set in. "That's not killing, it's murder," he said. "That's not how we're trained and it's not how Marines believe themselves to be. Honor above all," he added.

The retired Marine says today he's not proud to have had those thoughts, and says they have "plagued my memories of that moment ever since." But he also says he understands that such emotional reactions reflect "the truth of the infinite possibilities of the horrors of combat."

Following the March 25 battle in the trench, Lance Corporal Robert Kerman told Chontosh that he thought what they had done was "really cool." Chontosh sharply disagreed. "No, that wasn't cool." Kerman recalls Chontosh lecturing him. "That sucked. We killed them. We did our job." Chontosh was telling him, Kerman told me later, that there's no glory in killing.

If that was the first time Chontosh expressed that opinion, it certainly wasn't the last. On numerous occasions since then he has made clear that killing in combat is a necessary evil, not something desirable, or "cool."

For his book *The Kill Switch*, author Phil Zabriskie interviewed Chontosh about the March 25 battle and his later combat experiences. He told Zabriskie that at the time he "wasn't thinking in depth about what it meant to take another human being's life."

But since then, he's done a lot of thinking about it. "Killing is ugly, it's violent, it's disgusting. I wish it wasn't part of what we had to do," Chontosh told Zabriskie, continuing: "In the moment yeah, maybe you think you enjoy it, the excitement. But as the tempo slows down, a maturity kicks in. Yeah, I didn't really enjoy taking your life, seeing you die. I didn't really enjoy that."

Sergeant Nathaniel Donnelly

They were zealots. They believed in the cause. I had no problem killing them.

Nathaniel Donnelly says he was born to be a warrior. That is why, he believes, he has no negative feelings whatsoever about killing enemy fighters. It's in his DNA. He killed an Iraqi political officer, one of Saddam's henchmen, in the first firefight in 2003, and was so pleased he kept his helmet as a war trophy.

Donnelly was also proud to kill numerous Fedayeen fighters who, according to several Marines, were to Saddam what the Gestapo was to Hitler. Donnelly says he knows from personal experience that they were well-paid zealots and drug addicts, as evidenced by the wads of cash and bottles of drugs he found in their pockets after killing them.

But he makes one exception to his positive feelings about killing enemy fighters. He says he took no joy in shooting conscripts, many of whom were on the battlefield only because Saddam's henchmen told them that if they didn't fight, they and their families would be killed. Conscripts could be identified by their civilian clothes and their frightened, tentative behavior in battle. "I remember wounding a couple of guys who were conscripts," Donnelly told me. "I was relieved that they didn't die."

Sergeant Colin Keefe

> The mother of someone I killed probably has a picture of him on her mantel, and she might have looked at it yesterday and felt sad. So, it is still happening in a way, and that troubles me.

Sergeant Colin Keefe's reaction to combat and killing has changed over time. "I remember being more exhilarated at the beginning and then the stress building over time," he told me. At the root of his stress, he said, was "empathy for the guys on the other side."

The 2003 invasion of Iraq was, as it was for almost everyone in 3/5, Keefe's first time in combat. "There was a certain level at which I certainly enjoyed it at the time," he told me two decades later. "We were generally beating the stuffing out of the guys we were fighting. It was a culmination of years of training." His specialty in Iraq was shooting a Mark 19 automatic grenade launcher. "There's an element to that which is just inherently fun," he said.

Keefe had a close call in the same ferocious battle that claimed the life of Corporal Erik Silva on April 4. They were closing in on Baghdad when hundreds of Iraqi troops flooded into the road a good distance ahead. Keefe immediately fired his grenade launcher, which was mounted on a Humvee and had a range of more than a mile.

Suddenly, seven Iraqis emerged from a canal about ten feet ahead, too close for the grenade launcher to be effective. His driver sped backward about 20 feet, and Keefe opened fire. He then exited the truck with his rifle and quickly flanked the Iraqi position. As the dust from his grenade launcher cleared, he saw an Iraqi aiming directly at him. Keefe and the Iraqi opened fire simultaneously. The Iraqi was killed. Keefe was not hit. Of the seven Iraqis in the trench, all but one had been killed. One of the dead was the lone survivor's younger brother. "He was very upset, as one can imagine, and that sticks with me," Keefe said.

Keefe has thought a lot about the war in the years since, and the people he killed, and has doubts about whether all the death and destruction were warranted:

> I certainly do feel empathy for the guys on the other side. It was a war that was somewhere between blatantly unjustified and thinly justified. And these guys [Iraqi fighters]were kids. They were younger than us a lot of the time. They were just defending their country from an invader. It's not like they were invading a foreign country. We were invading a foreign country. They were defending their homes.

Keefe told me that almost twenty years later he still feels remorse. He wonders about the families of the men he killed, and if the men had wives and children. "The mother of someone I killed probably has a picture of him on her mantel, and she might have looked at it yesterday and felt sad. So, it is still happening in a way, and that troubles me."

His feelings are not debilitating in any way. He's "generally fine" so long as he avoids certain TV shows and movies. For example, his wife watches *Criminal Minds*—a TV drama about FBI profilers who track down psychologically twisted perpetrators—but he can't watch it, or anything else that "realistically depicts the emotional aftereffects of violence."

He once attended a group therapy session, but mostly has dealt with his stress issues on his own. "I have a mutual non-aggression pact with my demons," he said. "I don't bother them, and they don't bother me."

Lance Corporal Robert Kerman, Silver Star Recipient

> You don't kill people, and then the next day you're just fine. It does have second and third order effects on your mentality.

The Presidential Citation for Robert Kerman's Silver Star states that he "exhibited exceptional bravery" on March 25, 2003, as he and Team Chontosh helped turn an Iraqi ambush into a quick American victory. "As enemy soldiers fired at him," the citation continues, "he fearlessly plunged towards them firing his M-16 with lethal accuracy." Kerman estimates that he killed ten or more men in a matter of minutes.

As someone who had been trained to kill, Kerman says: "That was my job. I did it without questioning. And I thought it was really cool at the time." When Brian Chontosh made clear to him that there's no glory in killing, "It was lost on me at the time," Kerman says.

Over the years, Kerman's tone has changed: "You don't kill people, and then the next day you're just fine. It does have second and third order effects on your mentality. Don't get me wrong, I would do it again because that's what the job requires. And if it's not them it's me, or people around me. But it's hard to swallow."

"When you personalize things, none of us are ready to kill," Kerman says. "It's not human. We're born sinners, don't get me wrong. But in the meantime, there's regret."

Lance Corporal Joe Perez, Navy Cross Recipient

> I don't think it's natural for guys to kill other people.

Joe Perez's Navy Cross citation says he "led the charge down a trench destroying the enemy," then "threw a grenade into a trench that the enemy was occupying," and "fired an AT-4 rocket into a machine-gun bunker, completely destroying it and killing four enemy personnel."

What allowed him to kill so efficiently, he says, was not a desire to kill, but his training. "The Marine Corps does a really good job of hammering home the basics and the fundamentals. And I think that bears out in combat because those are the things that you fall back on whenever you get stressed out, whenever you're in tight situations. It all just kind of comes together."

"I don't think it's natural for guys to kill other people," he says. "It's just not a normal thing." But the training allows Marines to overcome their natural reticence.

In 2004, during Perez's second deployment with 3/5 in Iraq, he remembers the commanding officer, Colonel Patrick Malay, giving the Marines some words of wisdom before entering the violent hotbed of Falluja: "I want you guys to be killers, not murderers."

"Man, that still sticks with me today," Perez says. "It's the difference between a killer, someone who can kill to accomplish the mission or to preserve life, versus someone who commits war crimes, or kills people just for the sake of killing people."

Lieutenant Mike Prato

There was a hesitation there. I think more from a perspective of being a Christian, to be honest. You're about to kill somebody.

In March 2003 I interviewed Mike Prato while the battalion was camping in northern Kuwait, shortly before crossing the border into Iraq. As commander of Second Platoon, Kilo Company, he had the responsibility of getting his young Marines ready for war. In the interview he delivered this made-for-TV soundbite that I used in that night's story on NBC Nightly News: "We're training them to find the bad guys and kill them. There's no nice way to say that."

When I interviewed Prato again, nearly twenty years later, he told me that the men under his command had been extremely successful at finding and killing bad guys. Prato was, once again, extremely blunt on the matter of killing: "I love fucking killing bad guys," he told me. "I'm not going to lie. It's the only thing I was ever good at. I say this with no ego. The only thing in my life I've ever really been good at is finding and killing the enemy."

Prato agrees that it takes special training to make most people want to kill. Most humans today, he says, are not part of a "warrior society" as they were eons ago when death and killing were a part of everyday life, and it was kill or be killed. "There's definitely a switch that needs to be pulled when humans today—most humans, normal people—take life," he says. Marine Corps training is part of what pulls that switch he says, but "your responsibility to the man next to you is really what allows you to do that. Because if you don't, their life is at risk."

But I was surprised when he described his role in all that killing. He told me he drew his weapon only one time in the entire 2003 deployment. As an officer, his job was to command his Marines in battle, not to pull the trigger. "Even in those ambushes where I could see the enemy straight in front of me, only one time," he says. His memory of that one time is vivid. They were clearing the town of Aziziya, about 55 miles from Baghdad on the Tigris River. They were "looking for bad guys" and spotted a platoon of Iraqi Republican Guard troops dug in by the side of the road about 50 yards ahead.

Prato yelled an order to the heavy machine gunner in the turret of his Amtrac to suppress them with fire, giving his men a chance to exit the vehicle and prepare to engage on foot. But the machine gun jammed, a victim of the sand and dirt in the desert air. Prato saw that an Iraqi was preparing to fire an RPG at his men as they exited the Amtrac. He grabbed his rifle, aimed, fired, and saw the Iraqi fall back into his spider hole.

Years later, though, he remembers that he hesitated. "I was about to take a life, and that was the only time I ever put my sights on another human being and pulled the trigger," he says. "There was a hesitation there. I think more from the perspective of being a Christian, to be honest. You're about to kill somebody."

Under his command, he says, his men killed "a whole bunch" of Iraqis. "I gave the orders. If I saw enemy, I said yes, kill them," he says, "and it became very natural. Sometimes with a cup of coffee in my hand."

For the most part, commissioned officers such as lieutenants, captains, majors, and colonels, rarely fire their weapons. Their job is to find the enemy, deploy their men to the optimal position, and decide when and how to attack. Of course, there are exceptions, like Navy Cross recipient First Lieutenant Brian Chontosh, who was both an officer and a trigger puller. But for Prato and most other commissioned officers, the job was to make decisions and communicate those decisions to their men, not to participate in the shooting.

If he had made a habit of firing at the enemy—except when necessary—it would have detracted from his ability to effectively command his troops, he says. And that could put everyone in danger. Prato was not worried about getting the Marines under his command to pull the trigger. The training worked—they did not hesitate. "They could turn that on very easily," he says.

After the fall of Baghdad, however, the rules of engagement (ROE) changed, and Prato became concerned about something else: after he had helped teach them to kill the enemy without hesitation, he now had to teach them to dial it down—and sometimes not to shoot at all.

During the march to Baghdad, the Marines were operating under rules authorizing them to shoot anyone in an enemy uniform or brandishing a weapon. But later, the rules of engagement changed to SAS—Stability and Support operations—in which the authorization to shoot was significantly curtailed.

As an example of how difficult it was for his men to dial it down during SAS, Prato told me about an incident in the middle of the night in which he and his Marines came across a group of Iraqis carrying AK-47s.

"My guys wanted to mow them down, all forty or fifty of them," Prato told me. "And I had to have the judgment to say 'No, guys, this isn't one where you pull the trigger,' because that would have been a slaughter. By the new ROE standards, we could no longer call them hostile and just kill them," Prato says. "The guys did very well with the changes, not pulling the trigger when they shouldn't, and I was very proud of them."

Corporal Jeremy Thomas

> It was just part of the job of being an Infantry Marine. When the killing happened, it was like training, just a task to get done.

If one goal of Marine Corps senior officers is to make men under their command "emotionally ready to kill," they clearly succeeded with

Corporal Jeremy Thomas. "I have no emotions tied to killing Iraqis," he says. "It was just part of the job of being an Infantry Marine. When the killing happened, it was like training, just a task to get done."

He doesn't like to talk about Iraq with friends and family anymore because they don't react well when he says how he feels. "I tell them it is nothing like movies and it is pretty boring, really. They ask me what it is like to kill someone, and I tell them it is just like shooting a target, but the target is a person who is now shot and either dies or will die soon." Killing in war, he says, is "banal."

On the other hand, he says: "I have never owned a gun and will never own a gun because I have seen what a gun can do, and I don't ever plan on killing anything ever again. There is absolutely no glory in war or killing."

CHAPTER 8

Post-Traumatic Stress Disorder and Post-Traumatic Growth

Post-Traumatic Stress Disorder (PTSD)

Navy Cross recipient Brian Chontosh retired as a major in 2013 after 21 years in uniform. His passion for aiding his fellow Marines led him to create the Big Fish Foundation, which helps veterans and law enforcement officers suffering from stress and trauma related to their service. The name comes from his Marine call sign, "Big Fish."

Through the work of his foundation, he has learned how unpredictable PTSD can be. Two Marines (or soldiers, or police officers) can experience the same event and one might be traumatized while the other is barely affected. "Everyone is calibrated differently," he says. "Everybody's stress thermometer is graduated in different increments."

One factor in that calibration, according to many Marines I've interviewed, is age. Marines who were in their teens or very early twenties when they were in combat seem to be affected the most. Barely out of high school, their brains were still developing, and they didn't have the life experience that older Marines had.

The youngest Marines are also more likely to be on the front lines. They do most of the shooting and killing, are most likely to be seriously injured, and most likely to see fellow Marines killed in action—all of which can contribute to PTSD. However, as I discovered, Marines who are in older age groups can also fall prey to PTSD.

I was initially surprised at how willing—even eager—Marines who have been diagnosed with PTSD were to talk about it. But it didn't take long to figure out that they found it therapeutic to talk—with therapists, fellow Marines, family, friends, even me.

On March 25, 2003, five days after roaring across the border into Iraq, the Marines of 3/5 engaged in their first major battle. It was the first real combat experience for almost all of them. Afterward, a young Marine who had been in the thick of it described it to me as "the adrenalin rush from hell." Little did he know then that, for many Marines, that adrenalin rush would endure for years to come.

Adrenalin is a stress hormone—a key element in the "fight or flight" reaction to danger. Dr. Bessel Van Der Kolk, in his best-selling book about trauma, *The Body Keeps the Score*, writes: "Under normal conditions people react to a threat with a temporary increase in their stress hormones. As soon as the threat is over, the hormones dissipate, and the body returns to normal. The stress hormones of traumatized people, in contrast, take much longer to return to baseline and spike quickly and disproportionately in response to mildly stressful stimuli. The insidious effects of constantly elevated stress hormones include memory and attention problems, irritability, and sleep disorders." Those are all common symptoms of PTSD. So are nightmares, sleeplessness, explosive anger, hyper-vigilance to danger, survivor's guilt, and depression.

One very common PTSD symptom was first explained to me by Colonel Craig Wonson. In 2003, as a major, he was 3/5's operations officer, and now teaches at the Naval War College. He did not suffer serious stress symptoms himself, but after 30-plus years working with, teaching and mentoring Marines and Sailors, he says many who struggle with stress can't stop thinking about the moment when a brother-in-arms was killed or seriously injured. They run it over in their minds constantly, tormenting themselves with thoughts that something they could have done might have saved their fellow Marine. "If you let it, it will eat you alive," he said. After he alerted me to that symptom, I noticed that Marines brought it up frequently in my interviews.

PTSD has been common among warriors throughout human history. Among the many examples of PTSD symptoms in ancient literature, the *Epic of Gilgamesh*, written in approximately 2100 BC, tells of Gilgamesh's torment and nightmares after witnessing the death of a close friend in battle. Written in the 8th century BC, Homer's epic poems *Odyssey* and *Iliad* contain detailed descriptions of the stress of combat, including survivor's guilt. And in 440 BC Herodotus wrote of an Athenian warrior who suddenly went blind after seeing a friend killed in battle.

Stress resulting from combat trauma has had numerous names over the centuries. In the 1600s in Europe the term "nostalgia" became a common diagnosis for soldiers suffering from symptoms such as anxiety, sleeplessness, and despair. "Nostalgia" had a lengthy run. The term was still being used during the American Civil War, when it was also called "feeble will," a condescending term that reflected the belief among many—including many doctors—that it was the result of personal weakness. In the years after the Civil War, veterans who had undergone extreme personality changes were described as having "soldier's heart."

During World War I the term "shell shock" was commonly used to describe symptoms now associated with PTSD, and in World War II the terms "battle fatigue" and "combat fatigue" were among several terms in widespread use.

In 1952, the American Psychiatric Association (APA) included the PTSD precursor "gross stress reaction" in the DSM-1, the first Diagnostic and Statistical Manual of Mental Disorders. Finally, in 1980, after much scientific study of trauma endured by groups including war veterans, sexual trauma victims and Holocaust survivors, the APA added Post-Traumatic Stress Disorder to the DSM-3.

Most of the Marines I interviewed for this book described some level of stress that they attributed, at least in part, to their combat experience. Quite a few had been diagnosed with PTSD, and most of those Marines did not object to that label and had no objection to talking about it. The experts who study trauma say PTSD has little, if anything, to do with weakness. This is how Dr. Van Der Kolk, the expert quoted earlier, puts it: "We now know that the behaviors of those with PTSD are not the result of moral failings or signs of lack of willpower or bad character—they are caused by actual changes in the brain."

But PTSD has a long history of controversy. Some of the Marines I interviewed were critical of the concept and how it has been diagnosed. Some Marines object to being told they have a "disorder" and prefer to use the term "post-traumatic stress" or PTS. Many said that medical professionals—especially in the early years of the wars in Afghanistan and Iraq—made diagnoses of PTSD too easily. Several Marines told me it was almost automatic in the early days of those wars that any admission of stress symptoms would lead to a diagnosis of PTSD.

It's not surprising that many Marines who experienced the chaos of combat later experienced at least some stress symptoms. The National Center for PTSD says that while events such as divorce, illness, a death in the family, or financial ruination, "might" be traumatic, depending on the circumstances, events such as severe war zone stress, torture, and rape are experienced as traumatic by nearly everyone who experiences them.

Many of the Marines I interviewed who experienced symptoms did not seek help at an early stage. Some waited five, ten, even fifteen years or more. Several said they didn't want to be "branded" with the stigma of PTSD while they were still on active duty, because it was seen as a sign of weakness and could harm their career or reputation. Some continued to resist seeking help long after they retired.

Post-Traumatic Growth (PTG)

After I decided to write this book, my first call was to Lieutenant General Sam Mundy, who had been commanding officer of 3/5 in 2003 as a lieutenant colonel. I had done numerous reports on various therapies for PTSD during my career as a TV news correspondent, and when I mentioned PTSD to Mundy, he encouraged me to look at the other side of the coin too—Post-Traumatic Growth, or PTG. After doing some research I was shocked that I had never heard of the concept. I wanted to kick myself for never having reported on it.

The theory was developed, and the term Post-Traumatic Growth was coined, by psychologists Richard Tedeschi and Lawrence Calhoun in the mid-1990s. As they consulted with trauma survivors, they were struck by how many had experienced positive changes such as a renewed appreciation for life, a newfound sense of purpose, greater inner strength, enhanced spirituality, stronger relationships with others, and a newfound desire to help other people.

PTG (like PTSD) has been around for as long as war and other traumatic human experiences have existed. There are numerous examples in ancient literature and religious tomes.

Over the past couple of decades, numerous books and articles have been written about PTG, some focusing on combat veterans, others dealing with such traumas as child and sexual abuse, violence and other forms of victimization, natural disasters, even divorce and family separations.

Any traumatic event can trigger post-traumatic stress. But getting through the long tunnel of PTS or PTSD all the way to PTG—the light at the end of the tunnel—is not easy. It does not happen automatically, the experts say. It requires effort, and it is rarely accomplished alone. It usually starts with a survivor's decision to communicate what's going on inside—with fellow Marines, with a spouse or other family member, or with a therapist. Tedeschi estimates that 30 to 70 percent of trauma survivors eventually experience at least one aspect of Post-Traumatic Growth.

For a deeper understanding of the concept of Post-Traumatic Growth, Brian Chontosh encouraged me to speak with Richard Goerling, a retired police lieutenant who spent 27 years in the U.S. Coast Guard Reserve.

Goerling founded a company called "Mindful Badge" which works mostly with first responders but has also worked with Chontosh and his Big Fish Foundation to help veterans dealing with stress and trauma. Goerling emphasizes that PTG does not happen passively—one must choose to take that path after a traumatic experience.

Humans have been going through terrible things throughout history, Goerling says, and there are countless examples of people working their way through deeply stressful or traumatic experiences and coming out on the other side wiser and healthier.

But he cautions that some therapy techniques don't work well with military and law enforcement personnel, many of whom are instantly put off by "the condescending, super-sensitive sing-songy voices" of people who may sound too eager to help. That is not a productive way to approach a Marine with PTSD. There's a much better chance of success, he says, if you approach it more like this:

> This is a predictable trauma injury. This is an injury. So, no shit, this is rough. But you've got to take action—with intervention—to move forward. It's a tough journey. It's your journey. You can do this. But it requires you to act. I'm here to support you in your actions. And as you move through this, you will find the possibility of coming through this stronger than when you started.

Most of the Marines I interviewed for this book had never heard the term "Post-Traumatic Growth" before, but after I explained the basic concept, many of them immediately recognized it as something they had experienced, and they were eager to share the ways in which they had grown because of their struggles with PTS or PTSD.

One perceptive Marine cut through all the medical jargon during our interview: "Isn't Post-Traumatic Growth just another name for 'what doesn't kill you makes you stronger?'" He was partially correct—but there's one big difference. "What doesn't kill you makes you stronger" just happens, while PTG takes sustained effort.

CHAPTER 9

Marines Tell Their Stories

Corporal Thomas "Tank" Franklin

> I've traveled a road that other people are starting to travel and they're looking for advice, how to get through to the other side.

Thomas "Tank" Franklin was the machine gunner in Brian Chontosh's Humvee when their team turned the tide in the battalion's first major battle on March 25, 2003. Armand McCormick, who drove the Humvee and received the Silver Star, says that if Franklin hadn't done such a spectacular job with the .50-caliber machine gun that day, they would all be dead. Franklin, McCormick insists, deserved the Silver Star just as much as he did. "Tank was underrated and unnoticed," McCormick says.

Franklin got the nickname "Tank" in boot camp. "I was one of the bigger guys and carried a lot of stuff," he says. "A lot of stuff" is probably a wild understatement. When I interviewed him he was in his late 40s and said he still squats about 455 pounds, and deadlifts about 550. He's a beast in the weight room, and on the battlefield, but face to face—at least on Zoom—he comes across as the gentlest of gentle giants.

Franklin spent a little more than four years in the Marines. He was scheduled to leave active duty in December 2002, but the Pentagon triggered the "stop-loss" clause in his contract, as it did with thousands of other Marines. His four-year term was extended because his services were needed in Iraq. He had no objection. He wanted to fight with his Marine brothers. "They couldn't have stopped me," he says.

Franklin and the other stop-loss Marines were sent home in May or June 2003, a few months ahead of the rest of the battalion. There was little opportunity to plan for what would come next. "When I first got out of the Marines, I didn't really know what to do," he told me. "Because there's not too many jobs out here for machine gunners."

When he applied to a south Florida fire department, though, he found his dream job. "I fell ass backwards into an amazing career working for a premiere fire department. I won the lottery," he says. "We were doing things in the street that they weren't even doing in ERs." He takes pride in the huge number of lives he and his colleagues saved during his 15 years with the department.

He was assigned to a very violent area, which made it a very stressful job. All that stress was piled on top of what he had already experienced in Iraq. "I went from war to looking at bodies again," he says. He and his fire department colleagues joked that it wasn't a full day until they had seen a dead body.

Soon after leaving the Marine Corps, he says, he started to realize that something was wrong. "I didn't realize I had PTSD." He says it was cumulative, starting in Iraq and becoming steadily worse during his time with the fire department.

"I lost my family over it," he says today with evident sadness, adding that the failure of his marriage was all his fault. "When I got home from Iraq it was hard for me to relate to my wife. There was a little distance, and I had a hard time closing the gap." He became angry too easily and was withdrawn to the point of being a recluse. "I just didn't want to deal with people," he says.

After six years of nightmares and other symptoms of PTSD, he finally sought help and was diagnosed with PTSD. "I probably should have been in treatment way before," he says. "But it's that alpha thing. You don't want to admit that there's something wrong. I hid it for a long time." With the help of therapy, he started to get his life back together. But then a series of horrific tragedies hit in rapid succession.

The first was Covid. "We were sometimes working a hundred hours a week," he says. He was constantly surrounded by utter misery. "Most with Covid were going untreated, they were getting it really bad. We were treating people who were on their last legs."

Next came a nightmarish span in which he responded to a series of calls so gruesome that some EMTs and firefighters don't experience so many extreme horrors in a whole career. In a short period, he responded to a 12-year-old boy found hanging from a tree; a car accident with multiple dead teenagers; and a 13-year-old girl, a victim of human trafficking, who was raped so violently she died on the way to the hospital. "It was like bam, bam, bam, bam," he says.

The final trauma involved a fellow firefighter who committed suicide with a gun in the fire station. Franklin was on his bunk napping, just a few feet away. "He blew his brains out all over me. I had to treat him, intubate him, medicate him, and transport him 40 minutes away to the hospital." Despite his valiant efforts, the firefighter died.

PTSD is not uncommon among firefighters and EMTs, who spend their careers on the front lines of human suffering, but Franklin's experiences caught the attention of the department psychologist. She worried about so many horrors in such a short time, added to his pre-existing PTSD from his combat experience. The department decided—for his own good, they said—to end his career. Instead of working in the job he loved for 25 years, as he had planned, he was involuntarily dismissed after 15.

More than a year later he does not seem bitter. It helps that they gave him a very generous pension, threw him a big party, and often invite him to dinner at the fire station to spend time with old friends. "They took care of me," he says.

The balance in his life has been shifting recently, he says. There's less Post-Traumatic Stress, and more Post-Traumatic Growth. He feels much more resilient and has a strong need to help other people, two common symptoms of PTG.

He gets calls from fire department colleagues who are having difficulty with the extreme stress of the job. He tells them he can't be their psychologist or therapist but tries to point them in the right direction to get help. He explains that their feelings are understandable under the circumstances—and are nothing to be embarrassed about. "I've traveled a road that other people are starting to travel," he says, "and they're looking for advice about how to get through to the other side."

Sergeant Elber Navarro

> If I hadn't gotten help, I'm pretty sure I'd be dead. I think I would have taken my own life.

My interview with Elber Navarro left me mentally exhausted. I don't know how many times I thought to myself "I can't fucking believe this guy." Heroism, trauma, and recovery all bound up in one courageous, highly intelligent, and incredibly eloquent Marine, who is utterly devoted to his brothers-in-arms.

Navarro almost didn't join the Marines. At 18 he initially decided he should go to college. But he had long dreamed of being in the military, and he couldn't stop thinking about it.

A friend who was a year older had joined the Marines the year before and told Navarro that if he decided to go into the military, he should join the Marines. Navarro asked why. Because, his friend said, it's the hardest of all the services. For someone who loved to be challenged, that was all Navarro needed to know. If he joined the military, he would be a Marine.

During high school Navarro's after-school job was at a Subway restaurant. While at work one day, a co-worker, who was also a close friend, said he was going to the Marine Corps recruiting office after work and asked Navarro to join him. "Really?" Navarro replied. "Yeah, you should go with me," his friend said. Navarro thought for a moment and said: "You know what? I'll go with you." It was a spur of the moment decision that would completely change his life.

At the recruiting office he took an entrance exam and scored well. The recruiter asked what he wanted to do. He looked at a poster on the wall with a photograph of infantry Marines and replied: "I want to do that." The recruiter said: "Are you sure? You have options." Navarro said: "I want to be in the infantry. That's all I want to do."

Navarro was involved in two of the most traumatic events that the Marines of 3/5 experienced along the road to Baghdad. The first was the death of two Iraqi girls on the night of March 25. The second was the death of two Marines, Staff Sergeant Riayan Tejeda and Lance Corporal David Owens Jr., in the April 11 nighttime ambush in Sadr City.

Navarro's four-year term of service ended after he returned home from his 2003 deployment in Iraq. He quickly enrolled in college again. But he felt like his fellow Marines were tugging at his shirt—and at his heart. After agonizing over it and talking it over with his mother he said: "You know what, mom? I don't want to get out of the Marine Corps. I love what I do."

Making that announcement to his mother was one of the hardest parts of his decision, because his 2003 deployment had been especially hard on her. When he came home, she had lost thirty pounds. She said she felt guilty eating because she didn't know what her son was eating, or if he was eating at all. His mother had refused to eat for days at a time.

But Navarro couldn't imagine abandoning his brothers-in-arms, who were scheduled to do another tour of duty in Iraq in 2004. He re-enlisted, and soon found himself in the middle of the bloody battle of Fallujah, where he earned a Bronze Star for valor.

The presidential citation accompanying the medal says that while clearing a house suspected of holding enemy fighters, his squad came under "a heavy volume of enemy fire… with enemy bullets impacting all around him, he bravely suppressed the room with fragmentation grenades and semiautomatic rifle fire … and personally eliminated multiple insurgents as they attempted to escape. Sergeant Navarro next led the assault force, spearheading the strongpoint's destruction and the rescue effort for a fellow Marine."

Navarro left the Marines after nearly nine years of service, a lot of heavy combat, and much more than his fair share of traumatic experiences. He struggled to adjust to his new life almost as soon as he arrived home. "I was going through some really, really hard times," he says. "Almost cost me my marriage. I couldn't adapt. I couldn't find my place in the civilian world."

Navarro was resentful that Americans didn't seem to appreciate the enormous sacrifice he and his fellow Marines were making. While in Fallujah he and his Marine buddies used to say: "America is not at war. We are at war. America is at the mall." Now that he was home, it was clear to him that they had been correct. Nobody seemed to care.

He started drinking heavily and soon found himself "in a really dark place," he says. He had an acute case of PTSD, and it was not only hard on him. In a marriage, PTSD can be "almost contagious," he says. "You have all these thoughts, but you don't know how to address them, so it kind of trickles down to your spouse."

I asked Navarro where he'd be today if he hadn't sought help. "I'm pretty sure I'd be dead," he replied. "I think I would have taken my life. It was almost easier to take that route because I didn't want to deal with the struggle, and the guilt of coming home when all those other Marines I served with didn't come home."

Hearing him say that was extremely difficult for me, because I remember him from 2003, at age 22, as one of the most exceptional young Marines I had met. He stood out. Two decades later, he has even more to offer the world. What a tragedy it would have been to lose him by his own hand.

Sadly, many veterans don't have a magical awakening, a moment of clarity that saves their lives. Fortunately, Navarro did, and it came without warning. "One day something just clicked in my head." He says he told himself: "If I don't get help, my marriage is going to end. My life is going to end. Everything I've worked so hard for and everything that I sacrificed so much for, I'm going to lose everything."

Navarro got over his reluctance to get professional help and now sees an individual counselor, and a marriage counselor with his wife. He proudly told me that he had a counseling session just two hours before our Zoom interview.

Navarro is now working in Los Angeles County as a firefighter-paramedic, a job that has given him a profound sense of purpose. He finds fulfillment in serving people in a more localized way. He thinks of the Marine Corps as "America's 911 force" when there's an emergency overseas. Now when there's an emergency, or even a catastrophe, in his hometown, people turn to the fire department. "It's filled a void that I thought I was going to be missing when I got out of the Marines."

In terms of mental health, Navarro says he's doing a lot better now, largely because of his fellow Marines. "They are my support system," he says. "They are the ones I can talk to about my experiences because they went through it with me." He still talks to most of the Marines he was close to in 2003 and 2004 and speaks to some of them weekly.

When he talks to Marines who are struggling, he always tells them the same thing: "Don't wait. Get help now. Because you don't want to be on your second divorce when you decide." Certain days or months of the year—anniversaries of Marine buddies' deaths—are still hard for him and all his fellow Marines. That's when they need each other the most.

Navarro says the other vital part of his support system is his wife, Crystal. He calls her his "foundation." "She helped me through all of this," he says. And he's deeply grateful that she never used his PTSD against him, never pinned the blame on him. They both understand that the counseling will probably have to continue indefinitely because, he says, "the thoughts of war, the thoughts of the Marines that we lost, will never go away."

Through it all, Navarro's love of the Marine Corps has never wavered. "I could become the President of the United States or the Fire Chief of the City of Los Angeles," he says, but aside from his wife and two young daughters, Lily and Kaysie, serving as a United States Marine will always be his "greatest pride, joy and honor."

Corporal Rob Gilbert

> Having chewed the same dirt and been to the same places, hopefully I can help them out and be there, just an ear to listen or a shoulder to cry on.

Rob Gilbert considers himself to be fortunate to have returned from Iraq without experiencing some of the post-traumatic stress issues that a lot of guys go through. Some of his close friends have suffered through the agony of PTSD.

Shortly after coming home from Iraq, he watched the movie *Band of Brothers*, which he says might not have been a great idea. His wife Kimberly was in the kitchen, about 20 or 30 feet away, and she told him she could hear him grinding his teeth. His dentist told him he needs a mouth guard, so he doesn't crack his teeth. But that's about the extent of his post-traumatic stress.

Gilbert is one of the fortunate people who have been spared the debilitating symptoms of post-traumatic stress, while experiencing the positive side of the ledger, Post-Traumatic Growth.

He has volunteered in his free time to help combat vets who have suffered from PTSD, understanding that he has a special role to play. "Combat vets won't necessarily open up to other vets, unless they are combat vets," he explained. "Having chewed the same dirt and been to the same places, hopefully I can help them out and be there, just an ear to listen or a shoulder to cry on, or whatever they need."

He brought up the topic of military suicide: "I think we (3/5) lost more Marines since we came home than we did while we were there in Iraq in 2003. If we can help and keep that from happening and keep those heroes alive, then that's a small effort that I can make."

Along with his wife of 21 years, he also volunteers in marriage ministries at their church, helping people avoid the "mistakes and roadblocks" that so many young couples experience.

Does Gilbert's desire to help others stem from the trauma of combat? It's hard to be certain. But I've heard similar stories from so many combat Marines who now have the urge to give back, that it's hard to believe they're not related. As Gilbert puts it, he believes his heart has grown because of his experience in war.

Staff Sergeant Fred Keeney

Combat is amazing. It's just unbelievable because it's the ultimate test of manhood.

War is the ultimate evil.

It might sound like a contradiction, but Fred Keeney is very passionate about combat *and* war. He *loves* combat. And he *hates* war.

The combat part isn't that surprising—a lot of Marines feel that way, and Keeney seems to have come by it naturally. One of the first things he told me about himself was that he "grew up in Irish bar fights." Case in point: he almost got tossed out of the Marines after getting thrown in jail for bar fighting at the University of Kansas. But brawling is for beginners. Combat is the pinnacle.

"Combat is amazing. It's just unbelievable because it's the ultimate test of manhood. There's no bigger test," he told me in an impassioned voice. "I don't freak out when I see guys wearing Super Bowl rings," he said. "I'm like, yeah, cool. You can play a game. But that's not the ultimate fucking test. The ultimate test is to go throw down in gunfights when other people are actively trying to kill you."

After one's time in combat is over, he says: "you'll never feel as alive again. Life is just fucking boring after it. We were running around shooting and now we're over here mowing the yard. Now you're Ward fucking Cleaver after you were one of the Viking berserkers."

But when he steps back and looks at the big picture—at war—he says it is absolute hell. To illustrate what he means he described a bizarre scene in Iraq that sounds like it's out of a dream—or maybe a nightmare.

As a Catholic, he remembers that it was either Good Friday or Easter Day in 2003, when gunfire suddenly erupted a short distance up the road. As his unit rushed to join the fight they came across a Marine chaplain—in this case a Catholic priest—in the middle of the road offering communion to Marines about to go into battle. "I ran out and said 'Father, you've got to get down,'" Keeney says. The priest replied very calmly: "Don't worry son. I've got this. We're fine."

He remembers that one Marine, after taking communion, asked the priest to bless his M16 rifle. The priest politely refused.

At that strange moment, Keeney says, the contrast between the goodness of the priest, who was wearing his vestments, and the horror of war hit him. "I could feel evil all around me," Keeney said. "And from a spiritual point of view, war is the ultimate evil, isn't it? I mean, it's fucking murder. And we killed a lot of people."

He says that feeling, of the evil of war being all around him, is one of his most intense memories of Iraq. "That feeling of oppression, of the heavy weight of pure and true malevolence. It was just in the air."

When Keeney came home from Iraq, he says the change from war to civilian life was so extreme and so sudden that "life didn't make sense anymore." His son Collin was born two weeks after he returned. "There's no transition. All of a sudden, you're back with the family, and I have a son." Looking back 20 years later, with some wisdom, he says, "It was way too much change."

He started drinking heavily and fell into depression. It destroyed his marriage, he says. The only explanation for his behavior that made sense to him was that in combat your brain becomes addicted to adrenalin and endorphins, and if your brain doesn't get what it wants, depression follows. "One way to fill the void," he says, "is with a bottle, because that kind of shuts it off." By 2008 his drinking was so excessive that he got a DUI and "was about to get thrown out of the Marine Corps."

It was then that he took the first step toward recovery. He stopped drinking—and hasn't had a drink since. But other symptoms of post-traumatic stress worsened significantly after he returned from Afghanistan around 2012. A close friend pulled him aside and told him: "You've got a big problem," Keeney recalls. The friend told Keeney that he had all the symptoms and signs of PTSD, including memory loss. Keeney had recently forgotten to attend his own promotion ceremony.

Keeney says he bristled in anger. But the friend then told him: "we can do this one of two ways. We can fight right now, and I'll drag you to the hospital. Or you can go on your own and see this lady I've been seeing."

Keeney's first response was to fight. But he considered the fact that such a good friend was telling him this and thought: "Thank God." So, he went to see his friend's psychiatrist at a nearby Air Force base. At first, he was deeply unimpressed. "What the fuck are you going to tell me about combat?" he asked her. Keeney says the vibe he was giving off was that of Cro-Magnon Man. The very petite woman calmly replied: "I'm not going to tell you anything about combat. I'm going to tell you how your brain has changed."

It didn't take long for his opinion to change too. He was diagnosed with PTSD, and she helped him "a hundred percent" in his recovery. What would he tell another veteran who's suffering from PTSD symptoms? "I would tell them go see somebody that deals with PTSD. Absolutely, unequivocally."

He also believes "one hundred percent" in the theory of Post-Traumatic Growth. His appreciation for life is "orders of magnitude" greater than it was before. He says he's "a thousand times more compassionate about life and trying to understand somebody else's plight."

Here's a case in point, that Keeney revealed to me. When Keeney's son Collin was 14, he bought a winter coat for a friend named Jaylen who lived in poverty and couldn't afford one. Keeney was very proud of his son. "Very Catholic of him," he says. Jaylen lived in a violent section of Kansas City, and two of his family members had been killed on the streets.

Keeney made it his mission to help Jaylen escape that world. He welcomed Jaylen into his home and his family. He made it possible for him to attend the same prestigious Catholic school his son Collin attended, and then helped Jaylen get into college—something that had not even been on Jaylen's radar before meeting the Keeney family. "We made a lifetime commitment to him," Keeney says.

Keeney downplays the amount of compassion it took to help Jaylen. In fact, he says: "being a devout Catholic, what I do for Jaylen is selfish." That comment left me confused. Why would doing so much to help someone else be selfish? "Well, someday I'm going to meet my maker," he explained, "and he's going to say: 'I sent you Jaylen. What did you do?'" Now, Keeney says, he can give the answer that his maker wants to hear: he did everything he could to help Jaylen.

Lance Corporal Frank Quintero

> By the time word got back to my family they heard that I'd been shot by a sniper and had been dead for a week.

It seemed miraculous that only one member of 3/5, Hospital Corpsman Michael Johnson, was killed during the battle of March 25. Frank Quintero, known as Frankie in 2003, barely survived after being struck by the same RPG that killed Johnson. Unfortunately, Quintero's parents had recently moved, and the Marines had the wrong address. So instead of hearing that he had been badly injured but was alive, his family heard an entirely different story through the rumor mill.

"You know how the telephone game goes?" Quintero asked me. He was referring to the party game in which people whisper a message down a line from one person to the next, and it comes out completely different at the other end. "By the time word got back to my family they heard that I'd been shot by a sniper and had been dead for a week."

His first opportunity to call home came after arriving at the U.S. military hospital in Landstuhl, Germany. Quintero's brother answered the phone. Quintero said: "It's Frankie." His stunned brother didn't believe him. Quintero said: "Shut the fuck up and put mom on the phone." When his family finally realized that it really was Frankie, he remembers a cacophony of screaming and crying on the other end of the line.

Quintero's family was not alone in thinking he had died. Many years later he called an old Marine friend, Alvin Hudgens, known to his fellow Marines as "Huggy Bear," to reconnect. When Hudgens answered Quintero said: "Hey Huggy-Bear, it's Q." Hudgens angrily responded, "Who is this?" and hung up, after cursing what he assumed was a cruel prankster. Quintero called back and told him it really was his old friend Q. After a long pause Hudgens replied: "Son, I've been drinking to your memory for sixteen years."

Quintero was extremely lucky to survive, for several reasons. First, if the RPG had exploded it certainly would have killed him, and possibly everyone else in the Humvee. Second, the bullet proof "SAPI plate" on his chest had been melted by the RPG's burning propellent. If he hadn't been wearing the plate, or if the incendiary had hit an area not protected by the plate, it might have burned him to death. And third, his internal damage was massive. He had a lacerated liver, a collapsed lung, and lost a portion of his right rib cage. He also lost about two feet of intestine and has endured two complete abdominal reconstructions, plus multiple surgeries to remove scar tissue. At one point during his recovery, Quintero says, he was "living in a wheelchair and weighed 113 pounds."

The surgeries continued for years. In 2008, five years after the incident, doctors removed a painful three-inch bone shard that was fused in his intestines. He still lives with a lot of pain, but he's a typical Marine—he doesn't like to talk about the pain because he doesn't want to sound like a whiner.

Quintero is more likely to use his injuries as material for gallows humor. It's been said that Marines can make a joke out of anything, and Quintero is proof of that. Here are some examples from our interviews:

1. Shortly after being injured Quintero realized that his excruciating pain was so low on his abdomen that the RPG might also have

hit his, well, let's just say organs that are not internal. He was too afraid to look, so he turned to Staff Sergeant Fred Keeney, who was tending to him while they waited for the medevac helicopter. "Is my shit still there?" he asked Keeney. Keeney lifted Quintero's shorts and took a quick look. "Yep, it's all there, Frankie." "Thank God," Quintero replied.

2. Quintero's first surgery was in a field hospital. When he woke up the first thing he saw was a Navy nurse who was tending to him. "What's a beautiful thing like you doing in a place like this?" he asked. Hearing that, a nearby doctor said: "I think he's going to be just fine." Instead of asking the doctor about his condition, Quintero had a more urgent concern: "My next question was 'How are my tattoos?' because I have a tattoo on my stomach." The doctor responded: "Your tattoos are good," to Quintero's great relief.

3. Finally, Quintero told me that when he's shirtless people often ask about the long vertical scar on his abdomen from his many surgeries. "I had a C-section," he routinely answers.

Quintero's injuries were so severe that the Marine Corps tried to discharge him—but he fought to stay in. He worked doggedly on his physical fitness and passed every test they threw at him. "I wanted to prove to myself that I was still that hard-core Marine," he told me, "to prove to myself and those around me that I could still perform." But he was ignoring another challenge. "My emotional state wasn't matching my physical state," he said. "I wasn't doing anything for that. I was just feeling sorry for myself."

Quintero had been diagnosed with severe PTSD. The symptoms included frequent nightmares, most of which involved getting hit by the RPG. He was also full of anger and anxiety, and was hypervigilant—always on the lookout for danger. And he avoided crowds—not a good trait for a guy whose wife loves Disneyland.

Quintero also had a bad case of survivor's guilt stemming from the death of Michael Johnson, who had been sitting next to him when the RPG hit them. "Something that I had to deal with is the fact that you have this great person, a Christian, very, very kind, very, very funny, just an amazing human being and he didn't make it. And me, a little punk asshole, I did survive, so survivor's guilt really hit me hard for many, many, many years."

Quintero won't say he's "gotten over" his PTSD, but he has learned to cope with it. "That's why it's so easy for me to talk with you about it," he told me. "I've learned that the more I talk about it, the easier it is for me to cope with it."

His wife Lindsay, he says, has been "phenomenally important" in his recovery. "This is something I'm not proud of, but I used to drink a lot," he told me. "For the longest time I would find excuses and blame the rest of the world for acting certain ways, making bad choices, and just being stupid, and she was at the forefront of that blame. But she stuck around. She understood. She listened." When he awoke during nightmares, she calmed him down. He says he's extremely lucky that she stayed by his side: "I count my blessings every day."

Quintero continued his service in the Marines until 2020, mostly doing counterintelligence and human intelligence work. He now serves in a civilian capacity with the Marines. But his life revolves around his family—Lindsay and their twins, Frankie, Jr., and Lucie. "I've come to realize that the purpose of life is to have a purpose," he says. And that purpose is his family.

Lance Corporal Robert Kerman

> When you go through something traumatic you tend to escape. It was very famous back then to say: 'It sucks dude. It's horrible. Here's a bottle.'

The up and down path of Robert Kerman's life might be as dramatic as the March 25 battle in which he earned a Silver Star as part of Team Chontosh.

Kerman's father and grandfather had both been Marines, in Vietnam and World War II respectively, but as a rebellious teenager his attitude was "I'm not joining the military, no way." So, he went to college instead. For two whole weeks. That's when the terrorist attacks of September 11, 2001 occurred.

Kerman had already concluded that college was not for him, and by a stroke of luck he happened upon two Marine Corps recruiters in the campus cafeteria. His Marine Corps family's DNA suddenly kicked in and he decided to enlist. In short order he was at boot camp, and soon after that in Kuwait, waiting for the order to invade Iraq.

If he had continued the trajectory that his life was on before joining the Marines, he guesses he would have dropped out of college, returned to his hometown in Oregon, where he had already been in "a bad situation," and would be working smalltime jobs just to survive. "And doing meth somewhere," he adds, noting that two of his friends from home died from heroin overdoses.

After his heroics in 2003, Kerman deployed to Iraq again in 2004. But this time he came home feeling like he had a heavy weight on his shoulders. For one thing, the many men he had killed took a toll. In addition, he had helped convince a close friend from home to join the Marines. That friend was killed in Iraq in 2004. That left him with a colossal case of survivor's guilt. Finally, as he put it: "Alcohol was readily available."

Alcohol abuse after a combat deployment was a theme in many of my Marine interviews. "I did it because everybody else did," Kerman says. "It's a staple in the Marine Corps." He says one fellow Marine who was struggling with PTSD was told by his platoon sergeant: "Just drink as much as you can. It'll go away."

"When you go through something traumatic you tend to want to escape," he says. "We're not taught to deal with it in responsible ways. It was very famous back then to say: 'It sucks dude. It's horrible. Here's a bottle.'" He says that in recent years the Corps has done a better job at reining in excessive drinking.

But that was too late for Kerman. He says heavy drinking led to a divorce from his first wife, as it has done with so many Marines after they come home from war. He says he went through more than a decade of alcoholism. During all that time, he denied to others what he knew to be true. "I was like, no, I don't have PTSD. But looking back now, it's just so obvious that I did, and do."

He didn't seek professional help for almost 20 years. Fortunately, he had non-professional help—from his second wife, Jessika, who also served in the Marines. He describes her as loving, accepting, supportive—and tough. Exactly what he needed. "The grace of God, and my wife being a total badass, pulled me out of that life," he says now. "She helped me through a lot of this, and it wasn't easy. But not drinking is key."

In recent years his life has been transformed. Instead of alcoholism and PTSD, he's living in a world of Post-Traumatic Growth. He completed two years of college, and at work he enjoys assisting young Marines with their issues and problems. He finds great rewards in helping his loved ones, and even strangers, a common trait of people experiencing PTG.

Perhaps most important, he says, he's "the best father I can be" to his six children. As an example, during our Zoom interview I still had a few questions I wanted to ask, but he had a higher priority. He told me he had to hang up. "My nine-year-old daughter wants me to go upstairs and tuck her in and pray with her," he said. "And I don't want to miss that."

Lance Corporal Chad Huffstutler

Chad Huffstutler's PTSD diagnosis can be traced, in part, to the accidental killings of two young Iraqi girls by 3/5 Marines, and the screams of their mother that have haunted him for years. Unlike many others with PTSD, he did not fall into drug or alcohol addiction. But because he worked in law enforcement, he also did not seek help. "With that job, you don't go seek help when you have issues like that, or you're not going to have a job," he says.

He was able to live with it for ten years, but not getting treatment "finally caught up," Huffstutler says. "You can't really hide PTSD issues. My wife knew I had it. Close, close friends knew I had issues. But you can only go so long pushing those issues aside."

It took a series of major blows for Huffstutler to finally seek help. "My divorce and losing everything, losing my career," he said. "I ended up in a Cincinnati psyche ward for eight weeks in an inpatient program. That's when I learned to talk about it." It was a VA facility, he says, adding that—unlike some Marines—he has nothing negative to say about how the VA treated him.

He takes full blame for his divorce and is glad he's no longer in law enforcement, with all its triggers for someone struggling with PTSD. He now lives primarily on his military disability, but he also makes leather products in a shop at his home. He and his second wife, Maria, sell the leather goods from their own store, Sew-N-Leather, in Newton Falls, Ohio. Leatherworking is an art he picked up several years ago as a PTSD coping skill. He also copes by connecting with fellow combat veterans. "There's still no medicine like talking with people I was there with," he says. He describes his recovery as "an everyday, lifelong kind of thing."

When I asked Huffstutler about the most important things he learned as a Marine, he said: "If I whittled it down to one word, it would be 'adaptability,'" which he describes as being able to adapt to new challenges "without going off the deep end."

He says he has no regrets. Being a Marine is what he always wanted to do. He graduated from high school on a Thursday and left for boot camp the following Sunday. Despite all his tribulations, he says it's still one of the best decisions he ever made, adding, "I miss it every day."

Corporal Al Lopez

> I think about different scenarios all the time, what I could have done different so Erik would probably still be here. It's like a fucking tape, I just rewind, rewind and rewind and rewind and it doesn't stop.

Al Lopez and Erik Silva were close friends. They lived next to each other in the barracks at Camp Pendleton. Sadly, like so many Marines when they lose a brother in battle, Lopez still agonizes over what he might have done to save Silva's life on April 4, 2003.

Lopez was "point" that day, the first man in his platoon to cross the small bridge over an irrigation canal that some Marines called Devil's Ditch. After walking a bit beyond the ditch, Lopez stopped. The Marine behind him, Lawrence Russell, stopped too. "I told Russell this doesn't feel right man, this doesn't feel right," Lopez recalls. At that moment the air around them erupted. "We started taking fire from everywhere," Lopez says. He hit the dirt behind a small berm. He could hear, and even feel, the bullets smacking into the berm, inches from his face.

Hospital Corpsman Jeff "Doc" Parnakian later told me an important fact about that moment in the battle—a fact that Lopez hadn't mentioned in our interview. An enemy shooter had Lopez in his sights, Parnakian says, and Lopez kept popping his head up. Each time Lopez did that, the enemy shooter would fire. "And I kept seeing Lopez stick his head up because he's trying to let us see where the fire is coming from. He was doing it on purpose. And I'm thinking, man I don't want to see him get shot in the face." Lopez's ploy worked. They were able to find and shoot the enemy fighter.

Lopez says the enemy on that day, more than any other, knew what they were doing and had prepared for this moment. "They were dug in," he says. Instead of firing as soon as the Marines were in range, they had the patience to wait until several Marines had entered the kill zone. "I thought I was going to get shot in the ass because we were taking fire from the rear too," Lopez recalls.

Above the cacophony of battle Lopez heard someone scream "corpsman up! corpsman up!"—the call for a Navy Doc to rush to the aid of an injured Marine. His close friend Corporal Silva had been shot in the chest, a fatal hit that barely missed his bullet-proof ceramic plate.

Two decades later, Silva's death still torments Lopez. "It's a day I can never forget. I think about different scenarios all the time, what I could have done different so Erik would probably still be here. It's like a fucking tape, I just rewind, rewind and rewind and rewind and it doesn't stop."

Lopez says he was diagnosed with PTSD but doesn't like going to therapy. "They want me to go to group therapy and sing Kumbaya and hold hands. It ain't fucking happening," he says.

The death of Erik Silva was not the only trauma Lopez experienced. He recalls another day in 2003 when he was leading a patrol and came upon an American tank in the road. He asked if it was clear to pass, and the gunner said yes. Seconds later the tank fired a round. Lopez was just five or six feet from the barrel. The explosive force sent him flying like a rag doll, landing on the back of his head. The impact herniated three discs in his neck and left him with a TBI, a traumatic brain injury.

That was 2004 and Lopez has been fighting with the VA ever since over the size of his disability payment. He believes he deserves 100 percent disability, but the VA has refused to give him more than about 70 percent. The pain is constant, and sometimes he loses all feeling in his left arm. "I take more pills than a 98-year-old man," he says.

Lopez left the Marines after the 2004 deployment but felt extremely out of place in civilian society. He tried to re-up with the Marines but was turned down because of his injuries. To deal with his pain—physical and psychological—Lopez started drinking heavily. His first wife took him to the doctor to try to deal with his painful heartburn. The doctor asked if he drank. He lied, he says, telling the doctor he drank "occasionally." His then-wife called him out—telling the doctor that he was drinking about 30 beers a day.

"I drank a 30-pack of beer every day for four or five years," Lopez says now. It got so bad he worried about ending up in a hospital bed with severe liver disease. So he went cold turkey for two years. Then, started drinking "moderately," and soon was back to his old ways. After another period of excessive drinking, he stopped again. Today he says it's not the problem it once was, "but on occasion I'll sit down and take back a good 24 or 30 beers."

When Lopez left the Marines, his plan was to become a police officer. He passed all the tests—until he was asked to do a verbal psychological evaluation. He had just returned from Iraq and was "pissed off and aggravated," he says. "The guy started asking me questions that I wasn't ready to talk about." He failed the test. "I chose the wrong time to go to the police academy," he added.

Lopez has a somewhat pugnacious attitude. Or as he puts it: "I have a little bit of a mouth." That might be an understatement. He did security work for a while but got in an argument with his supervisor. "I told him, basically, to blow me," he says.

After losing that job, he did car repossessions, which suited him well. "You're in the truck. You're alone. No one bothers you." But he grew tired of it after about twelve years, and got a job in the transport business, which lasted about eight years. Unfortunately, a few days before our interview his mouth got him in trouble again. "My boss decided he had to yell at me, and I had to tell him to fucking blow me," Lopez says. "So he fired me."

At the time we spoke, Lopez was doing personal security, "bodyguard stuff," as he called it. With his shaved head and his no-bullshit attitude it's a good bet that he's an intimidating bodyguard. "I don't give anybody a reason to talk to me," he says. "I'm not friendly with anybody." Adding to the intimidation factor is his very effective scowl.

Lopez has been divorced twice, which isn't unusual for Marines with PTSD, especially those who don't seek help. "My ex-wife says I'm just very moody," he says, and after 14 years she said: "I just can't do it anymore."

Lopez says now: "Ain't nobody wants to put up with me." In fact, that's not quite true. There's a lot of love in Lopez's world. He has a strong relationship with his young son and daughter.

And I've got to admit, as tough as he sounds, he's a very likeable, funny, self-deprecating character. When I asked if he prefers to be called Al, Albert, or Alberto, he said: "It doesn't matter to me. Dipshit, jackass, it all works." He's the kind of guy you'd want to have a beer with, or maybe even a few. But probably not 30.

Lopez has at least one source of unconditional love—his young dog Chesty, an American Bully. "He looks like Chesty Puller," Lopez says, referring to the most decorated U.S. Marine in history. And he's right. Chesty the dog is built like a tank with a big, strong head and square jaw, much like Chesty Puller. On several occasions Chesty demanded his owner's attention during our Zoom call. Lopez complied by doing high fives with him, hand to paw, making both smile.

Despite all he's been through, Lopez says joining the Marines was "a hundred percent" the best decision he ever made. "If I could, I'd go back and do it all over again," he says. His love of the Corps came through as he proudly displayed his many Marine tattoos. It was almost like he was showing off his collection of paintings by Van Gogh or Picasso.

"It's the brotherhood, the camaraderie," Lopez says. "I would drop anything right now for any of those guys. It's an irreplaceable bond that you won't find anywhere else in the world." Included in that bond is Erik Silva's family. Silva's sister, Gloria Silva, told me that Al Lopez is one of the big-hearted Marines she still depends on all these years later. "No matter where I am, or what Al is doing," she said, "if I need anything or anyone, Al goes out of his way to be there to help me."

Corporal Eric Olson

> I think that anybody who goes through trauma is going to have post-traumatic stress. You have to get it off your chest. The solace you get from being able to lean on another veteran is that you trust them because they've been there. They chewed that same dirt.

After 9/11, Eric Olson and his fellow Marines were furious. They wanted payback. "We were like a bunch of wild dogs waiting for somebody to let us off the chain." Very well-trained wild dogs, he added. There's something different about people, he told me, who seek out a profession in which they might kill or be killed. "That's the kind of people we are," he said of Marines. "We're not like other people."

Olson knew from a young age that he would go into the military, and there was no question which branch it would be. "I never knew that there was any other branch of service except for the Marine Corps," he says. His stepfather—who is also his mentor—was an infantry Marine in *Desert Shield* and *Desert Storm*. His father was in the Navy. And grandparents on his mother's side were both Marines. Interestingly, Olson's grandmother outranked his grandfather.

Olson loves the discipline, the self-sacrifice, and the teamwork. He loves the blood, sweat and tears. He loves the sense of confidence he feels because of what he's accomplished. And like most Marines, he loves the history, and the spartan existence. "We don't always have the most illustrious equipment," he says. "The Marines don't just make do. They do more with less."

Like most of the front-line combat veterans I interviewed for this book, Olson experienced post-traumatic stress after returning home from Iraq. "I remember vividly driving down the freeway at thirty-five miles an hour, dodging plastic bags that were drifting across the road, seeing berms that looked like fighting positions, and worrying about IEDs. I remember pulling off and saying: 'What the hell, man?! This is San Clemente, California. This is not Fallujah. You can relax!'"

But unlike some Marines, Olson did not put off dealing with it. As soon as he knew it was an issue, he decided to confront it. And that meant talking about it—especially with his fellow Marines. "I think talking about our experiences is cathartic," he says. "I think that anybody who goes through trauma is going to have post-traumatic stress." But the worst thing one can do, he says, is clam up. That approach, he says, is a remnant of "the bravado of the John Wayne era."

"You have to get it off your chest," he says. "The solace you get from being able to lean on another veteran is that you trust them because they've been there. They chewed that same dirt." Who better to talk to, he says, than the men in your brotherhood. "You're forged by fire. And you build trust with anybody who's shared that experience."

Of his traumatic experiences in war, Olson says: "The sting of it tapers off, but it never goes away." But because he has faced it instead of letting it fester, he's turned it into an opportunity for Post-Traumatic Growth. After 15 years working in law enforcement in San Diego County, he got an MBA, went into the mortgage business, and now works as a consultant on security and risk threat assessments for schools.

"I love the consulting work," he says, "because I can impart and share my failures and successes on the people that are protecting children in schools." After the tragic—and maddening—shooting in Uvalde, Texas, in 2022, which left 19 students and two teachers dead, Olson told me he was happy to be very busy working with other schools to improve their plans to keep children safe. "That's an awesome mission," he said. "And I think it's important for guys and gals that have served, especially in combat, to have a mission where they can impact society."

Navy Corpsman Jeff Parnakian

After five years as a Navy Corpsman, Jeff Parnakian rejoined civilian life. "It was a mess," he says. "I was drinking tons and I was living an extremely reckless life." One incident in particular, he says, was like a big warning light that something was wrong. He woke up one morning and his girlfriend was staring at him. He said: "What's going on?" She replied: "You don't remember?"

She described to him an incident that had occurred moments earlier, while he was apparently still asleep and having a nightmare. He had rolled over to her, put his hand over her mouth and told her to be quiet because "they're really close." "I didn't remember any of it," Parnakian says. "And it scared the shit out of me." He saw a therapist who concluded he had PTSD, and prescribed medication, but the pills made him feel worse, so he stopped taking them.

"I just needed to get away from drinking for a while and do my own thing," he says. "I was going to break. I was either going to end up in prison, or dead—or something like that." He eventually found an unusual type of therapy that seems to work for him: hiking. Not just any kind of hiking—extreme hiking. When I interviewed Parnakian he had just returned from a five-month hike on the Continental Divide Trail, from the Mexican border to the Canadian border at Glacier National Park. It was his third time.

He has hiked the Pacific Crest Trail twice, which also goes from Mexico to Canada and takes about five months. He's hiked from Florida to Maine, mostly on the Appalachian Trail, which can take six months or more. And he's hiked and climbed mountains from Mexico to Nepal. Soon after our interview he was heading to Ecuador for an extended mountaineering trip.

"I wish I had started hiking years before," he says. "Just having time out there to process things. I've never been to counseling. I just process things differently. It took a lot of time, and I'm still working on things. It's difficult."

Lieutenant Mike Prato, the Rogue Marine

> I thought the Marines was a joke in a lot of ways, to be honest. Just kind of brainwashed people, running around, institutionalized. I was never like that, and I never wanted to be like that.

Mike Prato says he's "a pretty boring guy" who does "pretty simple stuff." He likes going out to dinner, riding his Harley, and going bass fishing with his dog. Sounds simple. But he's really not. In fact, he's pretty complicated. He's a good example of why writing this book was such a never-ending trail of discovery, with surprises around every corner. There is no such thing as a cookie-cutter Marine—they're all different.

And in Prato's case—a lot different. And I don't think he would be the slightest bit offended to read that.

In a world where everyone takes orders, he struggled to conform to the demands of his superiors. And he has some unusually rebellious feelings about the Marine Corps itself. Early in our first interview he told me: "I was often called rogue. I didn't follow the rules. I didn't run around saying 'oorah.'" That, of course, is the Marine battle cry, and taking pride in *not* saying it is unusual.

"I didn't care about having a pressed uniform," Prato said. "I thought the Marines was a joke in a lot of ways, to be honest. Just kind of brainwashed people, running around, institutionalized. I was never like that, and I never wanted to be like that. I was a guy who didn't always comply," he continued, and mentioned again that he was often seen as "rogue," especially by people above him in rank. "I didn't do it belligerently," he said, "I just wanted to be myself, to solve problems and deal with people the way that I felt was best, not what the Marine Corps said was the best way to do things."

Prato took pride in being the first to do something, setting a new example, if he saw a better way. "And sometimes it meant I had to break some rules. I don't wear the institution on my sleeve," he said. "If you come to my house, you won't see any plaques or any Marine garbage on my walls. It's all broken in boxes upstairs. I'm probably going to throw it away. I don't want it hanging around my neck for the rest of my life."

But there was a dramatic change in tone when Prato was asked about the Marines he served with, especially those he commanded in battle. He was fiercely devoted to his men and took great pride in mentoring and shaping them. When talking about that role, the stubborn resistance to Marine Corps tradition disappeared, and he sounded like a dyed-in-the wool, hard-core Marine.

"The memories and the times I had with the guys in the mud were the best times of my life," he said, reeling off his combat tours in Iraq and Afghanistan: "2003, 2004, 2011, 2012, those were the best times, influencing people, changing their lives, helping build them as men and women, as officers. I love that stuff. Suffering with like-minded people, doing what other people would never want to do, and being with men that you really love and care about." But putting a Marine Corps bumper sticker on his car or an award on his wall? Fuhgeddaboudit.

Despite those mixed feelings, though, Prato stuck with it and had a long career in the Marines. He enlisted right out of high school in 1996. "I saw how the Marines carried themselves," he recalls, and he wanted to be like that. The other military recruiters were "kind of boring," but the Marines Corps guy was: "Type A, let's go kill 'em. And I took it hook line and sinker. I was drawn to the idea of being a badass and being part of something bigger than yourself."

After boot camp he decided he could have a much greater impact as an officer, so he went into the reserves while he completed his college degree. Upon graduation he became a commissioned officer. Later, at the Corps' insistence, he earned a master's degree in aerospace engineering. Yes, there's a lot of brain power lurking under Prato's rogue exterior.

He was injured during both Iraq deployments in 2003 and 2004—including a shrapnel wound in his knee from a grenade. Later in Afghanistan, his vehicle was destroyed by a roadside bomb, injuring some vertebrae in his neck and, as he puts it, "probably" leaving him with a traumatic brain injury.

He was so beat up—he says his joints were "falling apart"—that he spent his final year in the Marines in what's known as the Wounded Warrior Battalion, which helps Marines recover and transition to civilian life. That has not always been easy. After more than 20 years in the Marine Corps, he told me, "I didn't know what I wanted to be when I grew up."

Prato wasn't ready to jump into the workforce. So, to "decompress" he went to the Massachusetts Institute of Technology, a school known for its brain power, in a 12-month executive MBA program. "I felt like a million bucks," he says. "I slept better. I was playing softball again. My joints felt better. But as the stress notched up, I started going through a lot of the same issues."

And Prato did have issues—symptoms of PTSD that he didn't deal with for years. During his first marriage, after work he would retreat to his basement where he lived mostly alone—spending much of his time reliving his experiences in Iraq. "The situations I was in, the decisions

I made, and I kept running through it. Could I have done things differently? And what makes it PTSD, is the emotions you relive. You get the adrenalin rush, you almost feel like you're there again, and you desire to be back."

He still struggles with survivor's guilt stemming largely from the night of April 11, 2003. He was the senior officer on the night patrol in Baghdad when Staff Sergeant Riayan Tejeda and Lance Corporal David Owens were killed. They were his men. "I was right next to them. It could have been me." He says he had been ready to die. But in the ensuing years it's not his close call with death that bothers him—it's his persistent memories of Tejeda and Owens that just won't leave him alone. While waiting for the medevac helicopter to arrive he vividly remembers standing close by as the Navy Docs worked and "just watching them kind of fade away," he recalls. "To this day, I think about them a lot. I think about that situation a lot. I wonder about what their families are doing. I wonder where they are in the afterlife."

His PTSD was at its worst soon after coming home from Iraq. "I was reliving those feelings over and over again. I was not letting go. Like a broken record, I just kept going through it." He did this for months—didn't talk to anybody, didn't go anywhere. He remembers his then-wife telling him: "You've got to start interacting again because this isn't healthy."

Eventually they divorced. "I got very depressed and angry. I'd break things and blame people for my problems, and I destroyed relationships," he says now. "I was not in a healthy place. I stiff armed everybody. I didn't let anybody get close to me."

Prato eventually sought help for difficulty sleeping. He says eighty percent of his dreams were either violent or heartbreaking. The doctor read him the riot act. "I see a million of you guys," he said, referring to veterans struggling with traumatic stress. "You destroy your lives, you ruin your relationships, and then you come in and seek help. Over and over again I see this," the doctor said, "because you guys don't deal with it."

His next serious relationship also had an ugly end. After that, he finally sought therapy for more than just his sleep issues. "I really

Lieutenant Colonel Sam Mundy, commanding officer of 3/5, speaking to his Marines in northern Kuwait shortly before crossing the border into Iraq. (Permission from Baltimore Sun Media. All Rights Reserved)

Senior officers of 3/5 in northern Kuwait shortly before the war began. Bottom row (left to right) 1stLt David Valentino (S6—Communications Officer), Major Kevin Nave (Battalion Executive Officer), Major Craig Wonson (S3—Operations Officer), Captain John Howard (S4—Logistics Officer), 1stLt Travis Holland (S2—Intelligence Officer), Evan Hume (S1—Battalion Adjutant). Top row (left to right): Captain Robert Piddock (Weapons Company CO, Battalion FSC), Captain Mario Schweizer (H&S Company Commander), Captain Ethan Bishop (India Company Commander), LtCol Carl (Sam) Mundy (Battalion Commander), Captain Scott Meredith (Lima Company Commander), Captain Vance Sewell (AAV Company Commander), Captain Michael Miller (Kilo Company Commander). (Marine Corps photo)

Embedded reporter Chip Reid (blue flak jacket) riding with 3/5 Marines in an AAV shortly after the war began. The Marines' smiles reflect their exuberance at finally crossing the border and roaring toward Baghdad. The mood changed a few days later after the loss of Hospital Corpsman Michael Johnson and the Executive Officer, Major Kevin Nave. (Author's photos)

Lance Corporal Bill Rodriguez, who drove the truck Chip Reid often rode in on the road to Baghdad. Rodriguez had a bad habit of looking out for Chip when the bullets started flying. (Courtesy Tyler Watkins)

Hospital Corpsman Michael Johnson (left) in Iraq on March 24, 2003. One day later Johnson was killed in the first moments of the first Iraqi ambush. On the right is Corporal Scott Smith who was driving the lightly armored Humvee during the ambush near the city of Ad Diwaniya. (Courtesy Scott Smith)

Corporal Scott Smith sitting in the Humvee he had been driving when it was hit by the RPG that killed Michael Johnson on March 25, 2003. The RPG entered the lightly armored Humvee through the shredded door frame. Smith was devastated by the loss of Johnson, a close friend. (Courtesy Scott Smith)

Marines climbing the berm during the battle of March 25. At this moment, First Lieutenant Brian Chontosh and his team were clearing dozens of enemy fighters from the trench on the other side of the berm. (Permission from Baltimore Sun Media. All Rights Reserved)

Rob Gilbert after the seven-hour battle of April 4, 2003. "It was a hellish day. Finally a moment of down time. Get off our feet, grab a smoke, maybe a bite to eat, before moving on to the next one." (Courtesy Rob Gilbert)

Corporal Eric Olson, lost in thought after his first combat action in the battle of March 25, 2003. "I was trying to put together what happened. It happened so fast, but seemed to take forever." (Courtesy AJ Pasciuti)

General Michael Hagee, Commandant of the Marine Corps (left), presents the Silver Cross to First Lieutenant Brian Chontosh on May 6, 2004 for his heroic actions in Iraq on March 25, 2003. Chontosh eventually retired as a major. (Marine Corps photo)

Marines grieve during a brief battlefield memorial service for Hospital Corpsman Michael Johnson and Major Kevin Nave. (Permission from Baltimore Sun Media. All Rights Reserved)

Marines of 3/5 run toward the battlefield on April 4, 2003. A Marine Cobra helicopter fires from above while mortars fired by Marines explode below. The battle, near Salman Pak, Iraq, lasted approximately seven hours. Corporal Erik Silva was killed, and several Marines were injured. (Courtesy Mike Martinez)

Marines search for enemy fighters hiding in "spider holes" during the battle of April 4. (Permission from Baltimore Sun Media. All Rights Reserved)

Marines take cover behind a small berm during the battle of April 4, near Salman Pak, Iraq. Many of the fiercest enemy fighters came to Iraq from other countries, including Syria and Sudan. (Permission from Baltimore Sun Media. All Rights Reserved)

Corporal Erik Silva keeps watch on a bridge over the Tigris River on April 1, three days before he was killed in action. (Permission from Baltimore Sun Media. All Rights Reserved)

NBC News cameraman Joe Klimovitz (left) and correspondent Chip Reid in the waning minutes of the 7-hour battle of April 4, 2003. (Permission from Baltimore Sun Media. All Rights Reserved)

Marines in traffic as they entered Baghdad. The Iraqis were flooding back in because the Americans had taken charge. (Permission from Baltimore Sun Media. All Rights Reserved)

Iraqis celebrating the arrival of the Marines near the entrance to Sadr City, Baghdad, on April 10, 2003. (Courtesy Colin Keefe)

Sergeant Colin Keefe with Iraqi children during the celebration of the Marines' arrival in Sadr City, Baghdad, on April 10, 2003. (Courtesy Colin Keefe)

Lieutenant Mike Prato holding a hedgehog that 3/5 Marines adopted as a pet in Iraq. Some Marines also adopted puppies and other animals. Somehow, Prato also adopted a small hawk. (Courtesy Mike Prato)

Lance Corporal Chad Huffstutler, holding one of many skulls found in a mass grave south of Baghdad. Marines were told by civilian Iraqis that the site contained the bodies of people slaughtered by forces under the control of Saddam Hussein. (Courtesy Chad Huffstutler)

Mike Prato (left) and Riayan Tejeda (a few weeks before he was killed in action) in Kuwait before crossing into Iraq. Tejeda, who was 26 years old, was posthumously awarded the Silver Star for conspicuous gallantry. (Courtesy Mike Prato)

Navy Hospital Corpsman Jeff Parnakian in combat mode. Parnakian frequently joined the Marines in combat operations, in addition to fulfilling his duties as a medic. (Courtesy Jeff Parnaikian)

Lance Corporal David Owens working with other Marines to quickly build a footbridge over a deep canal on the road to Baghdad in late March 2003. Owens was mortally wounded while on foot patrol in Baghdad on April 11, 2003. (Courtesy Mike Prato)

Captain Mario Schweizer, with his wife Jenni and their daughter Grace at Camp Pendleton in early September 2003, minutes after he arrived home from Iraq. The "Marines" book I'm holding was filled with notes and letters to my NBC crew and me, thanking us for our daily—sometimes hourly—reports on their Marines. (Courtesy Mario Schweizer)

Corporal Mike Martinez holds his son Mike Jr., while his wife Stefanie holds their newborn son Scott. This photo was taken minutes after they were reunited at the 3/5 homecoming at Camp Pendleton in early September 2003. Stefanie was overwhelmed with joy, but Mike was very subdued. The vacant look in his eyes might well be due to exhaustion, but it also seems reminiscent of the "thousand-yard stare," a phrase coined during World War I to describe the eyes of soldiers with what was then known as "shell shock." (Courtesy Mike Martinez)

Mike Martinez (far left) at the wedding of his son Mike Jr. (center) on January 21, 2021 to his bride Melissa. Mike Sr.'s wife, Stefanie, is second from right and their son Scott is on the far right. After years of family stress due to Mike's PTSD, Mike sought help and experienced Post-Traumatic Growth, allowing the entire family to experience a new sense of contentment. (Courtesy Mike Martinez)

Eric Olson (L) and Travis Pollock in August 2020. Pollock took his own life in 2021 at the age of 39, a devastating loss for Olson and many other 3/5 Marines. Olson recalls that Pollock was "extremely esoteric in his thoughts and loved to question the 'why' of all things." Olson says he will forever cherish their long, thoughtful conversations. (Courtesy Eric Olson)

Travis Pollock (left), with Josh Pryor in Iraq. Pryor attended Pollock's funeral with Marines he hadn't seen in 17 years. During that long period he had struggled with PTSD, but his recovery began the day he reunited with his Marines. "There was this feeling washing over me of 'you've never been alone,'" Pryor said later. "That changed my life, and I owe it to my buddy Travis." (Courtesy Josh Pryor)

Sergeant Nathaniel Donnelly (left) and Corporal Travis Pollock in Iraq in 2003. Agreeing with Olson, Donnelly says Pollock was famous for his "epic, deep conversations." (Courtesy Nathaniel Donnelly)

Captain Vance Sewell manning the 240G, 7.62mm machine gun on top of his Amtrac. The steel lid of the hatch on right of photo was dented by bullets that amazingly missed Sewell. (Courtesy Vance Sewell)

Joe Harris and his wife Sara. He titled this photo "The Beauty and the Beast." (Courtesy Joe Harris)

Chad Huffstutler and his wife Maria. He drove an Amphibious Assault Vehicle (the Marines' version of a troop carrier) from Kuwait to Baghdad, among other duties. They own a custom leather store in Newton Falls, Ohio. (Courtesy Chad Huffstutler)

Ethan Bishop in his "office" on the Middle Fork of the Salmon River, which is within his jurisdiction as a Senior Conservation Officer for the Idaho Department of Fish and Game. (Courtesy Ethan Bishop)

Robert Kerman and family. Left to right: Gary, Taylor, Robert, Makala (top), Abby (bottom), Jessika (wife), Jasmine, and Jackson. (Courtesy Robert Kerman).

Brandon Bunch and family. Left to right: Kaden (middle name David, in honor of David E. Owens Jr., one of the Marines to whom this book is dedicated); Katie, Kenzie, wife Nicole, Kamie, Brandon. (Courtesy Brandon Bunch)

Mike Prato with his wife Merry and daughter Theodora. (Courtesy Mike Prato)

Armand McCormick with wife Sarah and sons Milo and Ice (kneeling). (Courtesy Armand McCormick)

Thomas Franklin with son Christian and daughter Elizabeth. (Courtesy Thomas Franklin)

Sergeant Major James Miles Thetford at his retirement party in 2014, with his son James Miles Thetford II, then a 21-year-old Lance Corporal in the Marine Corps Reserve. (Courtesy James Miles Thetford)

At a 20th year reunion banquet at Camp Pendleton in July, 2023. Left to right: Author Chip Reid, Rob Witt, Elber Navarro, Rob Gilbert, Robert Kerman, Scott Smith, Frank Quintero and Miles Thetford. (Author's photo)

(Left to right) Elber Navarro, Travis Icard, and Jason Arellano and other Marine veterans of 3/5 carry a steel cross to the top of First Sergeant's Hill at Camp Pendleton on August 19, 2022. "We want to suffer through this hike in honor of our fallen brothers," one Marine said.

Marines of 3/5 on First Sergeant's Hill wearing shirts that honor their 36 brothers who "gave all" in Iraq from 2003 to 2006. (Author's photo)

Dog tags of the 36 men honored on First Sergeant's Hill blow in the gentle ocean breeze, sounding like delicate wind chimes, or as one Marine described it: "The voices of angels."

Marine veterans of 3/5 and Gold Star Family members on top of First Sergeant's Hill, where they memorialized the 36 members of 3/5 who lost their lives in Iraq between 2003 and 2006.

needed to talk to somebody and just share. Because post-traumatic stress is not just combat induced. For me," he says, "combat was strike one. Strike two was divorce. Strike three was the second relationship that collapsed."

When I asked where he'd be today if he hadn't sought help, Prato said: "I would be this lonely hermit, living by myself, reliving my experiences, both the combat and the relationship drama."

He says he's a lot better today, but still has sudden outbursts of anger over "something stupid." But now he can deal with it because he learned in therapy how to "ground" himself during those moments.

Prato is not reluctant to describe his internal battles, but he is also a strong critic of how the VA and others in officialdom handled the issue. "The whole damn PTS thing is witchcraft to me," he said. "In 2004 and 2005, they medicated the hell out of everybody. All my guys (referring to his platoon members) were on some type of behavioral control medicine. It went from not knowing how to diagnose it to everybody has it. I just don't believe everybody has it."

Today, Prato says he's looking for his "second purpose" in life after the Marine Corps. He doesn't want to work for someone else. "I want to be my own master and build my own team and find a way to give back to society," he says, a statement that sounds a lot like Post-Traumatic Growth.

During our Zoom interview Prato introduced me to his girlfriend Merry. At that moment the curmudgeon disappeared and for the first time in our interview he broke into a big smile as he told me that Merry was pregnant. I could see and feel his joy. I half expected him to break out in song as he described seeing the baby's heartbeat for the first time a few days before our interview.

"I'm 44 years old and I'm finally gonna be a dad!" he exclaimed. "We're super excited and it changed my perspective on a lot of things." A few months later he emailed me with the news that he and Merry were now husband and wife and that she had just given birth to a healthy baby girl named Theodora Hazel Prato. So, that second purpose in life he's looking for? Sounds like he might already have found it—or at least a very significant part of it.

Sergeant Josh Pryor, the Philosopher Marine

To have become a deeper man is the privilege of those who have suffered.

—Josh Pryor quoting Oscar Wilde

During our interview I asked Josh Pryor if he would be the man he is today if he had not joined the Marines. It was the beginning of an intellectual rollercoaster ride with the man I nicknamed "The Philosopher Marine." He started out by summarizing the ups and downs of life as a Marine in one succinct paragraph:

There's no way I could foresee the kind of man I'd be without the guiding force of the Marines, especially after losing my dad as a teenager. I've had tons of surgeries, I'm physically broken for my age, and I went through a lot of PTSD stuff. And I haven't regretted it for a single day. I learned so much and met so many great, great men and women. And going through the combat aspect of it, one of the biggest things I took away was the value of human life.

Then Pryor shifted into philosopher gear. He first quoted Thomas Paine, one of the great thinkers of the American Revolution, who famously said: "What we obtain too cheaply, we esteem too lightly." The ride really got going as Pryor explained what that quote means to him:

Life is just given to us. We're just here. Until you're faced with losing it and seeing it lost on multiple fronts—including the innocent and enemy combatants. It doesn't matter who, it's a loss of life. And I think that experience helped me appreciate that every second we're here is a gift. If you think about it, not just on a personal level, but on a global level, the fact that we exist amongst the cosmos—it's a gift. Whether from a scientific or spiritual perspective, it doesn't matter. It's still amazing.

The philosopher was just revving up his engine:

What we do with that gift matters. Every choice we make, the actions we take, the things we do, they echo, they affect other people around us. And I think being a Marine helped me become the kind of man that wants to affect people in a positive way, to help my fellow man and be the kind of person who would not just go through life selfishly, but to value my life in every breath that I have, and to use it for good so that one day when it is my time, I can go without regret.

I told him that I had never heard a better description of Post-Traumatic Growth, which prompted Pryor to go even deeper, quoting Irish poet and playwright Oscar Wilde: "To have become a deeper man is the privilege of those who have suffered," which he then interpreted in the context of his experience as a Marine with PTSD:

> Growth and pain are very closely linked. And it's not easy when you're in that fight and you're trying to find your way through the darkness. But on the other side is a perspective you cannot buy, you cannot teach, it's not in the book. You just have to know it and experience it. And it's life changing.

Getting to this life-changing point, though, was not easy. For Pryor, going from trauma and stress to personal growth was a painful, years-long journey. His father passed away when he was 15, and for several years afterward he felt that he had lost his "guiding force." He was "rudderless," he told me. "I lost my way." Pryor tried college, but despite his obvious intellectual abilities, he lasted only a year. He found various types of employment, but nothing that inspired him.

When he was 20 years old, a co-worker told him he was going to enlist in the Marines. Pryor offered to give him a ride to the recruiting office. Out of curiosity he went inside. The recruiter, after speaking with his friend, looked at Pryor and said: "What about you?" Pryor hadn't actively considered joining the military. But as he chatted with the recruiter, he proudly told him that his grandfather had served in World War II as a chaplain and had earned a Bronze Star. He also mentioned other ancestors who had served in the military. Pryor told the recruiter he was "open" to the idea, and as the conversation continued he remembers the moment when, suddenly: "It just kind of hit me. It just kind of felt right. I needed direction." He told the recruiter: "I'll do it."

Pryor took the ASVAB (Armed Services Vocational Aptitude Battery), a test created by the Pentagon to measure potential in the military and earned a score high enough to open a wide range of opportunities. The choice, he says, was easy. He wanted the hardest path—the infantry. "I've always been a 'go big or go home' kind of guy," he told me. "There's something very appealing to a young man that, if I'm going to do it, I'm going to go all in. And if I'm going to be in the Marines Corps," he added, "I'm not going to work on computers." Pryor wanted the biggest challenge, and he got it: He would be a frontline combat Marine.

The Corps quickly became the "guiding force" that he had been missing since the death of his father. Mostly, he says, it was about the feeling of community. "You never feel alone in the Marine Corps. I can't remember a time when I felt isolated. You feel part of something, and you feel supported, and you feel like they're going to fight for me and I'm going to fight for them. It's us, it's we, it's together. Brotherhood is key."

That intense feeling of camaraderie among Marines is what gives so many of them newfound purpose. It feels like climbing a mountain together. But leaving the Marines is the opposite feeling—it's like falling off a cliff. "When you get out, when you're trying to heal, when you lose that sense of community, there's a loneliness that I can't describe," Pryor told me. "There's a separation from something you didn't even know was your heartbeat. It's what kept you going. It's what got you through. And when you lose that, boy, it's a feeling of being lost."

He was sent home soon after the fall of Baghdad because, as a stop-loss Marine, his discharge date had already passed. When he returned there were very few other Marines to connect with. His closest buddies were still in Iraq. Within two weeks his wife was pregnant. "I went straight from the battlefield to a father at 22," he says. He turned his attention to his young family and for many years lost contact with his fellow Marines. But filling his life with fatherly duties was not enough to keep post-traumatic stress from seeping into his life. Symptoms began appearing and became worse over time. His temper became explosive.

I asked him if there was a particular moment of trauma at the root of his stress. Pryor told me the day that stands out in his 2003 combat tour was the ferocious battle of April 4, 2003. He's one of several members of India Company who trace their PTSD back to that day—when Corporal Erik Silva was killed in action.

To put that day in context, Pryor said that he and Silva had formed a special bond the day before. Pryor was experiencing such severe back pain that he could barely lift his gear. He limped along behind his squad, and it was Silva who helped him get over a wall that he couldn't climb on his own. "I got you," Silva told him.

On April 4, Pryor and Silva were again in close company. Their squad was being fired upon by enemy forces who were well dug in. To confront them, they had to cross over a ditch on a short metal bridge that has become very familiar to readers of this book. Unknown to them, enemy fighters were hiding in the ditch. "I was really physically close to him when he was shot," Pryor says. "We crossed over the same bridge. So, I've had to live with the fact that I passed right by the people that shot him. They didn't shoot me. They waited for him."

Over the years he has been wracked with survivor's guilt. Why did Silva die instead of him? "There's one hundred ways I might not have come back," Pryor said. "I had rounds go between my legs and close to my face." Those close calls didn't register as significant moments at the time, he told me, but they became impossible to forget as the years wore on.

"When you're holding your baby for the first time," he said, "you realize how close this was to never happening." Or when you "send that beautiful life off to college," and you realize that "all the impact that she would have in the world wouldn't have been here at all" if one of the many bullets that missed him in 2003 had taken a slightly different trajectory.

He started second guessing his own worth: "Was I a good Marine? Was I a good leader? Did I impact people?" In addition to his post-traumatic stress symptoms, Pryor was dealing with significant back and knee injuries, and excruciating pain. At times it was almost impossible to walk.

Reluctantly, he went to the VA. They gave him a large bag of pain meds including Vicodin, Soma, Lodine and Flexeril. As happens in so many cases, he says, it became easier to numb the pain than to deal with it. "One Vicodin turned into two, and two into three, and three into four, really, really fast," he says. "As I slipped into that world a little bit, I got mad at the VA. They made it so easy. Drugs don't solve the problem. So I never went back."

He decided he had to fight his post-traumatic stress issues on his own. Friends advised him to try the VA again, but he refused. Looking back, Pryor says he now accepts a simple truth: "You can't do it on your own. You have to get help. And it's a hard thing to ask for, especially for jarheads." I asked if he had become addicted to pain meds. "I got to a point where I was taking far, far too much," he said. "And I'm grateful that I had the sense to say myself: 'Dude, this is not sustainable.' I knew the road that I was on. Because it would have ended me."

In retrospect, he says he understands why so many veterans take their own lives. "I think that loss of community is a huge driving force in veteran suicide," he told me. "And I think people get so tired of covering symptoms for so many years they decide there's no other way out."

It was the suicide of a close friend in 2021 that finally opened his eyes. Travis Pollock, a Marine he had fought with in Iraq, was not the first Marine in Pryor's unit to take his own life, but Pryor and Travis had been particularly close. "He was a Marine's Marine," Pryor told me. "A really good dude, full of life, loved life, embraced life. And it was so sad to see him give up."

Pryor took a big step out of his cocoon and flew to California for the funeral, which was attended by many of his old Marine friends. He was overwhelmed. "Seeing those men again after 17 years, it was like nothing had changed," he says. "There was this feeling washing over me of 'you've never been alone, you just haven't been connected to these brothers, but they're still your brothers.'"

"That changed my life," Pryor says, "and I owe it to my buddy Travis. I think about him a lot as I kind of bask in this new mindset of 'I'm not alone' and I need these men around me, and I need to be a part of their lives. I had felt so secluded and alone," he continued. "You have to be connected to people who understand, who've been in that dirt. Because they're the ones who are willing to reach out to pull you up, they're the ones who are going to show you how to get out of the hole you're in. There's a difference between support and brotherhood, and that brotherhood really saved me."

Pryor is seeing a therapist who has helped a lot but says he couldn't have made the transition without reaching out to his fellow Marines. It was like waving a white flag and saying: "I can't do this on my own." He finds it hard to believe that anyone could experience combat and not be affected by it. "I think it's very naive to think that our emotional and brain structures are made of titanium," he says, "and that we can watch people die or we can take a life," and not feel anything.

He claims there are two types of former combatants. "There are the ones that have realized and embraced that this affected me, and I need to work on it. And there are the ones who are like, 'Nope, not me, bro. I'm good.' And those ones tend to isolate more," he says. "And those ones tend to turn a blind eye, and then that damage just builds and builds and builds. Honestly, I wouldn't want to be a person that could go through that unaffected. I think there's a loss of humanity there."

Corporal Scott Smith

> There's PTSD. There's severe depression. There's social anxiety disorder. You pull out the DSM5 [Diagnostic and Statistical Manual of Mental Disorders] and you just go down the list and start marking them off.

Scott Smith has one of the strangest stories of joining the Marines I've ever heard. It's literally "comical." He says he joined the Marines "because of an online comic strip." The strip involved "battling a dragon with a sword and turning a person into a Greek statue of a Marine." I don't get it, but 17-year-old Smith says he was "completely enthralled" by the comic. So, he got drunk and walked into the Marine Corps recruiting office and said he wanted to join the infantry. He filled out a form and thought he had joined the Marines.

But the recruiter called him the next day and told him that, because he had been intoxicated, they gave him a fake contract to sign. And of course, you can't sign up at 17 without your parents' permission anyway. He was told that if he still wanted to join, he could go through the proper process and sign a real contract. Smith felt like he had already committed himself, so he said: "Sure, why not?"

It is ironic that something that began so comically could lead to something so tragic. On March 25, 2003, Smith was driving the Humvee in which Michael Johnson was killed and Frank Quintero sustained near fatal injuries when both were struck by an unexploded RPG.

Smith says he was "literally falling apart" in the immediate aftermath of Johnson's death, and he's not afraid or embarrassed to admit it. "I just started breaking down. I kept screaming too, when it happened, on the radio: 'He's gone! He's gone! Johnson's dead! Johnson's dead!'"

When he got out of his Humvee he sat down by the side of the road and cried.

A friend leaned down to comfort him, and said, "It's okay to cry in war." An instant later that same Marine jumped to his feet and screamed "Did you fucking see that?!" after another Marine destroyed a speeding, heavily armed, enemy pickup truck with a missile. Anguish, jubilation, and bloodlust, all mixed together in a cocktail called combat. "Crying and laughing at the same time," as Smith later described the surreal scene.

He was so overpowered by his emotions at that moment, he says, because he found it indescribably sad that the first person in the battalion to be killed was a Hospital Corpsman—a medic, whose job it was to save lives. And the fact that it was Johnson, one of his closest friends, added to the horror. They had shared a tent in Kuwait and had gotten to know each other on a deeply personal level. Johnson had shared stories about his family and about his devotion to Christianity, and confided to Smith that he, as an African American, had experienced racial encounters with white Sailors. He had even been called the N-word by older servicemen.

After Johnson died, Smith found his Bible, which Johnson always carried with him. Every morning as the convoy began to move, Johnson would read from the 23rd Psalm: "Yea, though I walk through the valley of the shadow of death, I will fear no evil." Johnson had written in the Bible about his time in Kuwait and Iraq, about his family, and about finding peace with God. Smith kept the Bible to remember him. Fifteen years later, at a ceremony to honor Johnson in his home state of Arkansas, Smith gave the Bible to Johnson's family. They were overjoyed to receive it.

Today Smith refers to Johnson's death as the moment in his life when "the big tree fell," the beginning of his trauma, the instant when everything changed. "That was the most surreal and aware moment of my life," he says today. "That is what hell looks like."

It took a while for the stress symptoms to appear. "The nightmares and sweats and tremors didn't happen until later on," Smith says. When they did start, the nightmares were usually about "a family member of mine being killed by Iraqis, or someone putting a gun to my head and pulling the trigger. It's like a recurring nightmare, you're being executed, and you feel the blast but you're still alive." He also suffers from survivor's guilt. "We got hit by the RPG, but I lived. I ask myself if I had driven two miles an hour faster, or slower, would he still be alive. There's PTSD. There's severe depression. There's social anxiety disorder. You pull out the DSM5 [Diagnostic and Statistical Manual of Mental Disorders] and you just go down the list and start marking them off."

Smith finds writing fiction—loosely based on his combat experience—to be very therapeutic. And he's very good at it. Here's an excerpt from his essay "Up in the Gun" published in *Public Space*, a New York literary journal:

> The Veteran missed his 16. He missed holding it at his side, one-arming it while running, or plinking hood ornaments on patrol. He missed how the selector switch clicked when moved from safe to single burst. And the muzzle break, like a sea creature, vented and gilled and stinging against your cheek. He missed the cold, polished bores and chipped plastic grips. The thought of it emitted a lightness in his step that he felt radiate from down in his heels to the bruised cuticle of his trigger finger.

I hate to admit it, but I find that very poetic paragraph to be a very pleasant break from my somewhat pedestrian prose.

First Lieutenant Dave Valentino

> Marine training is a double-edged sword. It trains you to identify threats and be ready for them. But years later, as a civilian you're still looking for threats everywhere you go.

Dave Valentino comes from an Army family—his father was in Vietnam and his grandfather in World War II. But when he graduated from college he wanted the maximum challenge, so he decided to see if he "had what it takes" to become a Marine. The way he got through boot camp, he says, was by telling himself every day: "I can survive this one more day." He retired in 2015 as a major after 15 years of service.

Valentino was 3/5's Battalion Communications Officer in 2003, an extremely high-stress job, and was diagnosed with PTSD while he was still on active duty. But because of the stigma attached to PTSD, he initially dealt with it himself instead of seeking professional help. Over time it became "a less sensitive issue," he says, and after he retired in 2015 he sought treatment.

His symptoms today still include nightmares, occasional angry outbursts, and hyper-vigilance in crowded places. "I have good days and bad days," he says. "I'm doing better. And my wife helps a lot when she sees me having issues."

Valentino believes hyper-vigilance, one of the most common symptoms of PTSD, may have its roots in Marine Corps training. "Training is a double-edged sword," he says. "It trains you well to identify threats and be ready for them." But the other side of the sword comes into play after a Marine returns home. Years later, as a civilian, "you're still looking for threats everywhere you go. It's hard to turn it off. You're always on a heightened state of alert."

But there's another aspect of his combat experience that he talked about at more length during our interview and appears to have affected him more deeply—survivor's guilt. He has long suffered with recurring thoughts about whether he might have done more to help two fellow Marines.

Major Kevin Nave, 3/5's Executive Officer, was killed instantly when he was run over by a Marine Corps bulldozer. Gunnery Sergeant Russell Cederburg was sleeping next to Nave. His legs were crushed in the same incident. Valentino, who had been sleeping nearby, knew both men well. "I'll always wonder what if" he says. "What if I delivered better guidance for refueling that night Nave and Cederburg were run over? What if I'd gotten out of my sleeping bag sooner, could I have maybe provided more assistance to Major Nave?"

Valentino also sometimes feels responsible for the death of Staff Sergeant Riayan Tejeda, who was killed when his platoon was ambushed at night while on patrol in Baghdad. As communications officer, Valentino was involved in getting Tejeda evacuated by a medevac helicopter. "I was on the radio trying to get a medevac for him and they kept telling me to 'hold, hold, hold.' I still carry that with me, that I didn't do enough to possibly save him," he says. "What if I was able to get that medevac sooner?"

There's no rational reason for Valentino to believe he was in any way responsible for any of those losses, and Valentino—at least intellectually—understands that. "I know it was not my fault," he says. "But things like that never go away."

Of course, the Marine Corps *wants* Marines to feel responsible for each other. Protecting "the Marine on your right and the Marine on your left" is drilled into them from boot camp on. It's the reason some hesitant Marines told me they pulled the trigger in battle—not to protect themselves, but to protect their fellow Marines.

Valentino says his PTSD also stems from non-combat sources. During one deployment he had the particularly stressful assignment of loading "fallen angels"—Marines who had died—onto transports heading home. And during a non-combat assignment late in his career, he delivered casualty notifications to family members and helped families through that process, which included everything from receiving the Marines' remains to presenting the American flag at the funeral.

Marine Corps training doesn't deal with such things, he says. "These are things you aren't prepared for. And they leave a permanent mark on you."

Captain Ethan Bishop

I just don't get it.

Ethan Bishop is highly skeptical about PTSD. "I don't understand PTSD to this day because it never really affected me. I almost see PTSD and things like that as guilt. I don't lose any sleep over it."

One reason for that, he says, might be that the Marines under his command did not violate the rules of military engagement, so there was nothing to regret. "I'm proud of the way they conducted themselves," he says. "I can tell you with a hundred percent truth that they did everything I asked them to do correctly. I don't recall any instances where civilians were killed by my Marines as collateral damage, or even hurt."

Another possible reason is age—he was 31 years old at the time. The younger Marines—the 18, 19 and 20-year-olds—bore the brunt of the combat, so they were affected more than senior officers like himself. "There's Marines that I know of that are struggling to this day," he says. But he questions whether it's necessarily due to their combat experience.

"I think society wants to place the blame for where they are in life on those experiences."

Everyone has some bad memories, he says, and even he finds it helpful to talk about it. But PTSD? "I just don't get it," he says. "I've read about it and people have explained it to me. And I empathize, but not fully. Because I don't understand how that could change somebody. But everybody's built different."

Sergeant Nathaniel Donnelly

> Certain people are just wired to be warriors.

Nathaniel Donnelly says he is one of the lucky front-line combat Marines who came home with little to no trace of post-traumatic stress, even though he had the kinds of combat experiences that have haunted others for years.

He risked his life single-handedly taking out an enemy machine-gun nest. He killed numerous Iraqis in battle, including one who was less than a foot away. And he's had a few near-death experiences—including one where an enemy fighter had a clear shot at him from close range but did not fire. Donnelly doesn't know if the Iraqi's gun jammed or if he just decided not to shoot. He sometimes dreams of combat, but does not have nightmares. He says the dreams are more exhilarating than frightening.

He attributes his absence of stress symptoms to his family's warrior past. He wanted to be a Marine since he was a child, and believes he was literally born to be a warrior. "I think it goes back hundreds if not thousands of years," he says. Even his last name tells the story—he says it means "brown-haired warrior."

But he admits he did struggle with one thing after coming home from the war in 2003—a sense of "entitlement." As a warrior who had fought for his country, he felt that he "should have been made a priority in society, or in other peoples' lives. And of course, I wasn't." His resentment, he says, affected his behavior.

For three years after coming home, he says, he drank heavily and had no direction. In 2003 he was arrested for DUI. His blood alcohol level was twice the legal limit. "I struggled with my place in society, and wanted to get back in the Marines," he told me. "But with a recent DUI that was never going to happen."

In 2004 he got in a fight that was serious enough that the police were called. They tasered him twice and he was sentenced to 30 days in jail but was released on his own recognizance after four days. "I was still in war mode probably through 2004," he says now. Finally, in 2006 he had another DUI. That was the trigger, he says. "I finally took responsibility for myself and made some serious changes." From that moment on he experienced a turnaround that is nothing short of extraordinary.

He earned a degree from San Diego State University, where he was "Top Male Student" one year and graduated with a "Top 25" award. He also earned an MBA. He was president of his fraternity and a co-founder of Student Veterans of America. He was invited to the White House on Veterans Day where he met President Obama and First Lady Michelle Obama. (He describes her as "probably the most impressive person I ever met.")

Now, he's a devoted family man. He and his girlfriend have two young children, a girl and a boy. He stays "grounded" by practicing Jiu Jitsu every day at 6am and competes in local tournaments. "I remember being less scared in combat than I feel when I go out on the mat," he says. "I know I'm not going to die, but it's scary. It's just me against that guy. There's no team." Jiu Jitsu, he says, has become very popular, and very effective, among combat veterans battling post-traumatic stress, and he does whatever he can to spread the word.

While insisting that he never had PTSD, Donnelly does believe that the way he turned his life around is an example of PTG, Post-Traumatic Growth. He agrees with the concept that experiencing a traumatic event like combat can have positive consequences—if you make a sustained effort to grow from it.

He gave a poignant example about growing up in a military family, where the men never used the word love. "I never told my dad I loved him," Donnelly says. "And my dad never said he loved me. Same with my grandfather." Now, he always tells them he loves them before he hangs up the phone.

"That changed our relationship. Just that simple little tweak changed those relationships super-significantly. It made all of us more vulnerable and we started talking more about real shit instead of just trying to be guys," he says. "And I think that was definitely Post-Traumatic Growth right there."

Corporal Wes Smith

> The idea of being a victim doesn't match with our natural identity of who we are, the protectors ... as Marines, yeah, we need to suck it up.

Wes Smith is included in this chapter on post-traumatic stress not because he has a notable case of it—he doesn't—but because he has an interesting and somewhat controversial point of view about PTSD.

I interviewed Smith twice on Zoom. The first time, he was surprisingly sarcastic, flippant, even somewhat insulting, about people with PTSD. I asked if it was okay for me to include those comments in the book, and he said yes. But later that day he sent me an email that included this:

> I wanted to make sure that I'm not too controversial in my PTSD statements. Also, I wanted you to know that I think PTSD is real and I know people suffer from it. I just feel the overall veteran community exaggerates it a bit publicly. Especially those who never saw actual combat. As for all my 3/5 brothers or anyone else who saw actual combat, I believe their thoughts and feelings on PTSD are warranted and honest.

In the meantime, I discovered that I had forgotten to press the record button before our interview. Smith graciously agreed to a second interview, in which he dropped the sarcastic tone and was a lot less critical.

But he stuck to his guns on one thing—that diagnosing so many Marines with PTSD gives people the impression that Marines are victims, and that doesn't square with their role as protectors. "I think it's our job, even after we leave the Marine Corps, to be the type of person that protects people and keeps bad things from happening," he says. "And you can't be that if you consider yourself a victim."

Smith thinks one reason PTSD is so prevalent in the military—and there is statistical evidence to support this idea—is that many have signs of PTSD even before they join. "Who joins the military? Who joins the Marines?" he asks, using himself as an example. "I was like, sure, I'll go get shot at. I'll sleep in the dirt and get sent to another country for barely any money at all. To be that kind of person is not a normal thing. So, I think there are some mental areas where we're already a little crazy anyway. And then you throw war on top of that."

Smith concedes that he's had issues of his own. He drank too much for years after returning from combat, until right before his wife gave birth to their first child. "That's just one of the things Marines do. They drink a lot," he says. And when you leave the Marines it's hard to stop. "So, you're a civilian now, but you're still drinking like you're an alcoholic, like you're a functioning alcoholic."

Smith also struggles with sleep. He says he's had trouble sleeping all his life but admits that adding violent combat memories to a pre-existing sleep problem can certainly make things worse. But that doesn't mean he's a victim: "How can you be a victim and a protector at the same time?" he asks. "Even if we do have PTSD, and even if something's wrong with us, our job is to be the protectors. It's not nice to say, 'suck it up' anymore, but as Marines, yeah, we need to suck it up."

Smith's life today revolves around his wife and four young children, his job, and his hobbies. But that doesn't mean he's left the Marines behind. "Just like a marriage takes work," he says, "keeping a long-distance friendship with a large group of guys takes work." He's on the committee that's planning the 20th reunion of 3/5 in 2023, and he also helped organize the ten- and fifteen-year reunions. And he takes trips every year with his Marine buddies.

Smith says Marine camaraderie is somewhat like being in a college fraternity, "but it's even tighter because we all fit that psychological profile of a Marine." Smith's wife occasionally joins him on his Marine vacations and tells him: "I can see happiness in all your faces. That only happens when you are all together."

For guys struggling with PTSD, Smith says, one of the most important things they can do is nourish the relationships they had when they were in the Marines. "Every time we have a reunion, I feel so good," he says. "But you can do this on your own. You don't need a reunion. Call your best three Marine buddies and go on a hunting trip or a fishing trip."

First Lieutenant Brian Chontosh

> There are so many veterans that are high functioning but they're still managing a lot of shit inside. We help those that are trying to help themselves.

Brian Chontosh has devoted much of his time since retiring, as a major, to helping his fellow Marines through his Big Fish Foundation. "There are so many veterans that are high functioning," he says. "But they're still managing a lot of shit inside. We help those that are trying to help themselves."

When veterans take their own lives, he says, the news is often received with comments like: "I can't believe so-and-so just committed suicide," or "There were no signs." Or maybe people see the signs, but only after the fact. "Why is that?" Chontosh asks. "Because they're high functioning. They're managing their shit really, really well. But they can't manage it infinitely."

To help them manage their issues, Big Fish invites veterans to camping retreats. He also invites law enforcement officers, who witness similar traumatic events and experience the resulting stress. "We camp for a couple of days and barbecue and go for hikes and do some physical training, eat breakfast, lunch, and dinner together, and share making the meals," Chontosh says. "That reignites a sense of camaraderie, and a feeling that you belong and you're accountable to somebody else."

Getting out in nature and enjoying the company of people who've had similar experiences, he says, leads to much deeper and much more authentic conversation. "When you help them let their guard down you can effect real change and you can help a lot of guys out. It also creates networks between people so that when they leave here, they've got their networks reconnected. I find that these retreats are amazing," he says. "We've been very successful at helping people."

CHAPTER 10

Marine Families Tell Their Stories

The Martinez Family

In early September 2003, 3d Battalion, 5th Marines came home from Iraq after a seven-month deployment. NBC News asked me to cover the homecoming of "my" battalion. I met Joe Klimovitz, who was my cameraman in Iraq, at Camp Pendleton in Southern California.

We waited for the Marines to arrive, standing with their wives, newborn babies, mothers, fathers, and other family members, who profusely thanked us for our reports. In previous wars, those with loved ones on the front lines often went weeks or months without hearing a word. With our live and taped reports airing multiple times every day, the families kept their televisions tuned 24/7 to MSNBC or NBC.

The Marines arrived in three waves with the last arriving at 2:30am. The families of the final group had waited in a state of nervous excitement for more than eight hours. When the Marines finally got off the buses, Klimo shot video of the emotional reunions and I did interviews for stories that would air later that day.

Looking at those stories years later, one of the lines I wrote stands out: "Many here say that after so long apart, getting back to normal will be hard work." That turned out to be an enormous understatement for many of the Marines and their families, including Corporal Mike Martinez, who held his son Mike Jr., while I interviewed him and his wife Stefanie, who held their newborn son Scott.

A photo of this moment is included in this book. Stefanie was overwhelmed with joy to have their family reunited, but Mike was stoic and distant. Looking at his eyes, he appears to have what is known as "the one-thousand-yard stare." (The famous painting by Tom Lea is titled *The Two Thousand Yard Stare*.) It's an expression that was coined during World War I to describe the unfocused gaze of servicemen with shell shock, known today as PTSD.

At the time, I thought that's just the way Marines are. They don't like to show their emotions. And of course, he must have been physically and mentally exhausted. In fact, though, as I later learned, the extreme disconnectedness of some of the Marines, including Martinez, was also a sign of difficult times to come.

Almost twenty years later, I interviewed Mike and Stefanie Martinez again, this time on Zoom from their home in California. Their son Mike Jr. is in the Air Force and joined us on Zoom from a USAF base in Italy. Son Scott, a Midshipman at the United States Naval Academy, joined us from Annapolis, Maryland.

My first impression of the family on the screen in front of me was of the quintessentially happy military family—the proud father wearing a shirt with the Marine Corps Eagle, Globe, and Anchor symbol, sitting next to his beautiful, smiling wife; the sons, Mike Jr. and Scott, both handsome young men proudly following in their father's military footsteps. And in fact, I was right. They are a happy family. But it took a long time, a tremendous amount of patience, and a lot of love to get to this point.

Mike had told me before the interview that he struggled mightily with PTSD for several years following his 2003 deployment in Iraq, so I approached the topic gingerly because his family was present. He told me not to worry about it. He was totally open to any question I wanted to ask. "They know 100 percent," he said.

All four members of this courageous family were not just willing, but eager, to talk about their struggle in detail. Their hope is that other families can learn from their difficult experience. Perhaps someone else who reads this—and is driving his family to the ragged edge because of PTSD—will seek help right away, instead of putting it off for 15 agonizing years.

Mike said he had several symptoms of PTSD, including explosive anger. Just about anything could set him off. He had such a short fuse that his family was always "walking on eggshells."

Mike Jr. said there was never any physical abuse—but the mental abuse was at times, severe. His father could explode without warning. He said it was like living with a drill instructor. "We were scared. I was always angry, hearing my dad going off on our mom. Why is he doing this? Why is he like this? I didn't understand at the time."

Younger brother Scott said: "It was something that we just had to keep going through and endure, despite the fact that we knew it was wrong."

There were some good times. Even some good years. "It wasn't 24/7," wife Stefanie said. "It would come and go in spurts." But the bad times always seemed to return.

Anger was not Mike's only PTSD symptom. Many veterans with PTSD suffer from addiction. Mike's addiction wasn't drugs or alcohol. He medicated himself with food, gaining an enormous amount of weight and peaking at 340 pounds. That made him even more frightening. Stefanie said his attitude was: "I'm big and intimidating, and I don't care what people think." Mike said his mindset, before he sought help, was: "This is just who I am. I'm the big bad guy. I'm right, you're wrong."

Much of that attitude was aimed at Stefanie, who says the hardest part was that she always doubted herself. "I always felt like there was something I did wrong. Everything I did was never right, and I couldn't keep him happy." She was often too frightened and confused to respond to his outbursts. "I would always shut down. I couldn't say anything."

Her job, she said, was to try to keep peace in the household. When Mike was angry, she would sneak away to warn the boys. "Just stay away from dad, he's in a mood," she would tell them. "I was always protecting them so they wouldn't get the brunt of the anger," she told me, as her husband nodded in agreement beside her. Mike's PTSD almost tore the family apart. "There were moments where I wanted to just give up and leave, take the kids and go," Stefanie said. "There were many nights I cried myself to sleep because I just didn't know what else to do. I was stuck."

She said three things kept her going: her sons, her faith, and her commitment to helping her husband climb out of the dark hole he was in. "Don't give up. He needs you," she would tell herself. "You have to stay. You love him. And I do. I love him to death. And I decided, I'm going to fight for him. I have to fight for him because he's not fighting for himself."

Mike had sought help at the VA in 2007, but says they weren't helpful at all. A nurse even told him he needed to "suck it up." Instead, he gave up. It took him another 12 years to try again. For most people, New Year's resolutions rarely meet with success, but on January 1, 2019, Mike's resolution was to get help. And it turned his life around.

He started seeing a mental health therapist who guided him through his time in combat and the horrors he had witnessed, zeroing in on one particular incident—the death of Michael "Doc" Johnson, the battalion's first fatality in 2003. For years Mike had privately blamed himself for Johnson's death, even though his reasoning made little sense. This is how he explained it: "When Johnson got hit, I felt like I failed. As a forward observer my job was to call for fire, to provide support for anybody who's in need. I broke my radio; I could not maintain communication. My one job was to maintain communications. I could not do that. Because I failed, Johnson died."

With the help of his therapist, and the strong support of his family, he finally accepted the fact that blaming himself was absurd. "It's the Marine Corps," he says now. "We've got shitty gear. Things break. It was absolutely not my fault that Doc Johnson died." That was the beginning of the end of 15 years of self-imposed torture over unfounded feelings of guilt.

Eventually he reached the light at the end of the tunnel—and turned PTSD into Post-Traumatic Growth. Stefanie, who attended some of Mike's therapy sessions, says his turnaround has been the answer to her prayers. He's growing in ways that amaze and inspire her. He's going to school, with the goal of trading his monotonous job at the post office for his dream job—teacher and sports coach.

"He's now in a very happy place," she says. "He's very content with his life now." Mike calls it a "positive place," a dramatic change from the constant negativity of just a few years ago. And he adds that there's no chance he could have made the change without the love and support of his family. "They were my rock," he says. He now has a new mantra: "Better every day." A vast improvement, he says, over his previous mantra: "Fuck 'em."

Scott sees a silver lining on the dark cloud of his father's PTSD. It taught him an important life lesson. "We saw firsthand what PTSD can do to those around you," he said. "I feel like we have a different understanding than what the average person has."

He believes his father's PTSD did not come about because his father did anything wrong. It happened because his father did something right: he chose to serve his country. And PTSD is one of the sacrifices risked by all who serve, especially those who serve in front-line combat positions.

With a military career in his future after he graduates from the Naval Academy, Scott noted that he could be sent overseas some day and return with PTS or PTSD. But if so, he said, he will be able to lean on, and learn from, someone who's been through it—his dad.

Corporal Brandon and Nicole Bunch

I interviewed several married couples in September 2003 at the 3/5 homecoming, including Brandon and Nicole Bunch. Nicole recalls that while she and the other wives, girlfriends and family members waited, spirits were high—they were nervous, but giddy. But for some, when the Marines finally arrived and filed off the buses, it felt like the air suddenly leaked out of a balloon.

Almost 20 years later, I interviewed them again, this time via Zoom—first Brandon, then Nicole, then the two of them together. Nicole vividly remembers waiting for Brandon, a 23-year-old Corporal, and when he finally arrived, how disappointed and confused she was at his low-key response. "I was so excited about seeing him. I knew there were going to be changes, but I expected him to be more excited," she said later. Some of the Marines were outwardly joyful, but others—including Brandon—were quiet and withdrawn.

All these years later, Brandon remembers the interview we did soon after he got off the bus—not because of what he said, which was very little, but because of how he felt: "dumbfounded" and "closed off," as he later described it. "I felt like I had to speak very carefully about what not to say, what to say, and how to say it. I put on a front that I was okay."

But he was far from okay. He knew that the war had changed him, and that he had no desire to share what he was feeling—not with his wife, and certainly not with me. Two decades later he told me that while he was in Iraq he felt it was essential to keep his emotions in check. He needed to show steely leadership to the Marines under his command. They were looking to him to be an example, to be "level-headed and positive," no matter how much chaos was going on around them.

That need to bury his emotions continued after coming home. "He had hidden all the issues he was having away from me," Nicole says looking back. "He was very closed off. He just wasn't happy." Those "issues" soon became more apparent. He started showing classic symptoms of post-traumatic stress. "Everything bothered me," he says now. "Being in crowds, talking to people, driving down the road, everything. Nothing felt normal anymore."

"I knew something was wrong," Nicole says. "I remember the first time he drove on the highway and everybody's going 80 miles an hour and he's going 40." Always in a hypervigilant state of mind, he was constantly looking around for danger. The only emotions he showed were "anger or frustration, or just kind of a blank canvas," Nicole said. "But he tried to act like nothing was wrong, and because he was trying to act that way, I was trying to act that way too. And it just festered."

Brandon did his best to stay busy, going to college and becoming a firefighter/EMT, often holding two or three jobs at the same time. Staying busy was one way to keep his mind off his stress-related issues. The more he thought about what was happening to him and what he was feeling, he said, the worse it got. "It was a whirlwind of emotions. I knew I wasn't the same anymore. And I didn't know how I was going to transition back to the civilian sector. Everything was different. I didn't get any enjoyment out of anything."

He remembered the war as if it had been a video game. "Somebody else was playing your character and you didn't always have control over what you were doing. It almost seemed like somebody else was moving through you and working through you."

What he worried about most was his marriage, which meant everything to him. "I had the responsibility of being a husband and being there for her. So that kept me out of a lot of trouble," he said. He avoided the party scene with the single Marines, many of whom dealt with their post-combat issues by getting drunk in the barracks or at bars every night, which often made things worse. With so much changing inside him, Nicole had become his anchor. But he couldn't stop wondering if Nicole would accept this new, different—and more difficult—version of the man she married.

For years Brandon refused to seek help. "Being mentally strong is what the Marine Corps is all about," he explained. Seeking help showed weakness. And even if he had wanted to talk to someone, there seemed to be very little help available.

In later years, as more and more servicemen and servicewomen returned from Iraq and Afghanistan with stress-related issues, including PTSD, the Pentagon and the Department of Veterans Affairs revamped their procedures to focus more on mental health. But in 2003, Brandon and Nicole—and several other Marine families—told me that it felt like they were on their own. No one had counseled them about powerful but common issues like survivor's guilt, or symptoms of PTSD they should be aware of. "There wasn't a whole lot of talk about the emotions you might experience," he said.

During the years before Brandon finally sought help, they had two daughters. Tragically, the second was stillborn due to a heart condition. "That's when things really went to an all-time low for us," Nicole said. They were both grieving but "I couldn't help him, and he couldn't help me, so it just spiraled down for both of us."

About six years after coming home from Iraq, Brandon hit rock bottom. He temporarily moved out of the house, and says he was "in a very dark place." He started drinking heavily, which triggered disturbing memories of Iraq. "Stuff that I hadn't dealt with snowballed out of control," he said. Finally, he tried what he calls his "last-ditch effort." He sought counseling.

I asked him where he would be today if he hadn't sought help. "I hate to say it, and hate to admit it," he responded, "but I would be dead, for sure." "By your own hand?" I asked. "Oh, yeah," he said, showing no doubt whatsoever.

While talking about those deeply distressing days, Nicole became very emotional. "I could have seen him taking his life at that time," she said, tears welling up in her eyes. "I could see the pain. I could see the tiredness. I could see the alcohol, the things that were basically killing him one day at a time."

Brandon says he pulled through it largely because of Nicole: "My wife was in my corner no matter what. I consider myself extremely lucky and grateful." Nicole credits their faith in God and their love of family. "When he hit his all-time low with depression, he would still come over and see the kids because being a father has always been his top priority. That's all he's ever wanted to do," Nicole said. They would eventually have five children. (In a touching sign of devotion to the daughter they lost, they include her in the five children.)

Brandon says he would not have recovered without seeking help. Instead of locking up his thoughts and emotions, he has made a dramatic transformation. He now calls himself "an open book," adding: "I've learned a lot about the idea of sharing and being vulnerable. I think it's been a huge part of my transition and recovery." He says Marines do need to be mentally tough, but they also need to be mentally healthy. And that means giving up the Marine propensity to keep everything bottled up inside.

Today Brandon is not only interested in dealing openly with his own mental health—he also wants to help others with theirs. After what he's been through, he feels he's in a perfect position to do that. He dreams of being involved with, or even helping to create, a veteran non-profit. "It's one of my passions," he told me. "Trying to figure out what exactly veterans need, and to fill that gap with the help they're not getting." That attitude is what psychologists call Post-Traumatic Growth.

Navy Hospital Corpsman Paul "Doc" Elder

> I looked back at his wife and said, "I promise I'll bring him back." That was the first promise I broke.

Hospital Corpsman Paul "Doc" Elder was devastated by the death of his fellow Hospital Corpsman, Michael "Doc" Johnson, his closest friend in the battalion. As one of the first corpsmen to respond to the scene of Johnson's death on March 25, 2003, Elder was distraught—first by the inability to find Johnson in the chaos of the battle, and second, to learn that Johnson's injuries were almost certainly fatal.

Six months later, when the Marines of 3/5 returned to Camp Pendleton from Iraq, I interviewed Elder and his then-wife Jessica as he held their newborn son. They had named him Michael in honor of Michael Johnson.

Nearly 20 years later I interviewed Elder again, along with his ex-wife Jessica, and their son Michael on Zoom. Michael had just turned 19. I asked Michael what it meant to him to be named after Michael Johnson. He said that as a young boy he didn't understand the significance. But as he grew up and learned more about Johnson's story, he came to see it as an honor to be his namesake. When people call him Mike, he corrects them. "It's Michael," he says, out of respect for Johnson. "He was my dad's best friend," he tells people. "He lost his life in combat. And I was named after him."

Elder and Johnson met in early 2003, shortly before shipping out to Kuwait. As corpsmen they found it easy to talk to each other. Johnson ranked higher than Elder, and in some ways became Elder's mentor. Elder vividly remembers the day in 2003 when he and Johnson departed Camp Pendleton. "I looked back at his wife and said, 'I promise I'll bring him back,'" Elder recalls. "That didn't happen." It was a promise that would haunt him for years. "That was the first promise I broke," he told me, adding that he never makes promises any more. Adding to the weight of his survivor's guilt, Elder says he was scheduled to be in the Humvee in which Johnson was killed on March 25 instead of Johnson.

When Elder returned home from Iraq, he cut himself off from the men he had served with in Iraq and didn't talk to anyone about what he was going through. For the next decade he couldn't stop thinking about it, constantly questioning why Johnson had to die instead of him. "I couldn't let it go," Elder says. "There's a point in time where you should stop crying and just raise a glass up and share a memory. But I was still crying. I didn't really let his death go until about 2012 or 2013."

Elder's post-traumatic stress didn't all stem from Johnson's death; there were other traumatic events. In 2004, for example, during a training exercise on a California Marine base, the Humvee he was driving flipped over and a 19-year-old Marine riding in the back seat died in Elder's arms. And in 2008–2009 he spent a year in Afghanistan, where a bomb left him with a traumatic brain injury, nerve damage in his spine, and migraine headaches. In the following years he was divorced from Jessica, his first wife, married again, and divorced again.

Adding to his woes, Elder was forced to resign from the military, due to the severity of his injuries. He pleaded to stay in, to be sent to Iraq or Afghanistan to continue his life-saving work. "I kept getting told, 'no, you're damaged, no, you're damaged, no, you're damaged,'" he says. "I had all this experience and all this education, and I could be helping people, and nobody wanted me." By 2015, things were so bad that he was contemplating suicide.

Today, Elder's life has turned around dramatically. That's due in part to another promise he made—this one to Michael Johnson himself. While in Iraq, they promised each other that they would finish their education when they came home. Elder has steadfastly kept that promise with relentless effort. He studied to become a surgical tech and a respiratory therapist. He earned a bachelor's degree in health care administration and emergency management. He has worked as a trainer in community emergency response. And he's working on a master's in history.

Today, Elder still gets "a little bit depressed" about Johnson in the days leading up to the anniversary of his death. He always has a small shot of whiskey and gives a toast to his good friend. Recently, Elder finally took another big step he had been putting off for a long time—he got in touch with Johnson's family and was welcomed with open arms and lots of tears. He regrets not having opened that line of communication years ago.

Elder still experiences some post-traumatic stress symptoms but adds: "I don't really think I have the disorder anymore." He's always been drawn to opportunities to help other people, and he's finding new ways to do that, a sign of Post-Traumatic Growth. He created a nonprofit charity to help homeless veterans find places to live. And he's saving money for a scholarship in Michael Johnson's name.

Elder and his ex-wife, Jessica MacDonald, told me they see qualities in their son that Michael Johnson also possessed. Johnson was extremely caring and nurturing, and so is their son Michael. Johnson had a "hero streak," and so does their son Michael. They told me about the time Michael witnessed a man shoplifting and gave chase, catching him even after the thief jumped on a motor scooter. The man punched Michael in the face, but he wore the bruise like a badge of honor. In another of many such incidents, Michael, as a young child, grabbed his father's medical bag to try to help a neighbor who had been injured. Elder describes his son Michael as "Spiderman-ish"—always wanting to help people in distress.

An aspiring musician, Michael started his freshman year at the University of Oregon soon after we spoke. It's a daunting time in a young person's life, but Michael told me he often feels like there's someone watching over him. That someone is the man he was named for, Hospital Corpsman Michael Johnson.

Captain Vance and Cari Sewell

While he was in Iraq, Captain Vance Sewell became convinced he would not come home alive. He survived, and today he and his wife Cari have seven children.

Sewell was the commanding officer of the company that included the drivers, mechanics, and other personnel responsible for keeping the Amphibious Assault Vehicles roaring across the desert toward Baghdad with their precious cargo of U.S. Marines. It was amazing that those steel leviathans, dating to the 1970s, made it to Baghdad and beyond. And it wouldn't have been possible without Sewell and his crews, to whom he gives the credit. "The guys were keeping them together with bubble gum, duct tape, baling wire and prayers," Sewell told me.

Sewell was a latecomer to the Marines, joining at 24 after earning a college degree and experiencing a brief, unsatisfying career in the business world. His landlord was a retired Marine colonel. Sewell had come to respect him and told him he was thinking about starting a new career—in the military. The colonel encouraged him to join the Marines. "If you're going to be a bear," the colonel told him, "be a Grizzly."

Sewell followed his advice and enlisted as a Marine in the infantry. His college degree would have entitled him to join as an officer, but he wanted to be a grunt on the front lines, so he went to boot camp with a bunch of kids straight out of high school, several years younger than he was. He instantly loved everything about the Marines—the camaraderie, the hard work, the sense of pride. Even grueling training in brutal conditions was a positive thing – as several Marines told me – "because it sucked for everyone."

Sewell had served a dozen years prior to 2003 and had been deployed overseas on several occasions, but the invasion of Iraq with 3/5 was his first "true combat." He was almost killed in the first firefight and says it took an enormous toll.

As the ambush began the morning of March 25 and bullets rained down on the Marine convoy, Sewell was in command of an Amtrac, manning the mounted machine gun. Firing the gun required opening the hatch and standing up in the turret, exposing himself to enemy fire.

After the battle, a member of the crew noticed bullet pockmarks in the steel lid of Sewell's hatch, just inches behind where he had stood. "Hey sir, when did you get shot at?" the crew member asked. Sewell looked at the dented hatch lid and, dumbfounded, said, "I don't know." He says it must have happened during the few seconds when he reached down to grab more ammunition. If he had not done that, he says, he almost surely would have been killed.

Sewell says that in all his gung-ho preparation for combat he missed one important thing: "That combat is extremely final. People die and don't go home." He says now that it "sounds silly" because it's so obvious, but before that moment it had not fully dawned on him that "the difference between going home and not going home is pretty thin."

The combination of his own near-death experience, plus the deaths in the first days of the war of Hospital Corpsman Michael Johnson and Major Kevin Nave, had a profound effect on his mental state. "I became absolutely convinced there was no way that I was going home. Absolutely no way," he says. He was utterly certain that he would never see his wife or two young daughters again. Making matters worse, his wife was pregnant. "I was never going to meet my son."

Even though he believed he was going to be killed, Sewell continued to perform at a high level in Iraq. He didn't slump down in the turret or take other measures to protect himself. His priority continued to be the safety of his men. But he couldn't shake the horrible feeling of his imminent death. "The emotional part of it was just extreme sadness, because I knew I wasn't going home."

When he did return home, he says he was very surprised to be alive, and was overjoyed to meet his infant son. He had some "little blips" of unusual behavior early on, but says it was years before he experienced the full brunt of PTSD, an example of what has been called "delayed-onset PTSD." His post-traumatic stress symptoms really started bubbling up in about 2010, after he returned from a deployment to Afghanistan. "I couldn't sleep. My mind was constantly rolling, rolling, rolling. Not playing back combat events, but just anxiety, constantly flowing."

"The other piece of it was the anger," Sewell says. The smallest family issues would make him explode. "When a normal person would have been about a three or four on an anger scale in response to incident X, Y, or Z, I was like a nine or a ten-and-a-half," he says. Other than some occasional spankings, "I can honestly say I never, never beat my kids or abused them physically in any way," he says. "But I definitely, one hundred percent, verbally abused them and probably mentally abused them."

At the same time, he reached a low point in his Marine career. When he left his office Friday afternoon he was already dreading going back on Monday. By Sunday, he could "barely function." And Monday morning, "it took everything I had just to get up and go in."

In retrospect Sewell says it's obvious what was going on, but he was in denial. "Even though we had all the information on PTSD out there, I was, like, 'I don't have PTSD.'" His wife Cari pushed him to see a therapist. He refused while he was still in the Marines, in part because of the damage it could do to his career. "There was absolutely no way," he says. "I thought therapy was a bunch of crap." The last thing he needed was the lasting stigma of being diagnosed with PTSD. As he put it, if you're diagnosed with PTSD, "they're gonna put you in a bucket." In other words, that would be his new identity. Another guy with PTSD.

Over time, what was going on inside him became unmistakable, even to him. After so many years, his turnaround finally began one day when he was heading to a doctor appointment. His wife suggested he ask the doctor about post-traumatic stress. Today he describes the doctor as a "holistic medicine type doctor, she was a little groovy, you know? Kind of a witchdoctor-type lady." But the witchdoctor lady came through.

Sewell mentioned his issues to her, "and she asked me some pretty pointed questions," he says. "And when I answered them it kind of hit me. It kind of woke things up in me like, oh, maybe I do have PTSD. And then the more I talked about it, the better things were. I still think some of it is crap," he says. "But it does help talking to people about it. They can educate you on why things are happening."

One thing he learned is that loss had always been a big issue in his mind and probably contributed to his reaction to losing fellow Marines. "I think the reason my brain hooked into it is that I lost my mom when I was 11 or 12," Sewell says. "She had cancer, so I already had a big loss in my life. I'm in a pretty good spot now. And I think what made it better for me was basically identifying what it was. You have this event, and it basically throws off the chemistry in your brain. And it doesn't mean you're a weak little bitch."

The other thing that helped was verbalizing his feelings. "I hate saying this because I argued with my wife quite a bit about it, but talking to someone is important." Talking with fellow Marines helped too—they helped him realize that all, or at least most, combat veterans have stress issues. That made it easier to accept it in himself.

Sewell had never heard the term "Post-Traumatic Growth," but he instantly grasped it when I described the concept to him—because he has experienced it. Today, when something goes wrong at home or at work, he asks himself: "What's the worst-case scenario?" When he was a company commander in Iraq, he says, it was that "we could all get blown up." Now, it's always minor by comparison. He uses mental tools like that to defuse his anger.

He's also working on being a better father and realizes more than ever how important his family is to him. "I'm still learning," Sewell says. "I'm a work in progress, especially with the anger. But I feel a lot better. And I think I owe my family an apology."

What would he tell another veteran who's going through what he went through? "You can start off talking with your buddies," he said. "But, definitely, talking to someone professional that specializes in PTSD is the best idea."

I asked Sewell's wife, Cari, a similar question: What would she advise a military spouse to do if her Marine was exhibiting signs of post-traumatic stress? "I would really encourage them both to try to get some counseling," she answered. During the long period that her husband refused to seek help, she wishes she had done so on her own because, she says, reacting to someone who explodes with anger over minor incidents is not easy.

"There are always things you can do to work on yourself so that your reaction to the situation can be better," she said. "I think if I had better skills at de-escalating a situation instead of coming back at him with guns blazing, it could have worked a lot better." It would have been easier on the kids too, she said, "because shit runs downhill, unfortunately, even in a family. As much as you try not to allow your emotions to affect how you parent, that's just not possible."

During my interview with Sewell, he described Cari as a "rock star" for the role she played in raising seven children while he was working full-time and dealing with symptoms of PTSD. Not only that: she also homeschooled those seven children. She and Vance decided on that path when the kids were young because they were moving so frequently that they didn't want them to be constantly changing schools. Cari had studied to be a teacher, so that made it less of a challenge. Eventually, they decided to homeschool them through middle school, then send them to high school.

Of course, it's no secret that military spouses make enormous sacrifices, and that point was made painfully clear when Cari told me about giving birth to their third child (their first son) in February 2003, two weeks after her husband left for Iraq. The doctor determined that the umbilical cord was around the baby's neck, causing his heart rate to drop. The only thing she thought about during the delivery, she said, was that she didn't want her husband to get a notice in Iraq that his son had died in childbirth. "Please don't let this baby die!" she told the doctor. While telling this story to me, her eyes filled with tears. "I knew that Vance would feel a lot of responsibility," she told me. "Like it was his fault because he hadn't been there."

Cari is not one to complain about the sacrifices she's had to make. I asked her what it was like for her when Vance was deployed to Iraq and Afghanistan, and she replied: "It is what it is. Just put on your big girl pants and go." I also asked Cari what it was like for her after he came home from Iraq. She said the Vance who came home was a more emotional person, not as stoic as he used to be, but at first there was nothing extreme about his behavior.

She agreed with her husband that his PTSD didn't really kick in until about seven or eight years after he came home from Iraq in 2003. "All we saw was anger. He was very, very angry. And I'm not a go in my room and cry person because you said something mean to me. I'm going to come out fists swinging." (She was speaking figuratively.) At that time, it didn't occur to her that the change in his personality might be related to his combat experience years before. "I thought it was more related to the chaos of our house," she said. "When you've got seven kids something's always going wrong."

Even after Sewell retired, the explosive anger continued. Cari admits she had her own issues too, so he's not fully to blame. But there were too many times, she says, when one moment their marriage was great, and the next he would blow up about a minor issue and she would wonder if they were on the verge of divorce.

That's when she decided to talk to him about post-traumatic stress. "We've got to help each other out here," she told him. "I think this might be something more than we thought. How can you go to war and *not* come back with some kind of PTSD?"

Sergeant Joe and Sara Harris

In our initial Zoom interview, Joe Harris's eyes filled with tears each time he talked about his incredibly supportive wife Sara. Later, I came to understand why he became so emotional at the mere mention of her name.

Harris told me in that early conversation that when he came home from Iraq he felt like he was "walking around on Mars." But with Sara's strong support (she was his girlfriend in 2003 but later became his wife and the mother of their two children) he never felt the need to seek professional help to deal with his post-combat stress. "I've gotten through emotions and stress with the help of my family," he said, singling out Sara for her ceaseless patience and understanding in helping him avoid the ravages of PTSD.

Months later I received an email from Harris in which he courageously revealed a deeper truth about his struggles.

Harris has been with a police department in Texas for 20 years, working in such high-stress fields as street narcotics and organized crime. He has spent most of that time "running 100 miles an hour" he said, adding that "just like many in law enforcement I would use alcohol to decompress." He says he served the police department with "great zeal and joy," but eventually realized that something was very wrong. "I was using my work as an unprescribed medicine to push away things from my military service that I did not want to cope with," he told me in his email. "Working hard for so long helped, but over time it was not enough. That is when I started drinking more and more. Stresses that I had pushed off for so long had reared their head." Like countless other veterans, he had spent years trying to bury and ignore the trauma of war.

In late 2022 he entered a 30-day inpatient treatment facility for substance abuse, but admits: "I only half-accepted that I could never have a drink again," and relapsed soon after completing the program. Several weeks later he checked in for another 30-day inpatient treatment. "The first time felt humbling," he wrote me. "Having to go back a second time was devastating. Up to this point in my life I had accomplished so much and been able to overcome many challenges. But this addiction was one thing I could not beat on my own."

Harris said his time in treatment gave him "the opportunity to sit with my thoughts. I learned to process and identify things that I had been trying to disassociate from for so long." To give a sense of how exceedingly difficult it was to reach that point, he wrote: "I would rather have fought another war than go through all this."

He had been out of treatment for a week when he wrote to me, and said he was feeling well. But recognizing that he has a long way to go, he added: "I have to be laser focused on my recovery if I want to save my career, my family, and be the man I know I can be."

His biggest regret is the effect all of this has had on those he loves the most. "After years of medicating with work and alcohol, I had begun to cause much damage to my family. It's shameful not to feel joy or happiness when sitting at home with your wife and two children."

He concluded his email the same way he had ended his Zoom interview with me several months before—by praising and honoring his wife. "Sara has shown me so much grace and has been so supportive," he wrote. "She's the same beauty that I fell in love with as a young Marine at age 19. The same beauty that stood by me through my service, the war, my time as a Detective, and now in this war against substance abuse." I'm certain that as he wrote this there were tears in his eyes—just as there were every time he mentioned Sara's name in our Zoom interview months before.

Harris also emailed a photo of him with Sara. She is 4′11″ and weighs about 98 pounds, and he is 6′1″ and 250 pounds. He titled the photo "The Beauty and the Beast," and noted that while she will always be a beauty, he is working very hard to be less of a beast.

Corporal Jeremy and Heather Thomas

Jeremy Thomas had a very unusual—and possibly unique—reason for joining the Marines. He says he did it, at least in part, because he was mad at his parents for not helping him pay for college. His mother had told him that one thing she never wanted him to do was join the Marines, and his father, a Navy veteran, had a very low opinion of Marines. So, he joined the Marines. "I joined out of spite." he says now. "And for the challenge."

Because joining the Marines was not something he had investigated previously, he was surprised by how difficult bootcamp was. "I wasn't in shape," he says now. But he was determined not to quit, and he rose to the challenge. Boot camp wasn't the only big surprise. "When I joined the Marine Corps in 1999," he says, "I never expected to go to war."

It is sometimes difficult to pinpoint the precise triggers that lead to the development of PTSD, but Thomas describes two events in Iraq in

2003 as "horrifying." The first was the accidental death of Executive Officer Major Kevin Nave. The second was being nearby as his friend Corporal Erik Silva was killed in action.

His primary symptoms involved hypervigilance. "I was definitely in combat Marine infantry mode for a while," after coming home, he says. "I was cautious and suspicious and needed to see exits and watch people closely." He started drinking heavily to "medicate" himself. "I drank to feel normal," he says, "but it got out of hand, so I cut back."

Initially Thomas refused to believe he had PTSD, but his attitude changed when he filled out a questionnaire, which clearly showed he had an assortment of PTSD symptoms. He enrolled in therapy at the VA and says that even with professional help it took three or four years to fully adjust to civilian life. He claims that he no longer suffers from PTSD and is showing signs of Post-Traumatic Growth. "There is absolutely no glory in war or killing," he says, "but I have found glory in being a father." He also finds glory in his work. As a disability claims processor at the VA, he enjoys helping other vets get money for disabilities resulting from their time on active duty.

Thomas says his struggle with PTSD might have been hardest on his wife, Heather, and considers himself very lucky that she stayed with him throughout their ordeal. I asked Thomas if Heather might be willing to share her story, and a few days later I received an email from her. It is so achingly beautiful, and paints such a vivid picture of what it's like to be the wife of a Marine who is away at war, that I've quoted from it at length:

> I can still remember that night they left. Hours of waiting. Hours of clinging to them before they boarded a bus in the middle of the night. Going to the Del Taco off base at 11pm to buy like 50 tacos because the guys were getting hungry. More waiting. Then it was time to say the final goodbyes as they boarded a bus. Watching them fade into the hills as we were now clinging on to fellow wives. Not knowing what lay ahead.
>
> Being a wife to a Marine actually helped me develop a "tribe" unlike anything I've ever had. You had a built-in community of people who knew and felt what you were going through. If anyone needed anything, you had a handful of people who were there in a heartbeat, no questions asked. We stepped in to help run errands, host birthday parties and baby showers, kept each other company on

the weekends, and I even stood in as the birth coach for a friend. I was there in the delivery room while her husband was deployed. We shared news anytime someone got a letter, email or the rare—but treasured—phone call from Iraq.

Jeremy never really got to experience how supportive the community, and the country, really was of these men and women fighting overseas. I feel like a lot of people were trying to make sure what happened to the Vietnam vets never happened to this generation, as well as the deep sense of unity following 9/11. Living near Camp Pendleton, there were flags, yellow ribbons, signs, and red, white and blue everywhere. Businesses donated to Marine Corps family events. Schools and churches "adopted" our Marines, sending care packages and letters. It was heartwarming. And a far cry from how divisive our nation is today.

Those were all the positive things. Now for the hard parts. Fear, worry, separation, sorrow. Everything you can imagine and more. I wrote Jeremy a letter or card every single day of his deployment, and he wrote as often as he could… but it was still a good 4–6 weeks before his first letter arrived.

Then there was the accident where Major Nave was killed. I had gotten to know his wife and his kids at various events… That's when things shifted. We suddenly found ourselves in the thick of it. I got a phone call late at night from Lt. Col. Mundy's wife Jenny. She had called each of the company leaders, and then we had to call other wives in the company with the news about the accident. It was a long night of "First, your husband is okay but…" and then talking with them while they each processed the news. A few days later, my first military funeral, and seeing his widow and children in the front pew. Nothing can prepare someone for that.

That's when we began to fear people coming to our door. We never showed up unannounced at one another's home. We called ahead and we had a "friendly" knock on the door. I did have one door knock one night and I had such a sense of dread wash over me. I didn't want to answer the door. I stood at the door and yelled through, asking who was there. It was some package delivery, and I broke down crying as I answered. The poor delivery guy felt horrible when I was able to choke out that my husband was in Iraq, and I thought he was someone else.

Then Erik Silva died. Erik had been to our home a few times before the deployment. The night they left he gave me a package that he wanted me to mail his mom. And he gave me her phone number and asked me to check in on her while he was gone. When he hugged me at Camp Pendleton that night, he whispered 'I'll make sure Jeremy comes home.' I did mail that package, and I spoke with his mom Gloria frequently.

The day it happened, we had heard there was a firefight and some 3/5 Marines had been injured. While we were waiting, a few of us wives went out to dinner at Ruby's at the Oceanside Pier. We had just been seated when my cell phone rang. It was Gloria and Erik's brother. His brother spoke first, and then I heard

Gloria wailing that her baby was gone. They told me about the officers coming to her home to share the news.

Several of us drove out to Holtsville, CA for the funeral and to visit the Silva family home. The whole town was honoring his life. There were signs and billboards, and we had so many hugs from strangers when they found out who we were ... that we were there representing our husbands, Erik's Marine Corps brothers, who could not be there in person. Unfortunately, while we were out of town, that's when Jeremy finally had an opportunity to call home... but he called home instead of my cell phone and I didn't get to talk to him. Those were gut-wrenching moments. A missed call. Knowing he only had a couple minutes and you missed it. You never knew when the next one would come. I saved that recording for months and listened to it over and over.

After a few more weeks, the intense fighting was finally over. We could send care packages. We'd heard that the guys needed seasoning packets because the MREs and chow hall food was terrible. So we'd mail boxes of salt and pepper, ketchup, hot sauce, etc. We heard showers were hard to come by and baby wipes were needed. Done. My grandma had mailed homemade cookies and she heard all the guys inhaled them. So she started mailing more and more cookies, trying to perfect the shipping. She would freeze them rock hard, pulling them out just before packaging them up to the post office.

Finally, it was time for Jeremy to come home. There is NOTHING better than a military homecoming. It felt like tracking Santa through NORAD... monitoring their movements or getting quick calls from this airport or that airport (Dublin, Ireland and Dover, DE). Hearing that they had touched down at March AFB. They were finally on buses. The bus was getting off the freeway. The bus had gone through the Pendleton gate. And then we saw the buses pulling in... but having to wait until they turned in their weapons at the armory. Trying to pick out your Marine in a sea of camouflage. Finding each other, locking eyes and then in each other's arms. Pure joy and relief. He was home.

I thought it was over. But again, we were not prepared for what came next. It suddenly dawned on Jeremy during the car ride from the base to our apartment that he was really home and broke down. Jeremy wasn't able to sleep in our bed for several nights because the bed was too soft, he wasn't used to pillows (Oh my god, why didn't you tell me you didn't have a pillow? I could have MAILED you a pillow!), it was too quiet, he was used to being awakened every couple hours, etc.

We were at a mall several weeks later and there was construction going on. Something fell and clanged to the ground, causing Jeremy to jump, and needing a few minutes to relax again. It was months before Jeremy could sit somewhere with his back to the room. He always needed to see people and the exits.

The Marine Corps and war changed my husband. In many ways for the better, but in some ways, it took more than it gave. While his case is not acute, PTSD still rears its head. He has seen the worst in the world and seen what death and violence can do in a split second. That leads him to be less trusting with strangers and overly protective with our kids. And every now and then, a movie, game or a veteran's claim at work hits a nerve. It's too real. Too raw.

We've been through a lot, but we're still pushing forward together. I am incredibly proud of Jeremy and his Marine Corps family. For many years I had an e-signature on my personal email that said, "I pledge allegiance to the flag... and my heart to the Marine who protects it." Twenty years later, that's still the case.

If you can read that without getting tears in your eyes, you're tougher than the author of this book.

CHAPTER II

Lives Transformed by the Marines

All the Marines I interviewed for this book said they're better men because of being Marines. They cited various traits they learned as Marines that improved their lives, including leadership, discipline, confidence, and courage.

But for many—including those profiled in this chapter—becoming Marines did more than make them better men. It gave them a whole new start and transformed their lives.

Sergeant Enrique (Rick) Alaniz, III

> The Marines gave me a new life. I stopped my old life and restarted and became a totally different person.

Growing up in Brownsville, Texas, on the Mexican border, Enrique Alaniz knew he wanted to be a Marine when he was 14 years old and would have joined then if it had been possible. He had to wait until he was 17 to sign up—with his parents' permission. He then had to wait—impatiently—until he was 18 to join.

For some, the desire to become a Marine at a young age comes from watching war movies, for others it's family history. For Alaniz it was one person, his role model, an ROTC (Reserve Officers' Training Corps) instructor at his school, First Sergeant Ernest Bond. Alaniz was mesmerized by his stories and his combat history. He had been a Navy Corpsman (a medic) with the Marines in World War II, then joined the

Marines and served in Korea and Vietnam. "He was the greatest guy I ever knew," Alaniz said. "He put me on my path." Bond died in 2012 at the age of 84.

Alaniz still remembers, almost verbatim, what Bond told him, words that would change his life:

> There's a place you can go when you graduate high school where they don't care what you look like. They don't care who your parents are or how much money they make. They don't care, for the most part, about mistakes you made in the past. They only care about what you're capable of doing. And they're going to trust you with responsibilities and men and equipment. And it's going to be a great life if you decide to do it.

"After that I was hooked," Alaniz told me. It was the first time he had dared to dream about something beyond the community where he grew up. The Marine Corps was his ticket out.

His ROTC instructor was right—Alaniz had a great life as a Marine. After 22 years he retired in 2017 as a First Sergeant. When I asked him what the best thing was about being a Marine, he gave an answer I hadn't heard before. "It's a very simple life," he said. "It was basically, am I going to eat today? Am I going to sleep today? Am I going to die today? Am I going to shoot somebody today? And then it's rinse, cycle, repeat. Life gets broken down to its basic components. And it's basically just you living. And that's it. The stuff at home doesn't bother you anymore. You're only concerned with the here and now. And life becomes very, very simple."

That was especially true when he was in combat: "My two combat deployments were probably the best deployments of the seven I did simply because of that. The hardship part of it sucks. Having guys get killed sucks. Having guys get wounded sucks. But in the very generic sense of hardship, it's not really that hard. It's actually very simple. And life's a lot cleaner that way."

Alaniz goes so far as to say that he was "born again" when he became a Marine—and not in the religious sense. What he means is that his life was completely transformed. "Growing up, I was very shy, a very, very shy kid. I wasn't physically gifted and didn't play sports." But everything changed in the Marines, he said: "I went into my military career determined that I was going to come out better than when I went in. The Marines gave me a new life. I stopped my old life and restarted, and became a totally different person. My attitude now is different than when I was growing up. I'm much more outgoing, much more energetic, much more confident."

Alaniz talked about how eye-opening it was for a kid from Brownsville, Texas—where, he says, most residents stay for their entire lives—to see the world. "The Marine Corps gives you life experiences that you can't get anywhere else. A whole different perspective on life, how all the different cultures live."

Like nearly all the Marines in 3/5, Alaniz had never seen combat before 2003. "Some of the guys had been in the Marine Corps eight, nine, ten years and had never seen combat," he told me. He knew of only three Marines in his unit who were battle-hardened. Those Marines tried to prepare the others for what was about to happen.

"Not to sound like a warmonger or bloodthirsty," he says, "but every young man who grows up playing G.I. Joe in the backyard wants to go to war, you want to experience it. We trained for this invasion, but we had never done it for real. And once you experience it, nothing ever quite feels the same afterwards." Alaniz had only seen combat in movies, and says the real thing is nothing like that. "Hollywood sexes it up a bit," he says. "When you get down to the nitty gritty, it's a lot dirtier in real life, and it's not black and white. There's a lot of gray."

He gave some examples of the "gray":

— You roll into a firefight and need to make a quick decision whether to shoot somebody, but you can't tell if he's armed. If he is armed and you wait too long to decide, he might shoot you first, or he might shoot another Marine.

— You see an enemy fighter who's already down but appears to be alive, and he has an AK-47 pointed in your general direction. Should you shoot him?

— Immediately after a firefight you see people wearing women's clothing. Why are they here right after a battle? Are they armed? We've been warned about men wearing women's clothing to hide their guns. Could these be men hiding guns? What should we do?

There were other times when it was black and white—what needed to be done was clear, and he did it without hesitation. "That's a bad guy, I'm going to kill that guy," he would think. "That guy's got a weapon; I'm going to kill him. That guy just shot at us; I'm going to kill him." At times, Alaniz says, combat was exactly what he expected—it was just like training. At other times it was necessary to make life or death decisions in the fog of war, something that training can't replicate.

The kid who wasn't physically gifted and didn't play sports became a fitness standout in the Marines, winning a battalion-wide pull-up contest—but he's still so modest he won't tell me how many pull-ups he did. The kid who "ran a little" has completed several marathons and a couple of ultramarathons as an adult.

Today, Alaniz is a police officer in Austin, Texas, a job he loves. All his success, he says, can be traced back to one moment—when he decided to join the U.S. Marines.

Corporal Jason Arellano

> One day I'm going to be there and I'm going there as a Marine.

Jason Arellano remembers the day he decided to become a Marine like it was yesterday. He was 13 years old, sitting on the floor of his mobile home in New Mexico watching the TV news with his mother, who was sitting behind him on the couch.

It was January 16, 1991, and President George H. W. Bush had just announced the launch of *Operation Desert Storm*, a U.S.-led effort to expel Saddam Hussein's Iraqi forces after they had invaded and annexed Kuwait. (Today it's generally known as the Gulf War.) Both of Arellano's grandfathers had served in the Army, and an uncle and two older cousins were in the Marines. He looked up to all of them.

While watching reports of U.S. troops preparing for war, Jason turned to his mother and said: "One day I'm going to be there and I'm going to be there as a Marine." Without hesitating his mother responded: "If that's what you want to do son, I support you." That's all it took to set Jason on his course. But it would be a much longer and bumpier road than he had expected.

As a senior in high school his parents divorced, and he took it hard. His grades suffered and he started getting in trouble. He was "spiraling" as he puts it now. Eventually he was kicked out of school.

Arellano lived in a small town where, he says, you either get stuck forever, or you move on and do big things. His parents thought he was in the latter category. He was going to join the Marines. Until, that is, his father got a call from the Marine recruiter. "Mr. Arellano," he informed him, "your son is not going to graduate from high school. If he doesn't graduate, he can't join the Marines." Arellano had been knocked off his pedestal. He continued to dream of being a Marine, but as time passed it seemed to slip more and more from his grasp.

His uncle, a Marine, invited him to live with him in San Antonio, where he tried to get Arellano back on course. Progress was slow. "For four years, every night I laid down and I would ask myself, what are you doing Jason? You should be pursuing the Marines. That's what you want. What are you doing?"

Finally, at age 21, he graduated from high school. But he still felt stuck. He needed a push. It came from a friend who one day knocked on his door. "Come on in," Arellano said. "I just rolled a joint." The friend saluted him and said no thanks. He was on his way to join the Marines. Arellano dropped the joint. At long last, his wake-up call had arrived. They went straight to the recruiter and signed the paperwork. "I never looked back," he says. "I have my Purple Heart and my Navy and Marine Corps Commendation Medal because I never looked back."

In boot camp Arellano was consistently put in leadership positions. He claims it was because he was older than the new recruits, most of whom were 18. But you don't have to know Arellano very long to know that he is a natural-born leader. Having spent four years failing to pursue his dream, he was making up for lost time. He had a burning determination to succeed. "I just gave it my all," he says. "I wanted to prove to myself and anybody else who ever doubted me that they were wrong."

Arellano experienced some traumatic events during his first combat deployment in Iraq in 2003. He was present when two young Iraqi girls were killed on the pitch-black night of March 25. He believes they had been used as human shields by the Iraqis. And he was part of the night patrol in Baghdad on April 11 when two of his fellow Marines were killed during an Iraqi ambush.

Those experiences deeply affected him but did not deter him. He decided to stay in the Marines and make it his career. Following the usual protocol, he would have re-enlisted at the end of four years of active duty. But if he had done that he probably would have been transferred to a different unit. He didn't want to leave his men. He wanted to stay with 3/5, which was scheduled to re-deploy to Iraq in 2004.

He asked his senior officers if he could get a six-month extension with 3/5. "Let me go to Fallujah with you guys," he pleaded. His wish was granted, but as the saying goes: "Be careful what you wish for." Arellano's decision to go to Fallujah almost led to his death, and left him with injuries that ended his dream of building a life in the Marine Corps.

The Second Battle of Fallujah, in late 2004, was the bloodiest Marine battle in the Iraq War, and 3/5 was one of the hardest hit battalions. In November–December 2004 the battalion lost 19 men in combat. On December 12 alone they lost five, and Arellano came very close to being the sixth.

The citation for his Navy and Marine Corps Commendation Medal says that while clearing a building on December 12, Arellano threw a grenade into a room where insurgents were believed to be hiding. He took a quick glance inside the room before it exploded, and to his stunned surprise, it was near the doorway where he stood, only several feet away. He shouted for his fellow Marines to get back.

Had the insurgents thrown the grenade back? Or had it hit something and bounced back on its own? The only thing he knew for sure was that it was too late to throw it back. The grenade exploded.

This is Arellano's recounting of what happened next, which he wrote in his journal in the third person, as if describing it from someone else's point of view:

> Arellano saw everything clearly. The curtains rose in the room from the concussion... The loud boom seemed to echo, and everything became slow motion. The explosion spun Arellano onto his hands and knees... had he saved his Marines? He had, he had kept them from the door and taken the brunt of the blast.
>
> 'I'm hit, I'm hit!' he yelled. A Marine approached and told him he was okay. Arellano tried to move, but his palms slipped in a pool of his own blood. Dazed,

breathing hard, and feeling weak, Arellano told the Marine 'What do you mean I'm okay? Can't you see I'm bleeding to death?' Arellano felt the blood coming from his neck, and others rushed to help him to his feet. He crumpled to his feet like a rag doll, as he lost feeling in his legs.

Arellano's fellow Marines finished clearing the house of enemy fighters and carried him outside where a Navy Corpsman tended to him. It seemed to be a miracle to Arellano that the grenade hadn't killed him. He was "on the razor's edge between survival or death," his commanding officer later said. Arellano remembers looking to the sky and asking God if this was it.

They put him in a vehicle that sped to a U.S. medical unit outside Fallujah. When he awoke from his first surgery, he was told by a senior officer that he and his men had fought a good fight, but that not all had made it out alive. Arellano wept as the officer read the names of the five men—all close friends—who had died.

A few hours later back home, Arellano's girlfriend Lindsey (now his wife) received word that he had been hit by a grenade, but that was all—no word on whether he was alive or dead. Frantic, she tried to prepare for the worst. Emotionally drained, she eventually fell asleep. At 6am the phone woke her. Lindsey remembers saying hello and hearing the sweetest sound she could have imagined. It was Arellano, the love of her life, whispering "hello."

The grenade had sprayed shrapnel all over his body, narrowly missing vital arteries. He might have been able to continue with the Marines as a career, but he worried that his injuries would slow him down, putting his fellow Marines at risk. "I just felt like my time in the Marines was up," Arellano says now. "I could hold my head up high."

He and Lindsey married in 2006 and after a year living in the paradise of La Jolla, California, moved to Kansas City, in the region where she grew up. After successful stints in a few different careers, including one in which he trained Navy anti-terrorism units, he and Lindsey decided in 2022 to do something completely different.

They bought a business that makes use of his artistic skills—designing and welding metal chandeliers. "We've served others and we've served them well," he says. "Now it's time to do what we want to do."

Jason and Lindsey have four young children. Their eight-year-old son announced one day that he was going to join the Army when he grows up. Flabbergasted, Arellano asked "The *Army*? Why?!" "Because my friend's father is in the Army," his son said. "But your dad is a Marine!" he responded in exasperation.

In fact, Arellano says, his son has exactly what it takes to be a Marine. "He's a little warrior, but he also has a tender heart. If he sees somebody hurting, it hurts him, and he wants to make it better."

Corporal Wale Akintunde

> There is probably a good possibility I might have ended up in jail.

As a teenager, Wale Akintunde had only a casual interest in the Marines. He was attracted to the "glamour" and "tough guy" images portrayed in movies like *Full Metal Jacket* and Clint Eastwood's *Heartbreak Ridge*. But his interest became more serious after his plan to go to college on a soccer scholarship fell through.

He was heading in a bad direction and needed a challenge—and some discipline. If he hadn't joined the Marines, he says: "There's a fair chance that I would've gotten arrested a few more times. There is probably a good possibility I might have ended up in jail."

After surviving boot camp, he didn't want to jeopardize what he had accomplished. "I walked a very straight and narrow path," he says. "I didn't do anything that would get me in trouble." When his unit deployed to Japan early in his Marine career, "I didn't go outside the main gate. I stayed in the barracks and kept to myself because I didn't want to get in trouble." The Marines taught him discipline and accountability for his actions. That, he says, made his mother very happy.

Akintunde had a quick answer when I asked him the best thing about being a Marine: "The shared misery," he said. I noted that misery is usually considered to be a bad thing. He said that might be true for most people, but not for Marines. "Whether a Marine is 18, 30, or 75, we all know how it is," he said. They all survived the most brutal boot camp of all the military branches; had drill instructors spew venom and saliva in their faces while they stood expressionless at attention; ate horrible, cold food; endured 25-mile hikes with heavy packs; and made it through several other types of physical and mental agony. "That shared misery is the thing that I smile about now," he says. "It's the most joyous part of being a Marine."

Another joy of being a Marine, he says, is that while he is of Nigerian descent, the only color that matters in the Marines is green. "I never felt like anyone looked at me differently. I never experienced any instance where someone was like, 'I'm going to treat you less because you're a black Marine.' They treated us all the same. It was probably one of the few times where race and all that stuff never mattered."

Of his decision to join the Marines he says: "It is the best decision I've ever made, by far. I don't think anything I've ever done in my life makes me feel the way that being a Marine makes me feel."

Corporal Rob Gilbert

> I wanted to be a dentist.

One of the most surprising answers to a question I ever heard as a journalist came when I was interviewing music legend Gregg Allman for a story that aired on *CBS Sunday Morning*. What would he have done, I asked Gregg, if he had not become a rock star?

I almost fell out of my chair when he told me that right up until he agreed to join his brother Duane in a new band, *The Allman Brothers Band*, his dream was to be a dentist. Yes, instead of writing "Whipping Post," belting out the blues, and marrying Cher, he would have been drilling teeth and playing golf at a country club.

Well, the surprise was almost as big when Rob Gilbert, a mountain of a man, told me that he too had planned to become a dentist.

"I'm 6'3" and about 265 right now and I've got huge meat hooks," he said, showing his massive hands. "I can't imagine trying to get these into somebody's mouth to work on their teeth, so I think it all worked out for the better." Indeed, it did. For him *and* the people who might have been his patients.

Gilbert played football, basketball, and baseball in high school, and got a lot of calls from college recruiters. "I had no desire whatsoever to go into the military," he says. But after three-and-a-half years as a biochemistry major at the University of Nevada, Reno, his grades were tanking due mostly to poor study habits and lack of interest. He needed to do something to get out of the hole he was digging for himself.

Gilbert thought some military structure and discipline might help. He considered the Air National Guard, then the Army, and finally met with a Marine recruiter. A week later he was sworn in.

In the early days he liked it so much he decided to make a career of it. His plan was to finish college, become a commissioned officer, and then a military pilot. (Though you can't help but wonder how he planned to fit in the cockpit.) Those plans were side-tracked, though, by his deployment to Iraq in 2003. After that Gilbert could have re-enlisted, but he and his wife had been together only 13 months during three years of marriage. His wife was too important in his life to spend that much time separated. He chose his wife over the Marines.

But Gilbert's four years as a Marine served him well. He had learned the qualities he needed to succeed in life: leadership and that previously missing element, discipline. With funding from the GI Bill, he completed college, majoring in criminal justice, and made the Dean's list—a dramatic improvement from his first try at college. He even got a master's degree. Today he's a sergeant with the Austin, Texas police department.

Joining the Marines, this former wannabe dentist says now, was life-changing, "one of the best things I've ever done." He and his wife have four young children. I asked if he sees any of them as future Marines. "I'm hoping," he said with a laugh. "Because that's the only way I'm going to be able to pay for college."

Sergeant Colin Keefe

> I knew I needed discipline. I knew I needed to grow up.

Colin Keefe was a self-described "frat-boy" at Lehigh University and dropped out after three semesters. "I certainly didn't apply myself in school, or in life generally," he says now. "I knew I needed discipline.

I needed to grow up." He didn't want to take any "half-measures," so he joined the Marines.

Prior to enlisting, Keefe says, he "wasn't big on authority." As a Marine he quickly learned that respecting the authority of your superiors is not optional. He learned the importance of hard work and discipline, and the feeling of accomplishment and self-satisfaction that comes from fully applying your abilities.

And, Keefe says, he learned how to function in a hierarchical organization. That means not just developing the ability to lead—but also the ability to be led. He learned how to be commanded—how to do what you're told without resisting or complaining.

A significant percentage of Marines seem to have naturally rebellious natures—but they learn to squelch that instinct (most of the time) very early on. For Keefe, the ability to both lead and to be led were not only essential in the Marines—they were also invaluable in his civilian career.

After almost five years in the Marines, including his 2003 combat tour, Keefe went straight back to Lehigh University and showed up on the doorstep of the dean of students. He explained to her that because of his experience in the Marines he was a different person than the one who had flunked out five years earlier. She believed him, and marched him to the registrar's office, where he signed up for classes.

Keefe says his transition from the Marines back to college was "weird" at first. "The Marines is the most bizarre culture on earth, one small step short of being a cult," he says. And to transition from that to a "fancy private university, a bizarre little bubble on the extreme opposite end of the spectrum," he says, was a dizzying adjustment. "There are pygmy tribesmen who now live in New York City who had less of a cultural adjustment than I did," he jokes. As he described his transition, it reminded me of Tarzan returning to England as Lord Greystoke. From loin cloth to three-piece suit.

After a period of adjustment, the discipline and determination he learned as a Marine kicked in. Compared to the Marine Corps, college was now "a piece of cake." He did well enough to get into a top law school—Georgetown University—then spent three years at a prominent New York law firm.

After he and his wife had their first child, they decided to escape big city life and settle down in the much more livable environment of Lehigh Valley, Pennsylvania, near the university where they had met. They now have three young children. Today, he's a partner at one of the largest and most prestigious law firms in the area, heading the mergers and acquisitions department.

It's not just his professional life that benefited from his years as a Marine. He also has a clear sense of contentment. "I don't need to go jump out of an airplane," he says. "I've done some crazy stuff. I've done dangerous stuff. I know I'm capable of doing that. And I don't need to find some ridiculous thing to do in my mid-forties to make up for something I feel I lacked or didn't experience. I experienced it all. The whole gamut of human experience lives in me." And for that, he thanks the U.S. Marines.

Sergeant Stan Laskowski

> The Marine Corps is great at showing you exactly what you are good at, and what you are bad at, and how to improve yourself. It's a constant process of making yourself better.

The Marine who recommended that I interview Stan Laskowski told me that Laskowski will give me his opinion whether I want to hear it or not. That turned out to be partly correct, but it wasn't so much opinions as it was a steady flow of insightful and unfiltered thoughts and observations, punctuated by a good sense of humor and a big, disarming smile.

Laskowksi grew up in a small town near Scranton, Pennsylvania. At age 21 he was rattling around, doing odd jobs like working on and off at an auto parts store and a local garage. He was stuck in neutral. "I wasn't really going anywhere. I wasn't really doing anything," he says now. He needed a path out of town. His father had been a Marine, so he decided to follow in his father's footsteps—the best decision he ever made, he says now.

When I asked Laskowski what he would be doing today if he hadn't joined the Marines, he said, after thinking about it for a moment: "I would probably still be in Pennsylvania, and I don't even want to know what the hell I'd be doing up there. Probably stealing air conditioners and smoking meth. That would probably be my occupation. So, thank God I got the hell out of there and got into the Marine Corps."

Today, instead of using drugs, he's studying them. Last year he graduated from the University of Nevada, Las Vegas with a major in psychology and a minor in neuroscience. And that's only the first step in his very big plan. The next steps are to complete coursework in chemistry, study for the MCAT (Medical College Admission Test) and apply to medical school. He's 45 years old, so if the dream comes true, he'll be about 50 when he starts writing "Dr." before his name.

It sounds like a wild idea, but it fits perfectly with the philosophy of self-improvement he learned as a Marine: "The Marine Corps is great at showing you exactly what you are good at, and what you are bad at, and how to improve yourself. It's a constant process of making yourself better." He sums up his quest to become a doctor in two words: "Nothing's impossible."

That's not to say it's been easy. His life following his eight years of active duty has been a wild ride. The highs include four children, now in their teens and early twenties. But the low points include a divorce and some extremely dark times after coming home from Iraq. "I had nightmares. I had a fear of going out," he says. But those common symptoms of post-traumatic stress were just the tip of the iceberg. "I've been very close to that 22-a-day a couple of times," he told me, referring to the often-used estimate that 22 veterans take their own lives every day. He's glad he's not one of them, he says now. "Damn glad I'm not."

Those periods were tough on his kids, he says. "It's got to be worse for them, seeing their dad go through something like that. But what I've got to focus on is that they see me good now. And whatever they saw in the past, that needs to be a memory. We're in the now, now."

Laskowski's children were a major factor in bringing him out of those dark days, but what kickstarted that process was getting back together with some fellow Marines. After his eight years of active duty, he says he didn't talk to any of his Marine buddies for years. "I just kept to myself, didn't really contact anybody."

Finally, in about 2016, more than a decade after coming home, Laskowski drove from Vegas to California for a get-together with "the boys"—the group of Marine friends he played cards with in Iraq. That simple social gathering turned into a life-changing experience. "After that, boy did I feel terrific. It changed my whole perspective. Being back with them, just seeing them again. More than anything, that's what started to bring me back out."

As with so many Marines I've talked to, Laskowski regrets waiting so long. "I still kick the shit out of myself for that," he says. "Like, why the hell did I wait?" He says that if he had done it a long time ago, he wouldn't be looking at going to med school well into his forties. He could have done it in his thirties. But he strives to keep a positive attitude and says "better late than never."

He tries not to get too far ahead of himself, but when asked how it would feel to become "Dr. Stan Laskowski" at age 50, or even later, he replies, "That would be terrific," as he flashes that big smile.

Lance Corporal Armand McCormick, Silver Star Recipient

I was a little fucking lost.

At the age of 21, Armand McCormick earned a Silver Star for his courageous actions in 3/5's first battle in Iraq, on March 25, 2003. It was quite a turnaround. Three years earlier, as a newly minted 18-year-old Marine, he says: "I was kind of a dipshit." During his early months in the Corps, he was "getting in trouble all the time," he says, and was busted down in rank a couple of times.

One of those times changed his entire Marine career—and probably his life. He was court-martialed for hazing and assaulting another Marine. "If I hadn't done that, my world would be totally different than it is right now," he says.

When his four-year term came to an end he decided to make the Marine Corps his career. He applied to the Marine Enlisted Commissioning Education Program (MECEP), which gives qualified

Marines the opportunity to get a four-year college degree while maintaining active-duty status and full pay. Once they have the degree, they become commissioned officers as second lieutenants.

But McCormick's early court-martial stood in the way. He pulled every string he could think of—including getting letters of recommendation from senior officers—but nothing worked. His Plan B was to go to college, which he did soon after coming home from Iraq, and get a degree that would lead to a career in federal law enforcement. But with a court-martial on his record, it was unlikely he would ever be hired. "I was a little fucking lost," he says.

The disappointment sent him on a six-month tailspin. He went on a binge. "Real bad drinking," he says. He crashed a motorcycle while inebriated, went to jail for alcohol-related incidents and a couple of assaults, and got married and divorced. He came close to dropping out of school, but as a last gasp effort spoke with a college counselor at his school, the University of Northern Iowa. She asked him what he liked to do. He said fitness had always been important to him. The counselor steered him to the university's program in Exercise Science.

It was a watershed moment in his life. He found a career—the exercise business—that wouldn't be affected by his court-martial. All he needed now was some discipline, and he knew where to find that—his Marine Corps training. He forced himself into a brutal daily routine: Get up each morning at 4am; ride his bicycle to the gym to work out; ride his bicycle to his classes; ride his bicycle to his job; ride home, arriving between 10pm and midnight. The next day—do it all over again. "That's what I did and it's kind of what I still do," he says.

Today, he's married and has two boys, earned a master's degree, and runs multiple businesses—including several gyms in Iowa and Florida. He even owns a car wash. "My passion is business development," he says. "I love giving other people the opportunity to own a business and be your own boss." Pretty good for a guy who, after learning he couldn't have a career in the Marines, was "fucking lost." (One other Marine trait has stuck with him—he can hardly speak a sentence without an F-bomb. Not that there's anything wrong with that.)

As for the post-traumatic stress he experienced in that first year after getting out of the Marines, he says all combat vets probably get it in some way. "Could it still get me today?" he asks. "Absolutely it could. So I do everything I can to stay busy, busy, busy. And if there's ever a time—and I'm not just talking about the war—that something gets brought up that might cause an issue in my head, I always try to figure a way to turn it into positive movement."

Private First Class Ben Putnam

> Putnam was so gung-ho he played the Marines' Hymn on his harmonica as his unit roared across the border into Iraq. Being discharged from the Marines crushed him.

Ben Putnam's life was transformed by the Marines—twice. The first time was joining the Marines and serving in combat in Iraq in 2003. The second transformation occurred after the personal devastation of being medically discharged from the Marines.

When the terrorist attacks of 9/11 occurred, Putnam was a senior in high school. He felt a calling to defend his country and shelved whatever plans he had for his future. When a Marine Corps recruiter showed up at his high school outside St. Paul, Minnesota, Putnam walked up and said: "Where do I sign?" The recruiter started to give a sales pitch using props—little wood blocks etched with the words Honor, Courage, and Commitment. "I'm not here for preschool," Putnam said. "I'm here to sign up."

The recruiter explained that it wasn't that simple. He was 17, so he needed his parents' permission, and he had to go to the local Marine Corps office to register and take the required tests. Putnam's father had been a medic in Vietnam, and his parents were proud to give him permission to sign up early. One other piece of family history also motivated him. Putnam takes pride in being related to General Israel Putnam, a hero of the Battle of Bunker Hill in the Revolutionary War.

After turning 18 and graduating from high school, Putnam made a beeline for boot camp. For his MOS (Military Occupational Specialty) he chose "assault man," which includes demolitions, rockets, and missiles.

"Sign me up to blow stuff up," he says. "What 18-year-old wouldn't want that job?"

But in early 2003, after arriving in Kuwait, his MOS was changed. His unit needed another machine gunner, not an assault man. It was impossible to predict at the time, but that change destroyed his health and ended his Marine Corps career.

Putnam had heard stories of Marines in earlier wars who saved the day by re-supplying machine gunners who were low on ammo. Putnam saw himself as a "save the day" kind of Marine, so in 2003 in Iraq he carried massive amounts of machine-gun ammo, just in case it was needed. "You can't come in and save them if you don't have enough ammo," he told me. He carried so much that he not only herniated some discs, he also "blew out some veins." Veins that were supposed to be *one* millimeter in diameter had dilated, or enlarged, to *ten* millimeters. "It felt like someone was always stabbing me," he says.

Marine Corps doctors tried medication, but it didn't help, so they gave him a choice. He could do two years of light duty, or he could take a chance at surgery. If the surgery worked, they told him, he might be back in the saddle in three months, possibly soon enough to rejoin his unit in Iraq in 2004. Putnam chose surgery: "Cut me open, tie it up, let's go." Sadly, the surgery failed. Instead of re-enlisting, Putnam was forced out of the Marines—a medical discharge.

"It absolutely crushed me," he says. It was especially hard to take because the Marines had been such a perfect fit. Putnam was so gung-ho that he played the Marines' Hymn ("From the Halls of Montezuma to the Shores of Tripoli") on his harmonica as his unit roared across the border into Iraq on March 20, 2003. And when he came home at the end of that deployment, he experienced no symptoms of Post-Traumatic Stress. "Everything happened as I expected. In fact, I imagined it was going to be worse," Putnam told me." He could hardly wait to re-deploy to Iraq in 2004. "Mentally, I felt I was prepared for it," he said.

After his medical discharge, Putnam moved to Texas for a vocational rehab program, but eventually returned home to Minnesota. That's when he came up with Plan B. And since Plan A—the Marines—was bold and adventuresome, it's not surprising that Plan B was too. When Putnam was growing up in Minnesota, once or twice a summer he took canoeing and camping trips in far northern Minnesota, an area known as the Boundary Waters. "I loved it, and I missed it," he said.

His plan to transform his life after the Marines was to explore the Minnesota wilderness, learn everything he could—from dog sledding to fishing to canoeing—and then start guiding. The plan worked. He eventually started his own guiding business. "It was exactly as I dreamed it," he says now.

Along the way he went to college and got married. He and his wife Nicole wanted to have children but that was another mountain to climb. Putnam had been told that, because of his vascular issues, it was unlikely he could have children. "Well, we found out that we could have children, because we got pregnant," he says. Sadly, his wife Nicole suffered miscarriages. They decided to keep trying and moved back to the Twin Cities to be near the best health care available. They were elated when Nicole gave birth to their son, Judah. More recently, they adopted a "precious" 11-year-old daughter named Nova.

Putnam says he never felt lower than when he was discharged from the Marines, but even in those dark days felt confident he could transform his life yet again. All he had to do was apply a basic rule he learned in the Marines: Never, ever give up.

Corporal Robert Witt

> I feel like I can be put in any situation, both physical and mental, and somehow I can get through it.

Rob Witt's Marine Corps transformation began at a very early age. In the eighth grade he joined the Naval Sea Cadets, which provided him with the eye-opening opportunity of training on military bases.

He didn't have much interest in school and was only an average student. He blames that on his habit of placing military books inside his textbooks, so he could secretly read them during class. He particularly loved the Marines, with its "esprit de corps" and heroic tradition of victories in crucial battles. He dreamed of being part of that illustrious history, and was dead set on becoming an infantryman, a grunt, "the backbone of the Marine Corps," as he described it.

By his senior year of high school Witt had accumulated enough credits to graduate early. He saw that as an opportunity to get a head start in the Marines, and arranged to spend part of his senior year at boot camp. By the time he graduated from high school, boot camp was already in his past.

Witt spent a little more than four years in the Marines and says he has not experienced severe symptoms of stress. The worst of it is occasional nightmares. He credits his wife Liz for helping him transition from military to civilian life.

I asked Witt what he does today to earn a living and his answer was something I had not heard before. "I can't talk about it," he said. He still defends and supports America in his job, he told me, but other than that he can't say a word about it. It took ten years of hard work to achieve that unidentified position, and he says there was a lot of rejection before he finally reached his goal. Whatever his mystery profession is, it is obviously very competitive—and extremely secretive.

Witt says he learned the traits that propel him now, as a Marine—perseverance, and mental and physical toughness. "I feel like I can be put in any situation, both physical and mental, and somehow I can get through it."

At this moment in our Zoom interview, Witt's very persevering eight-year-old son Jackson walked into his father's office for at least the second time to see how the interview was going. I asked him what he planned to do for his upcoming ninth birthday. He said he was thinking about having a pool party and ordering pizza, drawing a surprised laugh from his father.

After Jackson left, I asked Witt if he would like Jackson to become a Marine someday. "Yes, I would love him to do that. He's big into airplanes," he said. "He designed an airport in our basement." He has over a hundred model planes. Witt has tried to twist Jackson's arm a bit, telling him: "You need to think about the Naval Academy, buddy," which gives its students the choice of becoming Sailors *or* Marines. So far though, his gentle pressure campaign is not working. "He wants to be a Southwest pilot," Witt says. "I'm like, whatever you want buddy. Whatever makes you happy."

I'll put my money on the Marines.

First Lieutenant Brian Chontosh, Navy Cross Recipient

> Going into the Marine Corps I was supremely selfish. The Marine Corps taught me how to put others first authentically, and to do it with a dose of humility.

To many of his colleagues, Chontosh is the iconic Marine. That's why I was so astonished when I asked him why he joined the Marines. I expected to hear that he had dreamed of being a warrior ever since he was a boy, or that he joined out of patriotic duty, or because of his family history. Those explanations are not even close to the truth.

When he was a teenager, he told me, "I couldn't care fucking less about the military and couldn't care less about my country." His abilities were obvious—he was very athletic and got good grades without much effort. But he didn't feel challenged. He was bored with life and says he got into trouble doing "mischievous shit" with his friends. He found himself before a judge who sentenced him to community service—and then proceeded to save Chontosh from himself.

Judge Joseph Steinwachs recognized his potential, and his need for direction and discipline. An Army veteran, the judge told him he was not on a good path and suggested he join the military. "I don't want to end up in jail," Chontosh says he thought at the time. So he took the judge's advice and started walking a path he had never even considered taking.

He tried the Air Force but was turned down. The recruiter told him: "You're not what we're looking for." He was told the Air Force wanted "quality individuals." As he was leaving the Air Force recruiting office, he had the life-changing good fortune of bumping into a Marine recruiter. "I remember him to this day," Chontosh says. "Super, super jacked, Black Marine. Chest of medals, uniform just immaculate."

"Young man, what's wrong?" the recruiter said, apparently noticing that he looked dejected after his bad experience with the Air Force recruiter. "Come on in, let me talk to you for a second." It didn't take much of a sales job. Chontosh decided on the spot to join the Marines. Nine days later he left for basic training at South Carolina's Parris Island, made famous for the punishing nature of its boot camp in the movie *Full Metal Jacket*.

Chontosh says he wasn't a bad person as a teenager, he just had a lot of "misdirected, unchanneled energy." The Marine Corps gave that energy an outlet. Today, he says he's "very, very fortunate" to have come across Judge Steinwachs, with whom he stayed in touch for years, and the recruiter, whom he only remembers as Staff Sergeant Allen.

I asked him where he would be today if he hadn't joined the Marines. "Dead, or jail, probably," he told me. A stunning answer coming from someone who succeeded on the difficult path from enlisted Marine to commissioned officer, received the Navy Cross, and is revered as a "Marine's Marine."

When I asked Chontosh what he learned as a Marine that helped him succeed in civilian life, he hesitated for a moment, then replied: "I learned not to be selfish. Going into the Marine Corps I was supremely selfish. The Marine Corps taught me how to put others first authentically, and to do it with a dose of humility. I'm not saying I learned that in year one, and I'm not saying I learned it completely after 21 years. But I would say that I came a long fucking way."

There are of course many who join the Marines because of their family's military history, or to protect and defend their country, or because of some other heroic impulse. But there are also many like Chontosh, who join the Marines because they're lost, troubled, or unmotivated, and are looking for discipline and guidance. It might be one of the most common Marine stories of all.

CHAPTER 12

Marines Who Loved It So Much They Made It a Career

Marines who serve 20 years receive a pension for life. The Marines in this chapter made or exceeded that time of service. But for most it's not the money that motivates them to stick with it—it's that they can't tear themselves away from the Marines.

Captain Ethan Bishop

If you're looking out for number one, you're going to fall on your face and fail.

If the measure of success is the degree to which you fulfill your dreams, then Ethan Bishop is one of the most successful people I know.

Bishop had two dreams. First, to be a U.S. Marine, which he did for 20 years, retiring as a Lieutenant Colonel. And second, to be a game warden in the wilds of Idaho, which is what he does today as a Senior Conservation Officer for the Idaho Department of Fish and Game. He spends his "work" days patrolling the Idaho wilderness by jet boat, horseback, and snowmobile.

I put the word "work" in quotation marks because it doesn't sound like work to me. It sounds like getting paid to have a new adventure every day. In fact, it also doesn't sound like work to Bishop, who confessed to me: "I would almost pay to do this job."

And there's a third chapter in Bishop's book of success. There's a lot of divorce in the military, but Bishop has been married to the same woman for 26 years and has three sons, who were toddlers when he was in Iraq in 2003. "It's about quality of life and family," he says, "not making a lot of money."

The most important thing the Marines taught him is people skills, which allowed him to be successful in both careers. Basically, it's the Golden Rule, he says. "Treating people as you want to be treated, it's that simple. If you're looking out for number one, you're going to fall on your face and fail. Looking out for others and putting yourself last always worked out well." That, as I noted earlier, is an important Marine custom. In this branch of the military the grunts always eat first, and senior officers like Bishop, a captain in 2003, step aside in the chow line for anyone of lower rank.

Bishop chose the Marines for a reason that is not uncommon: family tradition. His brother, father, and two uncles were enlisted Marines. But for him, there was a change in the family path—his father didn't want him to enlist. He saw something bigger for his son. So Bishop went to college first. "Boy, I'm glad I did that," he says. Not only did his college degree allow him to start as a commissioned officer in the Marines, but it also gave him a big leg up in his second career as a conservation officer.

Bishop was 31 years old when the Marines invaded Iraq in 2003, making him one of the more seasoned Marines in the battalion. He had been on active duty since 1995 but had never experienced combat. Before the first battle, he says, "the ulcers were already starting to develop in my gut." He was worried about how the "kids" under his command—several were just 18 or 19 years old—would perform. He also fretted about the "stop-loss" Marines whose service had been involuntarily extended. "What kind of disgruntled Marines are we going to have here?" he wondered.

He needn't have worried. "Holy moly, they didn't miss a beat," he told me. "They were phenomenal." In a follow-up phone call, he described his Marines as "lethal and ruthless" in battle, as they were trained to be. Instead of having to push them forward, at times Bishop had to hold them back. "I was holding the leash," he said.

When I asked him what goes through his mind when he thinks about his time in Iraq in 2003, he gave an answer I hadn't heard before: "Oh, I don't, to tell you the truth, think about it much." He said he occasionally "talks about it and brags about my Marines' actions," but other than keeping track of some of the guys on Facebook, he seems happy to leave that part of his life in the past and focus on his life in the Idaho backcountry.

"I've lost contact with most of them because it's such a rural area where I live," he explained. "I probably spend more time with cowboys and elk than with anybody else."

Second Lieutenant Casey Brock

> I had no intention of joining the Marine Corps. I wanted to become a doctor.

Casey Brock calls himself "The Last Man Standing." After 21 years in the Marines, he was the only member of his platoon still on active duty. What's surprising about that is that he almost didn't become a Marine at all. "I had no intention of joining the Marine Corps," he says. Instead, he went to college. "I wanted to become a doctor."

But while in college he thought a lot about his family's military history and came up with a new plan. Brock's father, whom he greatly admires, was a Marine infantryman in Vietnam. And his grandfather was a Sailor on the *USS Enterprise* during World War II. During his college years, the magnetic pull of family tradition became too strong for Brock to resist. And the Marine Corps was the top option—because he saw it as the ultimate challenge. "I wanted to know if I could do it," he says. "And I didn't know if that was the case. I thought long and hard about it, and l realized I could always go back and be a doctor. You can't always go back and be a Marine."

Brock never did "go back and become a doctor." He was commissioned as an officer in 2001, and when I interviewed him 21 years later he was a lieutenant colonel and battalion commander at MARSOC, the United States Marine Forces Special Operations Command, based in North Carolina.

Brock initially wanted to follow in his father's footsteps by joining the infantry. But with a college degree he could make the dream even bigger. He set his sights on becoming an infantry platoon commander, which is exactly what he was in Iraq in 2003.

When Brock recalls that time in his life, he considers himself to have been extraordinarily fortunate. "What a unique experience the invasion of Iraq was in 2003," he says. "I don't know when that's ever going to happen again. Horizon to horizon it was just combat vehicles and tanks. I know I'll never see that again. Not many Marines in modern times have witnessed an entire Marine Expeditionary Force going on the offensive, moving as one, leveraging all the power that the Marines have to offer. It was surreal. It was awe-inspiring."

I asked Brock why he decided to stay in the Marines and give up the dream of becoming a doctor. He said he loved what he was doing—and the people he served with—too much to leave. "I liked the challenge, and the challenge didn't go away. It only increased."

And of course, as with virtually all Marines, there was the intense bond with this band of brothers. The importance of that bond is a sentiment I've heard from dozens of Marines. But Brock explained it more poetically than anyone else:

> Everyone says this, but that doesn't make it untrue. The best part of being a Marine is the Marines. You get to be part of this club, this clique, this group of people, this gang of thugs and miscreants and deviants. Part of a group of people that no one else understands. I've been blessed to have these relationships and get exposed to this fantastic group of people who I know will be there for me for the rest of my life.

Brock is a natural leader. Sergeant Nathaniel Donnelly says Brock was the best commanding officer he ever had. And Captain Ethan Bishop, Brock's superior officer in 2003, described Brock—who has a gentle nature when not commanding troops—as a "kick-ass platoon commander." Marines of India Company still get together every year on April 4, the date Corporal Erik Silva was killed in action in 2003. All these years later Brock still attends when he can find time in his busy active-duty schedule. Some Marines act like Brock is still their commanding officer—not by being obedient or subservient, but by showing him the quiet respect given only to true leaders.

When I asked Brock about the most important things he learned as a Marine, leadership was at the top of his list. In his usual poetic way, he said it's all about integrity, honor, and respect:

> I've learned the power and the importance of integrity. That integrity is not just a word. That honor is something that has to be earned. Respect is something that has to be earned and should be coveted, and is so hard to gain, but so easy to lose.

There's one thing about Brock's idea of leadership that is, if not unique, certainly quite rare. It doesn't necessarily end when Marines go their separate ways:

> Once you become a leader of Marines, regardless of rank, you have an obligation to those Marines. You're responsible for those Marines during that time of conflict and crisis in terms of combat, but that responsibility doesn't end when the deployment is over. It doesn't end when you move on, or they move on. It doesn't matter whether you're on active duty or if you've moved on to civilian life, that responsibility, that obligation, to your fellow Marines, in terms of leadership, in terms of health and welfare and looking out for them and having their back, that never ends.

Brock uses social media to keep track of Marines from his platoon in 2003. "If an individual is really struggling, I'll reach out to them personally," he told me. "If there's something that I feel I can do to help, I make the effort."

In what universe do leaders watch out for people who served or worked under them two decades ago? In Casey Brock's universe. And they return the kindness by treating him like their commander of old:

> It always brings me a little joy in my heart when those guys still call me their lieutenant. I'm 44 years old. I'm a lieutenant colonel in the Marine Corps, but I'll never be anything more than second lieutenant to those guys. I have this overwhelming sense of gratitude for who they are, for all their rough edges and their sins. I feel blessed to have been a part of their lives.

Brock's sense of long-term commitment also carries over to his personal life. His wife, now a charter pilot, was his girlfriend in 2003, and they have three children together. But he still regrets one aspect of their relationship. Instead of proposing to her soon after he returned from Iraq in 2003, he waited until right before he deployed again to Iraq in 2004, where he fought in the extremely bloody Second Battle of Fallujah. "I made her sweat it out," he told me ruefully. "I'm still living that one down."

Speaking of Brock's family, there's a footnote to his story that involves his paternal grandmother. When 3/5 returned home in September 2003, several months after I returned, I traveled to Camp Pendleton to do a story about their homecoming for NBC News.

While we waited for their arrival, some of the Marines' wives presented me with an oversized book with "MARINES" emblazoned in gold on the cover, above the Marine Corps emblem. Inside the thick book were dozens of letters to me and my NBC crew from the Marines' wives, girlfriends, mothers, fathers, sisters, and brothers, thanking us for risking our lives to report on their Marines.

One of the most touching letters was from Brock's grandmother, Gladys Brock. She thanked me for keeping her informed about her grandson's battalion, and then revealed this about herself:

> I have lived through six wars with someone I loved in each one. WWII, Korea, Vietnam, Somalia, and Gulf one and two. Too many for one generation. War solves some problems and creates others. It remains to be seen if the Iraqi war was worth the price. The only way to stop future wars is for every new parent in every country to teach their children to love and not hate.

I mailed the letter to Brock, who shared it with his father. They were very moved by what she had written. Brock told me that she had since passed on, adding: "She was a kind and loving woman but very private. She never shared those thoughts with either of us."

Gunnery Sergeant Octaviano "Gunny" Gallegos Jr.

One of my most vivid memories from my first days as an embed with 3/5 in Kuwait was watching Gunny Gallegos competing in pull-up contests. He was in his mid-thirties and his all-time record was an astounding 46 pull-ups. Even more jaw-dropping was his record of 15 one-armed pull-ups.

He wasn't boastful about it. He just believes everyone should make the most of their God-given talents. Many young Marines were in awe of him. He's the first person I heard described as a "Marine's Marine"—one of the highest compliments a Marine can give another Marine.

It was no surprise to anyone that when he retired, after 24 years, he had risen to the rank of sergeant major, the highest rank a non-commissioned officer can achieve. At the time of his promotion there were 485 sergeant majors in the Marine Corps, out of 195,000 Marines. That's one-quarter of one percent.

I asked if he had a big promotion ceremony. "I'm not into all that hoopla," he said, and told me a story that says a lot about him. During boot camp, he was on mess duty one day when he started to have doubts about whether he could cut it in the Marines. He was standing next to some dumpsters at Camp Pendleton after filling them with trash. He had a view of Interstate 5 and thought "I want to get on that road and go back home." Twenty-three years later when he was promoted to sergeant major he held his small ceremony at that same spot—right by the dumpsters where he had doubted his abilities.

If a Marine aspires to achieve that lofty rank, I asked him, how should he or she go about it? Gallegos said that if you even ask that question, you're doing it all wrong. He tells Marines not to dream about promotions. "It pisses me off," he says, "when people get up in the morning and think: 'What can I do to help me get promoted today?' I tell people 'the only damn thing you have to do, brother, is do your damn job.' If your job is to clean shitters, you better be the best shit cleaner there is.'"

His theory of leadership is also very simple: "The biggest privilege about leadership and rank is not your parking spot, it's not a pay raise," he says. "It is the privilege of having people under you who are looking up to you for guidance. Get up in the morning to serve your people."

Where did he get his work ethic, discipline, and selflessness? That's also simple—from his father, an immigrant from Mexico. From the time he was 11 years old Gallegos started working every day after school with his father in the fields around Las Cruces, New Mexico, picking tomatoes, cucumbers, lettuce, pecans, apples, whatever needed picking. As darkness fell, they headed home for dinner—and then homework.

That work ethic carried over to the Marines, as did his gratitude to his father. "During those long, 18- or 19-hour days in the Marines," he says, "I remember thinking that I'm used to this, I'm used to being in the field, I'm used to being dirty, I'm used to working long hours, because of my good papa."

Sometimes his father would have sit-down talks in the cargo bed of their Ford pickup truck with Gallegos and his siblings, to explain how much they owed to America. "My good daddy said we need to give back to America for what it has given us, which is the opportunity to have better lives."

Those talks planted a seed of patriotism. When he was 12, he decided how he would make that seed grow. It was during the Iran hostage crisis in 1980. He was looking at photographs of the American hostages in the newspaper when he noticed a familiar name: Marine Sergeant Gallegos. "I remember seeing him in his Marine uniform," Gallegos says. He had no reason to believe that he and Gallegos the hostage were related, but the fact that someone with his last name could serve as a Marine stirred him. He thought: "I want to do that." As soon as he turned 18, he joined the Marines. He spent the weekend before he left for boot camp working the fields with his family.

In Iraq in 2003, as a gunnery sergeant, he was a "trigger puller," down in the trenches with the privates and the corporals. He firmly believed the Marines were there to liberate the Iraqi people, not to conquer them.

One of his most difficult moments was when two young Iraqi girls were accidentally killed after a massive sandstorm led to an impossibly dark and chaotic night.

Gallegos never sought counseling or therapy and had only minimal post-traumatic stress symptoms resulting from his years in combat. A big reason for that, he says, is that he was much older than the youngest Marines and had a lot of life experience. The younger Marines tend to be affected much more by PTSD, he says. "They're young men doing something very noble, but they're still maturing. They're still developing mentally."

Gallegos engages in what he calls "self-therapy." "When I start marinating on bad memories, I find something else to do, or just think about other things that are more positive."

The best thing about being a Marine, Gallegos says, was "serving the American people, serving this grateful nation that gave so much to me and my family, my good mom, and my good daddy." There was a lot of sacrifice, a lot of time away from his family. "But if I could be 18 again today, I'd go see the recruiter right now. I'd do it all over again in a heartbeat," he says.

His pride in America is as intense as ever. "The Marine Corps made me realize how good we have it in America. One thing that made me realize what a great nation this is, is seeing how messed up other nations are."

He has two large American flags—one in his front yard, one in the back, with spotlights shining on them so they can fly 24 hours a day. He can see the one in the backyard through his bedroom window. "I go to bed at night watching that flag, and I get up in the morning watching that flag."

After retiring from the Marines, Gallegos found a job running the linen department in a hospital. When he arrived, he says: "It was a frickin' mess. No accountability, nothing. I decided to use the same leadership style I had in the Marine Corps—look after and invest in your people. Once they saw I'm looking out for them, just like in the Marines, they'll do anything for you."

Now his department is a model of efficiency, and he has been named leader of the year and employee of the year at the hospital. What he learned as a Marine, he says, is "one hundred percent" transferable to the civilian world.

During our interview Gallegos mentioned several times how thankful he is to his wife Carrie for putting up with so much during his long career, so I asked Carrie what it's like to be married to a Marine for more than 20 years.

"I love being a Marine wife," she told me. One big reason for that is that she so greatly admires her husband for putting his life on the line for America. But she cautions that it's not for everyone. "It takes a certain someone to be able to handle everything the Marine Corps will throw at you." They married when she was 20. "The Marine Corps will make you become very independent, very quickly," she says.

There's a well-known expression among Marine spouses, Carrie says: "If it is going to happen, it will happen while they are deployed." Gallegos was deployed during both of her pregnancies and missed the birth of their son. Their daughter, when she was two years old, spent a week in the hospital with a serious illness while he was deployed. And of course, Gallegos missed more birthdays, holidays, and anniversaries than they can count, all in service to the country.

But there's not even a trace of bitterness or regret. Carrie is grateful for everything the Marines have done for her and her husband, adding: "I am who I am today because of the Marine Corps."

Gallegos is a masterful storyteller, and one of his favorite stories is about the two or three days on the road to Baghdad in 2003 when MREs suddenly became scarce. The Marines were asked to limit their intake to one a day. Some Marines were so hungry that they caught chickens and cooked them over a fire. Another group claimed that they caught a large lizard and cooked it.

I asked Gallegos why a well-supplied Marine battalion suddenly had a food shortage. Apparently, he told me, the logistics train, which carries essential supplies ("beans, bullets and band-aids," for short), had fallen behind the quicker combat units on the front lines. "We were moving so fast that the enemy got in between the lead element and the log train," Gallegos explains. "I think the enemy had figured it out. You know, here comes the lead element, let it go by. And then attack the log train."

Gallegos remembers a time during the brief food shortage when some Marines were assigned to burn a large pile of trash, which included numerous MRE packages from previous days. When MREs were plentiful, it was not uncommon for Marines to leave unwanted items in the bags when they threw them away. The hungry Marines asked Gallegos if they could go through the pile and look for leftovers before they burned the packages. "They knew that there was good chow in there," Gallegos says, "and I said 'Absolutely.'"

They found plenty of discarded food. "So once everybody got their chow, they gave me a thumbs up," he recalls. In accordance with the Marine custom that the higher-ranking Marines eat after the grunts, it was now time for Gallegos and his lieutenant to see what was left.

There was nothing—except one thick slice of turkey that was covered with dirt. "We tried to wash it off with some nasty ass water," he says. "I remember getting my little Swiss Army knife and slicing it into little cubes."

They added some hot sauce, and Gallegos broke a twig off a tree to use as a toothpick, as if they were dining on a fine delicacy. "We hadn't showered in weeks. We smelled bad. We were freaking hungry. And I remember the crunchy sound from chewing on the dirt. But eating that turkey slice was like having a five-course meal."

Lieutenant Colonel Carl "Sam" Mundy

> That experience with 3/5 was top of the heap. It was a privilege to command that unit.

Sam Mundy is a combination of tough guy Marine and soft-spoken gentleman. "He always treated us with dignity and respect," one sergeant told me. He retired in 2021 as a lieutenant general (three stars) after an extraordinarily distinguished 38-year Marine Corps career.

After he returned home from Iraq, I invited Mundy to be my guest at the annual black tie television correspondents' dinner in Washington. He wore the Marine equivalent of black tie—the Evening Dress uniform, displaying a chest full of medals. I felt a good deal more pride about my guest than I had at previous dinners, when my guests were usually high-ranking members of Congress.

Mundy served in two of the highest positions in the Marine Corps (Commander, Special Operations Command, and Commander, Marine Corps Forces Central Command), but he doesn't consider either of those lofty positions to be the highlight of his career. For that, you'd have to go back two decades—when he was a lieutenant colonel, commanding 3d Battalion, 5th Marines in Iraq in 2003. "That experience with 3/5 was top of the heap," he told me. "It was a privilege to command that unit."

In combat, a commander is too busy with strategy, tactics, and logistics, and too valuable to the battalion, to be up front with the grunts shooting at enemy forces. "I fought mostly with the radio handset in my hand," he says. But as 3/5 moved inexorably toward Baghdad, usually at the tip of the spear, the nearly daily ambushes could strike anywhere along the convoy. With more than 100 vehicles it sometimes stretched out two or three miles.

During one ambush Mundy remembers getting out of the command vehicle to observe the battle. He was, of course, on the radio, helping to coordinate movements, when a fellow officer told him: "Sir, they're shooting at you. You probably want to get to the other side of the vehicle."

"Well, this is stupid," Mundy says he thought to himself. "They see a Marine get out of a Humvee with a radio handset, that's obviously the kind of guy they probably want to shoot." He moved to the other side of the vehicle.

The hardest part of being a battalion commander on a combat mission, Mundy says, was dealing with the avalanche of things happening simultaneously, especially during the frequent ambushes. "Once the action starts, it's very confusing, there's a surreal quality to it," he says. It fell to Mundy and his top officers to see through the fog of war and create a clear picture of what was happening and how to respond. "You can't allow all the input to weight you down," he says. "If you did, it could be devastating to forward momentum."

Mundy was, and still is, "extremely pleased" with how his Marines performed in combat. There was never any problem getting them to fight. They weren't always perfect, he said without elaboration. "No unit is ever perfect." But he was awed by the countless examples of individual courage and leadership under fire. He's also proud of the fact—as he was informed years later—that 3/5 in 2003 had traveled a greater distance inland under combat conditions than any Marine Infantry battalion in history.

The hardest part, of course, was dealing with the loss of life. As the commander there was an extra burden on him because it was his job to explain to grieving Marines that mourning would have to wait. "For the good of the nation and the Marine Corps and this operation," he told them, "we need you to compartmentalize that and move forward and focus on what's in front of you."

There's no question that 3/5 is one of the most legendary battalions in the Marine Corps, with a long history of grinding out victories in historic battles. "I would argue that it's the most storied battalion in the Marine Corps," Mundy says. He admits, though, that there's "a good, healthy rivalry" with 2d Battalion, 5th Marines over which one is the "most decorated."

Before I interviewed Mundy, other senior officers told me that he had been assigned to command 3/5 at a low point in its history. The previous commander had been relieved because of "toxic leadership," they said. The battalion was a "disaster, a soup sandwich," one told me. (Mundy declined to join the harsh criticism of his predecessor.)

Mundy turned it around, they said, and did it quickly, in large part because of his philosophy of leadership. "You're sort of a father figure as a battalion commander," he says, which requires different skills than those of the dictatorial disciplinarian. "These Marines hadn't had someone love on them. You need to love them as your kids or your younger brothers."

Mundy agrees that the Marines need some leaders who will "run through a blazing hail of machine-gun fire and laugh about it afterwards." But you also need people with an even keel who project a "positive spirit." The best way to inspire dispirited Marines is not to ratchet up the discipline. It's to remind them of the history of the battalion and instill in them a desire to live up to that legacy. Once he had accomplished that, Mundy said, commanding 3/5 was like "holding back the horses. They were ready to run."

Today, Mundy is enjoying life in Florida with his wife Jenny, doing some consulting, and spending time with family. When I asked how Jenny feels about having him around the house all the time after so many years of being away, he jokes that the wives of retired Marines like to say: "I promised to be with you in sickness and in health, but not for lunch every day."

Joking aside, he says they enjoy, at long last, their time together. But he also admits there are times when Jenny says: "You've got to go do something by yourself, I need my time. I need girls' time with my friends."

The best part of the day is when his toddler granddaughter, who lives nearby, comes to visit. He describes time with her as "all joy, all the time." I asked: "Might she be a future Marine and continue the family legacy?" "She's going to make that decision on her own," he answered. "She could do a lot worse." He then revised his answer. "Let's put it this way. She couldn't do better than to become a United States Marine."

Captain Bob Piddock

> We call it the Piddock Partnership. It's 50/50. I'm an active-duty Marine and she's doing her end of that. She's tough as nails.

As commander of 3/5's Weapons Company, Bob Piddock was Brian Chontosh's superior officer. He did not witness Team Chontosh's heroics of March 25—he was farther back in the convoy in the command vehicle monitoring and coordinating movements by radio—but Piddock was proud that men under his command had acted so decisively and effectively. It was one of many high points in a long and successful career.

Although his father had been a Marine, Piddock was not one of those Marine kids who felt the need to follow in his father's footsteps. He went to college on a basketball scholarship—he's 6′4″—and was planning to go to law school and then maybe join the FBI.

But the summer after graduating from college, Piddock took a bike trip from Upstate New York to California, which gave him plenty of time to think about his future. One thing he thought about a lot was his father. He had great respect for him and realized that many of his best qualities were learned in the Marine Corps. By the time he arrived back home he had changed course, deciding that he could go to law school later—but if he wanted to join the Marines, he had to do it now.

His plan was to enlist as a private, but his father convinced him to go directly into the officer ranks, which his college degree allowed him to do. He had no thoughts at that time of making it a career. Just four years, and then law school. However, there was a problem with his plan. He came to love the Marines so much he couldn't leave. After twenty-one years, as a lieutenant colonel, he at long last considered retirement. He would have stayed in forever, but there were other people to think about—his wife Kathy and their four children, two girls and two boys who were then between the ages of 6 and 14. After so much time away, his family needed him.

Piddock's description of how he made the decision to retire sounds like something from a Marine Corps tactical manual. First, he said: "I assessed the situation." Then: "I determined where I could best position myself to have the greatest effect on the outcome of the situation."

"I love the Marine Corps, the honor of my life," Piddock says. "But the equation had changed." And his wife Kathy had made enormous sacrifices in all those years of being a Marine spouse. To get a sense of what military spouses go through, especially those with children, imagine living through the following scenario—without complaining.

About 12 years ago, while stationed at Quantico Marine Corps Base in Virginia, Piddock was asked to be the operations officer of a battalion soon heading to Afghanistan. The family packed quickly, loaded into a Denali SUV, and drove across country to 29 Palms Marine Corps Base in the California desert. "A five-day adventure with lots of potty breaks for the kiddos," he recalls. When they arrived at 29 Palms, he settled his family at the base motel, the Sleepy Tortoise, and promptly left for training in a remote location, leaving Kathy and the four kids in the motel room. When he returned three weeks later, they were still in the Sleepy Tortoise. The base had been unable to find them a place to live. Piddock spoke to his commanding officer who found housing. They moved in quickly and Piddock was off again, this time to Afghanistan—for a year. Kathy was left to care for four young children—ranging in age from seven years old to an infant—all while worrying about her husband in harm's way on the other side of the world.

"It's a story that highlights the sacrifices and the flexibility of Marine families," Piddock says. "We call it the Piddock Partnership. It's 50/50. I'm an active-duty Marine and she's doing her end of that. She's tough as nails. She's a typical Marine spouse and mom, the one who really anchors everything. Kath and I have been together a long time. We stick together."

Somehow, in addition to her family responsibilities, Kathy found time over the years to bring in a second income as a Certified Public Accountant, and to serve as a volunteer at Marine Corps funerals and other ceremonies.

The family is now living happily together in Piddock's hometown of Watertown, New York, where he's Vice President of Sales for a local foodservice company. To lead his sales team, he applies a principle he learned as a Marine, which he calls, "genuine, concerned leadership." Piddock's mentor was one of the most accomplished leaders in Marine Corps history—General Joseph Dunford, who later became Commandant of the Marine Corps and Chairman of the Joint Chiefs of Staff.

Piddock says Dunford taught him that "genuine, concerned leadership" means making sure that everyone on your team is provided with an environment that allows them to be successful. That includes giving them the necessary guidance, knowledge, and resources. It also means taking care of your team members—and even their families. This approach to leadership is as applicable in business as it is in the Marines, Piddock says. "The two overlap in so many ways."

After a demanding, sometimes grueling, often dangerous 21-year career in the Marines, Piddock now has a satisfying job and spends his free time with his family. "Every day is gravy in my world," he says.

On their front porch a Marine Corps flag always flies next to an American flag. He replaces the Marine flag every year. A few years ago, when his oldest son Bobby was thirteen, he claimed the old Marine flag and hung it in his bedroom. Perhaps a sign of things to come. Like his own father, Piddock does not push his children toward the Marine path. "I let them do their thing, whatever they want to do." But if one of his children were to join the Marines, I asked, would he be proud? "I sure would," he replied.

Captain Mario Schweizer

> Marines are "people people." Most people wouldn't think that about Jarheads and Leathernecks. But the Marine Corps really taught me about people.

Mario Schweizer says that, as a devout Christian, he felt called to join the military. But he did not feel called to be a chaplain. His sacred call was to serve "in the line" as they say in the Navy, or in the ranks. To lead people in battle.

His grandfather had been in the Navy, so he followed suit. But after a couple years in a Navy program during college, he had a revelation. "I didn't see myself on a ship or flying a plane," he says. Schweizer loved leading people in the field, didn't mind getting dirty, and liked physical challenges. His true calling, he realized, was in the Marines.

"I shocked the world during my junior year and made a late transition from Navy to the Marines," he says, and became a commissioned Marine officer upon graduation.

In 2003 he was a captain and was asked to be 3/5's Commander, Headquarters and Service Company (H&S.) "That was a little disappointing," he says. "It is not what an infantry officer hopes and dreams of."

But overseeing 3/5's H&S was an enormous—and enormously important—job. With about 200 men and 30–40 vehicles, Schweizer nicknamed the company "Ugly Beast."

A battalion couldn't possibly be an effective fighting unit without a strong H&S Company. It takes a skillful leader to keep 1,100 men well-fed, well-armed, and well-supplied while traveling across a desert, and also being ready at any moment to defend against an ambush.

Being a senior officer in a combat battalion was one of the highlights of his career, Schweizer says. "I had the surreal realization that this is real. Exhilaration is a good word for it. This is what we trained for."

He says he clearly remembers the day my NBC News team left 3/5 for another assignment in Baghdad. It was a sad day, he says, "because I knew we were moving into a phase of the operation where we probably were not going to be in the forefront of American minds." He's one of several 3/5 Marines who noted how dispiriting it can be to fight a war when the American people aren't paying much attention. After 20 years, Schweizer retired as a major in 2014, got an MBA from Pepperdine University, and spent six years working in banking. Given the weighty responsibility he carried as a Marine, and the large number of people he oversaw, it's not surprising that he says leadership is one of the chief traits he learned. But he says it would be a mistake to think that leadership in banking and in the Marines are similar—or similarly fulfilling. It's not even close, he says.

Schweizer's wife Jenni tells him: "The Marine Corps ruined you for leadership," and he agrees. In the Marines it's about leading people, he says. Taking responsibility, setting an example, motivating the team, working past the challenges, applying the ingenuity Marines are famous for, and finding a way to get it done.

In business, at least in his experience, it's not so much about leadership as it is about management. "It's widgets, it's numbers, it's bottom line. They want to put everything on a spread sheet and get a number." He has a finance degree so he can do the numbers. But he prefers leadership when it's all about people. "Marines are 'people people,'" he says. He admits that might seem counterintuitive. "Most people wouldn't think that about Jarheads and Leathernecks. But the Marine Corps really taught me about people."

That's why he recently left a "perfectly good job" at a major bank to be the business manager of a law firm run by a friend, who is also a retired Marine. "I'm working alongside my former infantry platoon commander as his Executive Officer," he says. "It's almost like being back in the Marines."

First Sergeant James Miles Thetford

> I wasn't afraid because I had always been raised to believe that God's going to take care of me. And if it's your time, it's your time.

When James Miles Thetford was in the sixth grade, growing up in a two stop-light town in Texas, he had a favorite leather belt. Lots of kids wore them, and most had their names stamped on them. Not Thetford. His was stamped with the word "Marine."

Another early hint of where he was heading in life is that his father's name was also James, so his parents decided to call him by his middle name, Miles—which he liked because it means "warrior" or "proud soldier."

And one more indicator: Thetford remembers as a child his mother singing the lullaby "Little Man, You've Had a Busy Day" at bedtime. The words to one of the verses have always stuck in his mind: "Come along little soldier and put away your gun, war is over for tonight."

Like so many other would-be Marine teenagers, Thetford signed up at age 17, with his parents' permission. His mother resisted but eventually gave in. Today he's pretty sure there's still a "Proud Parent of a U.S. Marine" sticker on her car. After 33 years wearing the uniform, he retired in 2014 as a sergeant major.

In all those years, he says, he never fired a shot in anger. He was fired upon in 2003 and received a combat action ribbon for his service. But he was in his late thirties in Iraq, and it was his first real combat deployment. He was a bit farther back in the convoy than the young kids who did most of the shooting on the front lines. "I wasn't in the shit like they were," is how he puts it. "Those guys were hooking and jabbing, they were down there cracking heads."

But that doesn't mean his job was less important. In some ways it was more important. He was more like the coach of a football team than the running back. "A coach who makes sure they have the gear they need, tells them what the play is, and sends them in to win the football game." Being from Texas, Thetford also used a cowboy metaphor: "You get all the cattle together and you start pushing the dogies. And you never know what's going to be around the next bend."

What he misses most about the Marines is the camaraderie. Second, is "the never say die spirit," Thetford says. "You don't ever think there's something you can't do." There are some things he doesn't miss, like getting phone calls at 3am telling him that some young Marine did "something stupid" and it was Thetford's job to get him out of jail. "You owned those kids 24/7," he says. Ninety percent of them were no problem—it's that other ten percent.

Only a small percentage of Marines engage in front-line combat. Many Marines spend most of their careers in support roles. But that doesn't mean they don't have challenging jobs. Thetford volunteered for four long tours in one of the most difficult jobs of all—Marine recruiter.

Thetford says the Marine Corps Recruiting Command used to describe itself as: "The only regiment actively engaged with an opposing force on a daily basis." An opposing force that largely consisted of mothers who didn't want their teenagers to join the Marines. "I convinced mothers to allow their sons to fight in wars," he says, not a job for the faint of heart. But he knew how important it was and kept coming back to recruiting—because you can't win wars if you can't fill your ranks with the best people.

Thetford also volunteered for funeral duty, wearing his Marine Corps Dress Blues. "I buried more Marines from car accidents and other types of accidents than I ever did in three combat tours," he says. But perhaps his most difficult job of all was when he had to inventory a Marine's gear after he was killed or seriously wounded—as he did after the death of Navy Corpsman Michael Johnson in Iraq. "There are no bad days," he says, "as long as I don't have to do that."

Despite taking on difficult assignments, Thetford says he never struggled with stress when he returned home. He gives much of the credit to his religious beliefs. "I had a lot of peace," even in Iraq, he says. "I wasn't afraid because I had always been raised to believe that God's going to take care of me. And if it's your time, it's your time."

Today he has three children and five grandchildren. Thetford is a "warehouse fulfillment manager," which he describes as working for "a very tiny Amazon." It's a good job, partly because he has only one person to manage—himself.

But any civilian job pales in comparison to being a Marine, he says. "I impacted lives. I get to tell my grandkids that we liberated three countries and gave the people of those countries their freedom."

Major Craig Wonson

> I think seeing war up close can help reduce people's eagerness to seek war as the primary option for solving global issues.

Instead of doing a Zoom interview, Craig Wonson chose to answer my questions in writing. In recounting his personal history, he mentioned that he "began working on a commercial fishing boat out of Gloucester at an early age." Wait a minute, I thought. Is he talking about Gloucester, Massachusetts? The home port of the *Andrea Gail* fishing boat in the book and movie *A Perfect Storm*?

I wrote back to him and asked if that's what he was referring to. "That is correct," he wrote. In fact, he added, his family helped found the fishing industry in Gloucester. His great grandfather is referenced in Sebastian Junger's book. There's a Wonson Cove and a Wonson Street in Gloucester. And his family tied up their boat just a few docks over from the *Andrea Gail*. He sent me old photos of the *Andrea Gail*; his family's old boat; and a fifteen-hundred-pound tuna he helped catch years ago.

I asked him what he meant when he said he started working on the family's fishing boat "at an early age." "About 11 years old," he responded. "Worked summers and vacations on it every year until I joined the Marine Corps." He said that's where he first learned to work long hours in a harsh environment. I asked how it compared to being a Marine. "The Marine Corps elevates everything to a whole new level," he told me. "Hard work and long hours took on an entirely new meaning."

In addition to the Wonson family's fishing history, it is also a military family, through and through. Wonson has ancestors who served in the Civil War. More recently, his father and grandfather were Marines, and his mother was in a branch of the Navy known as the Waves—"Women Accepted for Volunteer Emergency Service."

But it wasn't pre-ordained that he would serve in uniform. Instead of enlisting in the Marines, he went to college after high school, in large part because his parents insisted. He signed up with the Marines after college, but not because of any sense of familial fate or inevitability. It was because he admired the example set by family members and other servicemembers he met over the years. It was also because he had come to believe that Marines are "a different breed," adding: "Standards and expectations in the Corps are higher than the other services and that always appealed to me."

For Wonson, the invasion of Iraq began with a bang. Literally. As the Amphibious Assault Vehicle in which he was riding passed through a minefield between Kuwait and Iraq, there was a powerful explosion. A white cloud engulfed the passenger compartment. "I honestly thought we had struck a mine and had all been killed," Wonson recalls. "I remember being disappointed that we didn't even make it through the breech before being blown up." He thought for a moment that the white cloud was "some kind of transcendental state the body enters after you die," until he heard another Marine angrily cursing.

It turned out that the halon cannister used for firefighting inside the AAV had exploded. The intense feeling of relief to be alive lasted only a few seconds. "My joy turned to panic when I suddenly realized I had inhaled a lot of the halon and I slowly began to suffocate." He started to black out as he struggled to open the hatch to get out. He hacked up white mucus for hours.

"Today I can look back and laugh at myself for thinking I actually died," he says, "and that the white halon was some kind of out-of-body, heavenly experience."

Wonson had an enormously important job in Iraq—he was the battalion's operations officer, responsible for: "Developing and issuing orders (based on the commanding officer's guidance and intent) for all battalion operations, along with supervising all operations inside the mobile Combat Operations Center."

Apparently, Wonson did his job too well, because while he was in Iraq in 2003, he was nominated for a military position at the White House. That might sound like a stroke of good fortune, but he was very unhappy about it, as were other Marines who had been called home for similar duties. "You never want to leave your unit early," he says. "We knew our fellow Marines would be apart from their families for at least a couple more months, so having the chance to see our families before they saw their loved ones didn't sit well with any of us."

As the war extended and intensified in 2004 and 2005, Wonson could hardly bear to watch his fellow Marines fighting and dying on the news. "There are few worse things than knowing your fellow Marines are in a fight and you aren't there alongside them," he says now.

Wonson did everything he could to return as soon as possible but wasn't able to do so until 2006. After a few weeks in Iraq, though, where the fighting had become even bloodier, he began to hear a subconscious voice telling him: "Be careful what you wish for." Wonson was fortunate—he made it home uninjured. As a senior officer, though, he readily admits that Marines on the front lines were exposed to far more danger than he was. He also feels fortunate not to have suffered serious psychological issues. He had trouble sleeping for a few months, and still has dreams he wishes he didn't have, he says, but adds that everyone goes through that.

One positive result of his time in Iraq, Wonson says, concerns how he views war in general. "People sometimes get lulled into believing that war is simply blue versus red, or good versus evil," he says, or some other simplistic notion. But Iraq helped him see war for what it is. "War is death and destruction. A lot of people die, both good and bad. The people caught in the middle are usually the ones that suffer the most, often in the form of orphans, widows, and grieving parents." And the "playing field" where war is fought is left in shambles. "I think seeing war up close," Wonson says, "can help reduce people's eagerness to seek war as the primary option for solving global issues."

There was another change in attitude resulting from his time in combat zones: "I certainly feel more grateful for everything I have in life now because of that experience," including the simple things in life most Americans take for granted, like hot showers and hot meals. "I sustained myself on crackers and peanut butter for nearly three months," he says, "and lost 20 pounds in the process. Needless to say, I'm not the guy who sends his steak back to the kitchen at a restaurant if it isn't cooked to perfection."

But it wasn't just the little things that he had previously taken for granted. He also learned to better appreciate what his family had been put through. "You sometimes forget how important you are to your family and the terrible toll so much time away takes on them. I became a much better father and husband later in my career when I was able to establish a better balance between work and life."

Wonson is one of the small number of Marines I interviewed who are still on active duty, though it's in the safe confines of the Naval War College in Newport, Rhode Island where he's a professor of military science in the college's Maritime Advanced Warfighting School.

He finds teaching, coaching, and mentoring mid-career officers deeply rewarding, but says he has one unshakeable feeling that is common among former combat officers. "I do miss being in the operating forces," he said.

CHAPTER 13

Opinions About the Iraq War Today

In the days before 3/5 crossed from Kuwait into Iraq, I interviewed several Marines about what was going through their minds as they waited for the order. I wrote a story for the NBC News website that included the line: "A few Marines have even questioned whether the war is the proper response to Saddam Hussein." They didn't want to be quoted by name at that time, but some wondered why they were in Iraq when there was no evidence that Saddam had anything to do with the attacks of 9/11.

The next time I heard that kind of talk was a few weeks later, when it became clear that Saddam's arsenal of weapons of mass destruction did not exist. The Bush Administration had largely based its argument for going to war against Iraq on the existence of those weapons.

Most Marines who were willing to talk in 2003 about the rationale for going to war (many had no interest in talking about it), said they were sent by their country to fight a war and were simply doing their duty. Many also said that whether there were WMDs or not, they were there on an important mission—to free the Iraqi people from a brutal dictator.

But as the weeks wore on, with no discovery of WMDs, a small number of Marines became increasingly skeptical about the war. Some also questioned the "save the Iraqi people" argument because so many Iraqi civilians had already become "collateral damage."

If there was any doubt about the existence of WMDs, it was eliminated in 2005 when the bipartisan Iraq Intelligence Commission found that Iraq had not possessed WMDs and concluded: "The Intelligence Community's performance in assessing Iraq's pre-war weapons of mass destruction programs was a major intelligence failure."

Almost twenty years later, opinions are mixed. Most of the Marines I interviewed said they had no regrets. Their country called on them and they answered the call. They did their job, and they did it well. But many others have mixed feelings and doubts about whether the war was justified, and about how it was conducted. Some now believe it was a tragic mistake.

What follows is far from a scientific survey or a poll. It is the opinions and feelings of some of the Marines who were willing to be quoted.

Octaviano Gallegos, who retired as a sergeant major, very concisely made the basic argument that I heard from many others:

> I'm not in a position to question higher authority. Why we went in, whether weapons of mass destruction were found or not found, that is above my pay grade. As Marines, we're taught to follow orders and the order was to go in and do what we had to do. I'm not a politician, I'm not running for Congress. I'm not going to sit here and question authority. No sir, that's not what I do.

Thomas Franklin, the machine gunner of Team Chontosh, made a similar point very emphatically:

> I have no feelings about the politics. We signed up to do a thing. We got asked to do a thing. We did a thing. All that stuff, politics, is out of our area of responsibility. That's not our wheelhouse. That's somebody else's wheelhouse. We got pointed in a direction. We got told to do something. We did it. We did our job. It doesn't matter what the politics were. If the politics are bad or good, it doesn't reflect on us whatsoever. In my opinion, we did our job.

Another member of Team Chontosh, Robert Kerman, plans to retire as a master sergeant in 2023. Still on active duty when we communicated, he spoke with passion, but seemed to choose his words very carefully. He directed these words to his fellow Marines, especially those who harbor doubts about their service in Iraq:

> No matter what happened politically, it was worth the sacrifice. Our country, in my opinion, is great. We have ideals that are just. There's a reason people love America and come to America. It doesn't matter if we technically lost this war or that war. It doesn't matter what political decisions were made that, some might think, made our sacrifice null and void. It was worth it. Our sacrifice

meant something. We did it right. And nothing else matters. You can't control what you can't control. You were there for the men or women on your right or your left. You were there because you have beliefs. And what you did, no one can ever take away.

Eric Olson says he has spent a lot of time thinking about whether the Iraq war should have been fought in the first place. He has shared his thoughts with friends, family, and especially fellow Marines. Like Kerman, his message was also intended for his fellow Marines—especially those who fought in Iraq:

> You weren't conscripted, you were a volunteer, and you were sent over there to do a job, do it as effectively as you can, and bring home as many of your men as possible. It doesn't matter why you were sent over there because that's going to drive you nuts. I'm not a politician. The nation called. My president called. And we were selected to go and do our job. And we did it very well. We were extremely effective at what we did. That's how I'm able to sleep with it at night. I did my job. And I was able to bring the vast majority of my friends home.

As a professor at the Naval War College, it's obvious that Craig Wonson has given an enormous amount of thought over the years to questions about the wisdom of the war and decisions that were made over its long duration. Mistakes were made, but his analysis finds that any blame rests on the nation's leaders, not on those who fought:

> I supported going to war at the time based on the limited information I had available. We had no reason to believe the conflict wasn't linked to WMD and/or terrorism. Regardless, the actual decision to go to war was outside our lane. When the president and national leadership say, "Send in the Marines," your focus is squarely on achieving the military objectives assigned to you. We assumed the tasks we were assigned were directly linked to the desired political end state. Our job was to defeat Iraqi forces and set conditions for a peaceful, follow-on transition of Iraqi leadership. I think we accomplished that and all other military-specific tasks we were assigned. I've had time to study the war in more detail over the years, and clearly there were a lot of mistakes and bad assumptions made by people across all elements of national power. At our level, however, we did exactly what we were asked to do, and I think we did it quite well. One of the positive things I will always remember is how many Iraqis... from all different backgrounds... came up to us and thanked us for removing

Saddam. Many Iraqis understandably grew upset in the coming months when it became evident there wasn't a good plan in place following major combat operations. Responsibility for developing a broader strategy for post-war Iraq and the Middle East as a whole, however, falls on national-level leadership, not the young men and women in uniform.

Several Marines I spoke with have serious doubts about whether the war was justified. Fred Keeney, who told me he *loves* combat but *hates* war, says his hatred of war applies to the war in Iraq. He says he understands on the strategic level why the U.S. decided to go to war. But from his point of view as an American citizen, he says:

It was a mistake. We should have left it alone, because we killed a lot of Iraqi people, good and bad, but nonetheless, a lot of people. And a lot of good Americans died for a big level game that we probably didn't need to do.

He became incensed while talking about whether the nation's leaders have learned from their mistakes:

I hope that some asshole up at the Pentagon or some asshole in Washington, D.C. will think twice, three times, ten times, before they start another fucking war. During all the mayhem of the last administration, I was like, if they start another war, I'm going to be right there with the fucking hippies with a sign. We don't need to be in another fucking war. You can tell me all the geopolitical bullshit, but at the end of the day, it's our kids that are going to be doing that.

Quite a few other 3/5 Marines, including Mike Meyer, who was shot eight times during the battle of April 4, 2003, have mixed feelings. Meyer began his answer with a story about some Iraqi children he came across while on patrol in the city of Al Diwaniya in southern Iraq:

There were these kids that kept poking their heads out from behind the corner looking at us. I'll never forget it. I pulled out some candy and I reached out and looked at the kids and said, 'you want some candy?' The biggest smile pops on this kid's face. He comes out. Grabs the candy. He looks back. His parents look at us. They come out. Next thing you know there's about 20 of them just coming out, shaking our hands. Very, very friendly. So that little kid and his reaction was probably what I hold as something that says it was worth it for Iraq.

But after sharing that touching story, he shared his doubts:

Honestly, it was probably a big waste of lives and money. If I had the power to go back and leave Saddam Hussein and his brutality in place, and save

Silva, Doc Johnson, all these other Marines, save all that money, et cetera, et cetera, I'd probably do it because, you know what? Saddam Hussein probably, as terrible as he was, made that region a little bit more stable than what it is now, especially with Iran. But this is coming from a pawnbroker, not a professional diplomat.

Having said that, he added that he certainly doesn't blame the people who supported the war, because "everyone had different information."

Enrique (Rick) Alaniz says Iraq in 2003 was an awesome time and place to be a Marine:

You were with your buddies. You were with your friends. You were doing the job we had trained to do. We thought, hey, we're going to go in. We're going to kick some ass. We're going to free the Iraqi people and we're going be out of there.

But he told me that he and his fellow Marines never imagined what the Iraq war would become over time:

We did our job and we got out. And then went back in again and again and again. I'm not trying to be political but it's always about the entry plan, never about the exit plan. What's the end goal? What do we want to accomplish? And how do we get out? And it's something that I don't think they really gave much thought to. And that's why it dragged on the way it did.

Navy Cross recipient Joe Perez has mixed feelings about whether the Marines should have been in Iraq—and Afghanistan—in the first place:

When a war has a purpose and there's a particular outcome that you're looking for, like if you're in World War II, they had a clear enemy. They knew what they were doing. They knew what they were fighting against. And so, when those guys come home, they feel like they've accomplished something. Or they've contributed to something. Whereas, I feel like Vietnam veterans, and our group of guys, what were we there for? And I think a lot of that stuff contributes to the mental health issues because you come back and you're like, oh, yeah, I went to Afghanistan, lost a couple of brothers. For what, you know? What were we trying to do?

I asked Perez if he feels the same way about Iraq:

I don't know if I feel as much that way about Iraq. But like, what did Iraq have to do with any of it? Especially knowing what we know now. It was built on a lot of false intelligence.

"The Rogue Marine"—AKA Mike Prato—demonstrated earlier in this book that he has strong opinions and doesn't hold back, and he didn't mince words when I asked him what he thinks about the decision to go to war in Iraq.

First, he noted the toll on U.S. forces and their families after the Marines he served with came home:

> When we came back from deployments, I couldn't count on my fingers and toes how many people hanged themselves or wrapped themselves around trees driving their motorcycles 100 miles an hour. And alcoholism and drugs. There were failed marriages, there were guys coming back to pregnant wives. What the hell? I mean, lives were just destroyed.

Then he lambasted the decision to go to war in the first place:

> It was stupid. It was a bad decision. It's hard to see today what we got out of these things [referring to both Iraq and Afghanistan, where he also did multiple tours]. We created more disturbance in these areas than we did solutions. I'm not antiwar or anything, I'm not a dove. But I'm definitely not a hawk either. As I've gotten older and I follow politics more and take a very strong interest in my government and what we're doing, I think in hindsight that those were not wise decisions. And I wonder if they were even justified. Not just because people died, but also because, strategically speaking, what did the United States get out of it?

When he makes that argument to other people, he says they often respond with: "At least we got Saddam out of there." His response to that is:

> Saddam brought stability, man. He might have been a bad guy, but the region was stable. Yes, he used gas on his own people. Okay. But people do this all around the world. Do you want to go all over the world and start stomping on heads and then leave these power vacuums?

Scott Smith drove the Humvee in which Navy Doc Michael Johnson was killed and Lance Corporal Frank Quintero was severely injured by an RPG. When he first returned from Iraq, Smith says he was very grateful to be home in America. "I wanted to kiss the ground," he says. But over time he became angry and turned some of his rage toward his country. "For a long time, I hated America," he says. In 2005 he moved to France where he taught English and did a lot of traveling. Asked why he hated the U.S., he says it was because of how many people died in the war on both sides, a toll that could have been avoided:

> Deep down inside, I wanted to be with my family. And I would say 100 percent, that's what the other side would think too. You think those people wanted to fight us and die? No, they didn't. They had families. So I think about their people who lost their lives, and about our people who lost their lives.

Smith wonders if he would have been happier serving in Afghanistan: "I felt that was a more just war." He also hated the "war" among Americans, the furious debates over the war, the people who insisted on calling French fries, "freedom fries." And "people calling you a communist if you didn't agree with the war."

When Dave Valentino looks back on his years on active duty he feels an enormous sense of pride. He is particularly proud of his time in Iraq, and of how his fellow Marines conducted themselves. "They did it well. They did it proud. They did it clean."

But his tone changes when he talks about the decision to go to war in Iraq. "This might be an uncommon opinion," he told me. "And if it is I don't give a crap. I love being a Marine and I hold that title in the highest regard." But he says he is "plagued" by one question: "Why the hell were we there in the first place?"

While he was in Iraq, he says, he was "gung-ho, all in, this is great." But since then, he's given the war a lot of thought, and has concluded that "as you start peeling the onion back, you're like, okay, we went there for one thing, and that wasn't the case. Now you read all these stories, and the pretense that we were there to begin with wasn't even true."

"If we need to go and do a job, and even if it gets bloody, by all means, let's go do it. But let's make sure we do it right and do it for the right reasons. That still bothers me today, that we went over there. The intelligence was bad, and we destabilized an entire region. We had no plan after the fact. We literally were making it up day by day as we went along."

One Marine who is still angry about the war asked to be quoted anonymously because of the effect his comments might have on his job. He was especially enraged at the devastating effect the war has had on those who fought in it:

> Looking back at these people who were protesting the war in 2004, I would now argue that they cared about us just as much as the people who were pro-war.

They wanted us home and safe. If I had it to do all over again, I probably would have been joining them in those protests. Our leadership wastes our sacrifice. Did we win Iraq? Did we win Vietnam? We wasted money and we wasted people. We don't go there to win wars. We go there for political or economic reasons. We didn't win in Vietnam. We didn't go there to win in Afghanistan, and we didn't go there to win in Iraq. Militarily we could kick anybody's ass. So why didn't we? And that's why you see the bitterness, and the drinking and the suicides.

I'll leave the last word on this subject to Sam Mundy, commanding officer of 3/5 in 2003 who retired as a three-star general in 2021. Mundy was the first person I called when I decided to write this book. He encouraged me to move ahead with it and, according to my notes, said during our first conversation: "I have an opinion now and I can voice it because I'm retired."

I followed up later during our Zoom interview. "In the early days of this conflict," he said, "this was still the good war. The American people were behind us. We had embedded reporters. There was trust being built up. It hadn't gone sour yet politically in the United States."

"I think you can second guess a lot of things and recriminate," he continued. "That's the job of the media. And I find it tiresome, frankly, to do that. I think, strategically, there's a reason to look back at it and say that might not have been the wisest action to pursue, especially in light of what was going on in Afghanistan. And we now know that we took our focus off the ball in Afghanistan to go to Iraq. That's a valid critique and a valid complaint."

"But since then, we've made lots of decisions at a national strategic level that would only reinforce the bad decision, withdrawing and then drawing back, only to allow Al Qaeda to be resurrected as ISIS, only to have to go back in. So we've committed mistakes after the initial mistake that I think could have been avoided in the aftermath."

At the same time, he wanted to be very clear that he is "very pleased with the performance" of the Marines under his command. "At the time, with what we knew and what we were tasked to do," he concluded, "we were doing the nation's bidding."

CHAPTER 14

In Memory

Hospital Corpsman Michael "Doc" Johnson

Mom, I love you, and don't be afraid if I don't return. Realize that I'm in heaven with God.

—From a letter written by Michael Johnson shortly before his death.

Michael Johnson was unlike the other members of Lieutenant Brian Chontosh's platoon, according to Staff Sergeant Fred Keeney, who told me: "We were a rough platoon. We were a reflection of Chontosh. We were fucking rough. But Johnson wasn't. He was easygoing, even keeled, a really kind person. He wasn't wrapped tight like the rest of us. He wasn't swayed by us. He was true to himself."

Frank Quintero, who was severely injured by the same RPG that killed Johnson, remembers talking with Johnson a few nights before his death. He asked Johnson: "Aren't you scared of something happening to you?" Johnson replied: "No, I'm not. I know where I'm going if something happens to me."

Quintero also told me that each day when the convoy started rolling Johnson would read Psalm 23 out loud from his ever-present Bible. Initially, the silent response from others in the Humvee was unenthusiastic. "Oh, he's doing it again," Quintero says he thought. But after a while that changed, he says: "It was expected, and it was welcomed."

Johnson grew up in Little Rock, Arkansas, and graduated from the University of Central Arkansas. He and his wife Cherice lived in San

Diego. He was a role-model for many Marines, including other African Americans in 3/5.

In his honor, a medical facility at Marine Corps Recruit Depot San Diego was re-named the "Michael V. Johnson Branch Medical Clinic." An American Legion post in North Little Rock, Arkansas was also named for him. His father, a veteran, attended the ceremony and, according to the Associated Press (AP), told the crowd: "In all my days, I'll never be prouder than for what he has done for his family and his country." Recalling the day his son told him he was going to Iraq, his father added: "I could only think, 'You're my hero.'"

A photo prominently displayed at his family's home portrays him just as the family remembered him, AP reported shortly after his death. "Grinning in Mickey Mouse ears and waving at the camera."

Shortly before his death Johnson sent a letter to his mother in which he wrote, according to AP: "Mom, I love you, and don't be afraid if I don't return. Realize that I'm in heaven with God."

Major Kevin G. Nave, Executive Officer

> He was the glue that held the battalion together.

Commanding Officer Sam Mundy says that as soon as Major Kevin Nave joined 3/5 as its executive officer (XO), he knew there was something special about him. "He was like a breath of fresh air," Mundy told me.

In some Marine battalions, the role of the XO was to be the "hammer," the enforcer. That's not what Mundy wanted, and it was not what he got. Nave didn't need a hammer. "He was bright, he was engaging, he was quick witted," Mundy says. "And he could persuade people with just the power of his personality and intellect."

Captain Mario Schweizer, commander of Headquarters and Service Company, says Nave was a great mentor, and a very personable leader. "He wasn't the hard kind of XO," he says. "Sometimes an XO could be a hard nose and drive the staff. Nave's style was much more effective. He would bring us in and say, 'I think this is what you probably should do. I think this is what the boss is looking for. Or you probably should go back and try that again.'" Nave, Schweizer says, was exactly what 3/5 needed at the time.

His loss was devastating to the battalion, not only because he was so beloved, but because of his indispensable role. During Nave's battlefield memorial service, Lieutenant Colonel Mundy called Nave his "right hand man" and "the glue that held the battalion together." And he did it all, Mundy said, "with resolve unrivaled by any officer in the Marine Corps, and always with a smile on his face."

In my logbook I wrote:

> Kevin Nave was killed overnight... A very sad day for the troops—and for us. A patient, kind, good, decent man—who has been extraordinarily good to me and to us. We could go to him any time and ask him any question, and no matter how stupid or uninformed we may have seemed, he was patient and respectful and never wanted us to feel bad for asking. A great man and a real Marine.

Kevin Nave was the first person from Michigan to die in the Iraq war and, as routinely happens in such circumstances, TV news transmission trucks soon started arriving at the family home in the Detroit suburbs, and reporters started knocking on the Nave family's door looking for interviews.

It's a practice I've been part of many times during my career. On the one hand, I understand that it can feel unseemly and invasive. But on the other hand, the purpose was to let people know that this brave Marine died fighting for his country. The stories the reporters were writing were about honoring him for his service and his sacrifice.

Quite understandably, though, Nave's father, Reno, had no interest in talking to reporters he did not know. I later learned from his family that he told them he only wanted to talk to one reporter, and he pointed at me on his TV while I was doing a tribute to his son on NBC News.

Soon after that, I received a message from members of Kevin's family asking if I might be able to visit them in Michigan after I came home. They said they hoped it would help "fill the hole" in their father's heart.

After returning home, producer John Zito and I flew to Michigan and spent a day with the Nave family. They were heartbroken, of course, but incredibly gracious. Meeting them, it was easy to understand why Kevin was such a good and decent person. It was a family trait.

They told us all about Kevin, his growing up years, and his intense desire to serve and protect his country as a Marine. Zito and I told them about the kind and caring warrior we knew Kevin to be.

I hope our visit gave the Nave family at least a little bit of solace. I know it helped me enormously in dealing with the loss of a Marine who had become a friend.

Corporal Erik H. Silva

> As far back as I can remember he always wanted to be a Marine. As a child, he always dressed in uniform on Halloween. He would even color his face with camouflage paint.
>
> —Erik's big sister Gloria

Several Marines were injured in the April 4 battle, but only one was killed—Corporal Erik Silva. His loss devastated his many friends in 3/5, several of whom still struggle with survivor's guilt.

Hospital Corpsman Jeff Parnakian recalls that when 3/5 was in Okinawa, a deployment prior to Iraq, Parnakian had gotten in trouble for drinking and carousing. After that, when he went into town he always went with Silva, who kept him out of trouble. "He was my buddy because he didn't drink," Parnakian said of Silva. "He was a good dude. He wasn't getting shit-can drunk like the rest of us. We became really tight friends. His death in battle couldn't have happened to a nicer guy."

There is perhaps no better way to honor Erik Silva than to hear his older sister Gloria talk about him. "From as far back as I can remember he always wanted to be a Marine," Gloria told me. "As a child, he always dressed in uniform on Halloween. He would even color his face with camouflage paint."

Gloria was three years older than Erik, and she always felt the need to take care of him—even after he joined the Marines. When he was based at Camp Pendleton, Gloria lived about 45 minutes away. Like clockwork he would bang on her door on Saturday nights at about 11pm after a night out with his fellow Marines. "Sis, can you please give us a ride back to the base? We've got to be there in an hour."

She would grab her baby boy, Ryan, and pile into her truck with Erik and another Marine or two and drive them back to Pendleton, arriving just before curfew. "I was always there to take them back," she says now. Even as a Marine, he was still her baby brother, and she was his protector.

In late March 2003, when Erik was in Iraq, Gloria was based in Memphis, Tennessee with the Navy. She had some leave time and traveled home to Southern California to spend time with her family.

On April 4 her mother drove Gloria and her son Ryan (then two and a half years old) to the bus station for the more than 24-hour ride back to Memphis. "I got this gut feeling not to leave," she says. "I had an intuition that something was wrong." It wasn't necessarily about her brother, she says, just a powerful feeling that something was wrong. "I'm usually not one to feel that much emotion when I'm leaving because I'm very independent. I've been all over the world with the Navy. But this day felt different," she says. "My mom and I couldn't stop hugging each other."

Less than an hour into the ride her cell phone rang. It was one of her older brothers. "Get off the bus," he told her. He wouldn't say why, but she instantly knew. "He didn't have to say a thing. I just froze. I had an out-of-body experience where I just knew something had happened to Erik."

She sat in a state of shock, holding Ryan, for more than an hour before the bus stopped in El Centro, California, where she saw some Marines in uniform waiting, along with members of her family who lived nearby in Holtville, California, where Erik and Gloria grew up.

Her tears started flowing at this point in our interview and I asked Gloria if she wanted to stop. She said no. She wanted to tell the story to honor her brother.

The uniformed Marines at the bus station confirmed what she already knew—her little brother had died in battle. Her memories after that, she says, are hazy. She remembers picking out flowers for the funeral. She remembers the enormous sea of people at the cemetery. She remembers saluting in front of the casket. And she remembers that her two older brothers played taps on the trumpet. All four siblings had played the trumpet, but Erik had taken it a step further—he was the drum major of the high school band.

Over the past 20 years, April 4, the anniversary of Erik's death, has been treated as sacred by Erik's Marine buddies. Every year they gather for a few days to honor Erik and reconnect. In April 2022 they invited me to join them at the reunion at the home of Alex Sheeley in rural Ohio. Sheeley, a retired 3/5 Marine with a very big heart, is known for welcoming Marines into his home who need a place to stay. It was an honor to experience first-hand the band-of-brothers camaraderie that I previously had seen only in Iraq. They seemed transported back in time, standing around a roaring bonfire, drinking beer and bourbon, renewing their bonds with stories old and new.

Several Silva family members also attend the annual get-togethers. The bond is so strong that it's hard to tell if the Marines have adopted Silva's family, or if Silva's family has adopted the Marines.

For years Gloria did not attend. "I had a lot of grief and resentment," she says. "I was bitter." About ten years ago she started reaching out to individual Marines, but it wasn't until about five years ago that she finally let down her guard. She attended the Marine Corps Ball in Las Vegas where she instantly bonded with a group of Marines who had been very close to her brother. "I had sort of a revelation," she says, and chastised herself for waiting so long. "Gloria, you've been missing this for the past 15 years," she told herself. "What are you so afraid of?"

"I wanted to get to know these guys that knew a side of my brother that I never knew," she says. Today, she and the Marines are like family. If she has a problem, they are there—by phone, or in person if possible—in a heartbeat. Gloria says they are a bit "overprotective," but she doesn't seem to mind. And she is every bit as overprotective of them. "I guess because I was the older sister," she says, "I feel an obligation to all of them, to protect them. Just like I did with my little brother."

Staff Sergeant Riayan A. Tejeda

> His last words were "Tell my daughters I love them."

Staff Sergeant Riayan Tejeda was posthumously awarded the Silver Star for conspicuous gallantry. Referring to the ambush in Sadr City on

April 11, the Presidential Citation states: "Taking charge at the head of the formation, he inspired his Marines and directed them to positions to counter the enemy's attack. While bravely leading and fighting beside his Marines, he was struck by enemy fire and mortally wounded." He was 26 years old and had been a Marine for eight years.

That was not the only honor he received after his death. He also became an American citizen, at a ceremony in his family's home in the Washington Heights neighborhood of Manhattan in New York City. He was one of more than 37,000 noncitizen legal residents serving in the U.S. military at the time, and one of ten to die in Iraq, according to the *New York Times*.

Tejeda had immigrated from the Dominican Republic as a child and grew up in Washington Heights. Near his home, a portion of West 180th Street was re-named in his honor. The sign reads: "Staff Sergeant Riayan Agusto Tejeda Street."

Tejeda had two daughters, who were six and three years old when he died. The day after he died, Lieutenant Mike Prato—the senior officer on the night patrol in Sadr City—found Tejeda's belongings. Knowing from personal experience that personal effects of Marines wounded or killed in action sometimes get lost, he held onto a recording of Tejeda's two young daughters singing. He knew how important the girls were to him.

A few years later Prato tried to get in touch with Tejeda's daughters but had no luck. He did, however, locate Tejeda's father, Julio Tejeda, in the Dominican Republic. He called and tried to have a conversation, but Prato's Spanish wasn't adequate, so he contacted Corpsman Arturo Adame, one of the Navy medics who had so valiantly tried to save Tejeda's life, and who was fluent in Spanish.

Together they called Tejeda's father. After learning who they were, the father exclaimed to Prato and Adame: "You are angels sent by God. I've been waiting years. I just want to know what happened to my son." He said he had only been told that his son died in combat, nothing more. They told him what happened. The father also wanted to know what Tejeda's last words had been. They told him the words were: "Tell my daughters I love them." In a story by the Associated Press, Julio Tejeda said of his son: "I will always love him until the end of time." He said his son had loved his mother and music—especially the Merengue music of his native land.

Sadly, two weeks after their call with Julio Tejeda, Adame texted Prato with the news that he had died. It turns out that he had been terminally ill, and what he wanted more than anything else before he died was to get answers about his son. During those two weeks, Prato told me, Tejeda's father had reached out to his estranged granddaughters and reestablished their relationship. And he sent them the recordings that Prato had given him, of the daughters singing when they were very young.

A family was reunited, and a father died in peace. Prato told me that being part of that was overwhelming: "There was an element of closure in that for me too," he said.

Lance Corporal David E. Owens, Jr.

Wale Akintunde, who was a roommate and close friend of David Owens, told me: "David had heart and never gave up," whether in training or on the battlefield. Owens, who was just 20 years old when he was killed in action during an ambush in Baghdad's Sadr City, was "a really, really lovable kid," Akintunde says. "I think a lot of people considered him to be like a little brother because he was so unassuming."

He was also extraordinarily generous. "He'd give you the shirt off his back. He'd give you the last cigarette in a pack, and the last dip in a can of dip. I can't say enough good things about him," Akintunde told me, clearly moved by the memories.

Owens played football and wrestled in high school in Winchester, Virginia. He had hoped that joining the Marines would lead to a career as a state trooper.

He was an only child. His mother Debbie told the *Winchester Star* newspaper after his death: "Our whole life was centered around him."

Owens' high school wrestling coach told Associated Press: "He did well, even surpassed his own ability, by giving it all he had." He placed fourth in the Commonwealth District Wrestling Tournament. "He had a good sense of humor and was a good, gentle person," the coach added. "This town was proud of him before he went to Iraq and we're even prouder of him now."

A friend told the paper that Owens was "a quiet, decent guy who will be considered a hero in our town." On an online memorial page, a Marine friend wrote: "He was the most genuine person I have ever known. He had a heart of gold."

Another friend from the Marines, Alex Maxwell, wrote on the memorial page in 2021: "You are still loved and remembered by everyone who ever knew you, David. You were my first friend when we both checked into the unit in 2001. It has now been 20 years since I met you. But I feel your hand on my shoulder even now, every so often."

Epilogue

An Emotional Mountaintop Reunion

During a combat deployment it's unusual to see Marines cry. There are wet eyes at brief battlefield memorial services, but with a war raging, there is precious little time to mourn. But on August 19, 2022, almost twenty years after 3d Battalion, 5th Marines' 2003 deployment to Iraq, I witnessed a veritable flood of Marine Corps tears. It happened on the summit of First Sergeant's Hill at Camp Pendleton in Southern California, where 3/5 has long been based. I was honored to have been invited to join them.

I arrived at Pendleton shortly after 5am (0500 in military time) in a van with several 3/5 Marines who served in Iraq in 2003. We drove to the foot of First Sergeant's Hill (better described as a small mountain) where an extraordinarily steep, well-worn dirt path began. From a distance it looked like the incline was almost vertical, and it wasn't much friendlier up close. It looked like one false step might send you tumbling backward, head over heels.

As dark turned to dawn, about 40 Marines, almost all retired, gathered at the staging area at the base of the mountain. Most were in their early forties. All had served one or more tours in Iraq with 3/5. The atmosphere was festive as brothers-in-arms reunited. Some hadn't seen each other in years. But as the time to begin the climb approached, the mood became much more solemn.

The summit of First Sergeant's Hill is the site of dozens of handmade memorials to fallen Marines. The mission on this day was to hold a ceremony at the summit honoring the 36 men—35 Marines and one

Navy Hospital Corpsman—who lost their lives while serving in Iraq with 3/5 between 2003 and 2006. Five of the 36 had lost their lives in 2003 while I was embedded with them.

The Marines wore black tee shirts specially designed for this day, with the 3/5 insignia on the front, and the names of the 36 men on the back, along with their rank and the date of their death.

In a gesture of generational unity, more than a hundred young, active-duty Marines of 3/5's Kilo Company soon joined us and lined up in two columns at the bottom of the hill. They were strikingly reminiscent of the Marines I had met in Kuwait almost 20 years ago.

A few vehicles were waiting to transport Gold Star Families (families of the fallen), and any Marines who couldn't make the climb due to wartime injuries, by way of a dirt road up the back side of the mountain. The vehicles could have transported all the equipment. But the retired Marines—the "alumni" as they called themselves—wanted to carry the burden themselves.

The hardware included an 8-foot-tall aluminum cross, with a large steel "3/5" emblem, weighing about 70 pounds; a steel base for the cross, about 80 pounds; a steel plaque with the names of the fallen, about 75 pounds; ten 50-pound bags of concrete mix; plus tools, including shovels, rakes, and post-hole diggers. For the Marines who volunteered to carry that heavy load, an already difficult climb would become much more grueling. "We want to suffer through this hike in honor of our fallen brothers," one Marine explained.

The cross was initially carried by the young, active-duty Marines but was passed up the hill to the alumni who took turns, four or five guys at a time, giving everyone who wanted to carry it a chance to do so. The only heavy item that was transported by a vehicle was a very large cooler filled with water and—we're talking about Marines here—beer. A lot of beer.

I had been warned that it was a brutal hike and—at age 67 with arthritic knees—I considered their offer to ride up in one of the vehicles. But while watching the Marines—old and young—waiting and talking in the fresh pre-dawn air, I caught a case of Marine fever. There was no way I could miss this climb. One motivating factor: a 40-something Marine was making the climb with a prosthetic leg.

It was a tough climb, but not as bad as I had expected. At the steepest parts, ropes were anchored in the dirt for those who needed something to grab onto. I don't think any of the active-duty Marines used them, but some of the alumni did, as did I. Most arrived at the summit covered in sweat, but the sense of exhilaration overwhelmed any feelings of exhaustion. The view of the Pacific Ocean was awe-inspiring, and on this calm, clear day it was true to the meaning of its name: peaceful.

The young, active duty Marines soon headed back down the hill, leaving the alumni to get to work. They dug two deep holes, one for the steel base of the cross, the other for the base of the large plaque. They filled the holes with concrete mix and water, took frequent measurements and made precise adjustments as the concrete hardened.

(While they worked, I wandered through the sea of handmade crosses and wondered why I couldn't find any other religious symbols. I kept it to myself since I was there as an observer, not in my former role of annoying journalist.)

In a final symbolic touch, Gold Star parents poured two small bags of sand onto the soil at the base of the cross. One contained black sand from a beach in Iwo Jima, site of the bloodiest battle in Marine Corps history. The other held sand from Fallujah, site of the deadliest Marine battle in Iraq, a battle in which most of the Marines present had lost close friends.

Before the ceremony began, two eloquent Marines who played major roles in organizing the ceremony set the tone with impromptu speeches. Jason Arellano, a corporal in 2003 who was almost fatally injured in Fallujah in 2004, held up the plaque containing the names and bellowed: "We carry their legacy, today and every day! If we don't forget their names, they never die—these are our brothers!" His words were punctuated by a loud chorus of "OORAH!"—the Marine Corps battle cry.

Elber Navarro, a sergeant in 2003 who earned a Bronze Star in Fallujah in 2004, was even more emotional. "This is our day. Let's enjoy it," Navarro shouted. "If you haven't cried and you want to cry, fucking do it right here. I'll give you a shoulder to cry on as long as you give me one to cry on as well."

His eyes filled with tears and his voice began to crack as he continued. "It's been the fucking greatest honor of my life to be a part of 3/5, and to have served and fought alongside of every one of you. This is a brotherhood that goes on forever."

Turning to the mother of Marty Gonzalez and the father of Michael Anderson, Jr., two fallen Marines whose names are on the plaque, Navarro said: "I *promise* you that these names, your sons, will never be forgotten. They live in our souls. They live in my heart," he said, pounding his chest. "Every single night before I go to bed, I remember those Marines." Choking up, he concluded: "I will remember them for the rest of my life."

Navarro was showered with cheers of "OORAH!" as he wiped away tears.

As the formal part of the ceremony began, Navarro read the names of the fallen Marines, one at a time. As each name was spoken, a Marine from the crowd walked forward carrying a dog tag etched with the fallen Marine's name and hung it from the horizontal beam of the cross. For those who had received the Navy Cross, Silver Star, or Bronze Star, Arellano read their presidential citations.

The commander of 3/5, Lieutenant Colonel James Greco, told the crowd that during the eight years of *Operation Iraqi Freedom* twenty-two Marines received the Navy Cross. Six of the twenty-two were awarded to Marines of 3/5. That means, he said, that a battalion representing one-half of one percent of the Marine Corps received more than 25% of the Navy Crosses awarded.

Marines occasionally interjected their own thoughts and memories during the ceremony. After the reading of one of the names, a Marine who had been a close friend spoke up: "He was killed the day his son was born," he told the crowd. Tears began to flow freely as Marines were moved by their own memories.

As Arellano read the Bronze Star citation of a close friend who had died while saving the lives of fellow Marines, he paused, overwhelmed by emotion. After a chorus of encouragement from his fellow Marines he continued.

One Marine, deeply affected by hearing one of the names, walked away to be alone. After a few minutes another Marine approached him, put his arm around him, and guided him back to his brothers.

The parents and other relatives of Sergeant Marty Gonzalez quietly wept and comforted each other as his Bronze Star citation was read. Michael Anderson, Sr., came forward to hang the dog tag of his son, Corporal Michael Anderson, Jr., who had been killed in action in 2004 at the age of 21.

In the distance the Pacific Ocean glistened in the sun and a gentle ocean breeze made the 36 dog tags clink gently against each other, producing the quiet music of windchimes. Or as one Marine described it: "The voices of angels."

The moment after the last name was read, we heard a thump-thump-thump sound in the distance. Everyone turned toward the ocean. A Marine Corps Cobra helicopter was heading straight for us. It roared low over our heads and, as the Marines cheered and raised their beers in salute, it made a dramatic turn over the valley and roared back up and over First Sergeant's Hill for a final pass.

The timing was perfect. In fact, there was only one glitch in the entire ceremony. They ran out of beer. A few Marines jumped in a van for a quick beer run. Problem solved.

Oorah.

Afterword

Lieutenant General Sam Mundy (Commanding Officer of 3d Battalion 5th Marines as a Lieutenant Colonel in 2003) sent this letter to the Marines of 3/5 on the occasion of their 20th anniversary banquet at Camp Pendleton on July 8, 2003. This letter captures—more poignantly than anything else this author has read—the essence of what it means to be a United States Marine:

Greetings fellow warriors—the Consummate Professionals of the 3d Battalion, 5th Marines:

Even though it pains me to be "UA," I'm grateful for the chance to offer a few words in this letter, as you gather.

To remember our youth, and the years we spent together in the uniform of our nation...

To remember our friends and fellow Marines, who forged a common, unbreakable bond based on shared hardships and triumphs...

And, especially, to remember those who signed a blank check to the American people... and, through their ultimate sacrifice, paid it in full.

There is something uniquely powerful about a gathering of Americans, like you, who understand deeply about the price paid for our freedom. Our former 1st Marine Division Commander, and now-retired Secretary of Defense Jim Mattis once said, "I believe the ultimate test of a man's or woman's conscience is the willingness to sacrifice something for future generations whose thanks they will never hear."

He's right. There is something transcendent, even noble about men like you who are willing to defend their country and its values without seeking applause or public appreciation. This is even more radical if you stop to consider the fact that you could have done almost anything other than serve as a United States Marine:

...when you might have chosen a different career, an easier livelihood, or one that offered a lot more money, or when you might have avoided the character-defining moments that are only revealed by serving a cause beyond self-interest.

No matter the personal reason that compelled you to join the Corps—and for all of us, the reason is unique—you knew then and you still know today that it's worthy to stand up and fight for ideals and sacred things...

...like love of country,

...like our fellow Americans—especially those on our left and right when we go into harm's way

...or simply to try and leave this world a better place than the one we grew up in.

Yes, it's worthy.

Writing about the Peloponnesian wars two thousand years ago, the ancient Greek historian, Thucydides said, "What you leave behind is not what is engraved in stone monuments but what is woven into the lives of others." And today, in the midst of your brother Marines, this is what really matters.

What is woven into my life is that I served with the best; I served with men in 3/5 who cared far less about grand strategy or personal politics and cared far more about their fellow Marines and sailors; who cared about living up to a standard that demanded courage, perseverance, and commitment. I served alongside men who honored their country by stepping forward and doing their duty.

I hope you have a great reunion and promise to make it to the next one!

And finally, please pray for the widows and bereaved family members and touch the memorials of our fallen Marines and sailors on my behalf.

Get Some and Semper Fidelis,
Carl "Sam" Mundy III
United States Marine Corps, Retired